Creative Writing in Health and Social Care

of related interest

**The Self on the Page: Theory and Practice
of Creative Writing in Personal Development**
Edited by Celia Hunt and Fiona Sampson
ISBN-13: 978 1 85302 470 2   ISBN-10: 1 85302 470 8

Writing Works
**A Resource Handbook for Therapeutic Writing Workshops
and Activities**
Edited by Gillie Bolton, Victoria Field and Kate Thompson
Foreword by Blake Morrison
ISBN-13: 978 1 84310 468 1   ISBN-10: 1 84310 468 7

Therapeutic Dimensions of Autobiography in Creative Writing
Celia Hunt
ISBN-13: 978 1 85302 747 5   ISBN-10: 1 85302 747 2

The Therapeutic Potential of Creative Writing
Writing Myself
Gillie Bolton
Foreword by Sir Kenneth Calman
ISBN-13: 978 1 85302 599 0   ISBN-10: 1 85302 599 2

Writing My Way Through Cancer
Myra Schneider
ISBN-13: 978 1 84310 113 0   ISBN-10: 1 84310 113 0

Writing Well: Creative Writing and Mental Health
Deborah Philips, Liz Linington and Debra Penman
ISBN-13: 978 1 85302 650 8   ISBN-10: 1 85302 650 6

Creative Writing in Health and Social Care

Edited by Fiona Sampson

Foreword by Christina Patterson

Jessica Kingsley Publishers
London and Philadelphia

Cover photograph taken by Fiona Sampson

First published in the United Kingdom in 2004
by Jessica Kingsley Publishers
116 Pentonville Road
London N1 9JB, UK
and
400 Market Street, Suite 400
Philadelphia, PA 19106, USA

www.jkp.com

Copyright © Jessica Kingsley Publishers 2004
Foreword copyright © Christina Patterson 2004
Printed digitally since 2006

The right of the contributors to be identified as authors of this work has been asserted by
them in accordance with the Copyright, Designs and Patents Act 1988.

Library of Congress Cataloging in Publication Data
Creative writing in health and social care / edited by Fiona Sampson ; foreword by Christina
Patterson.
p. cm.
Includes bibliographical references and index.
ISBN 1-84310-136-X (pbk.)
1. Creative writing--Therapeutic use. I. Sampson, Fiona.
RC489.W75C744 2004
615.8'515--dc22
2004012457

British Library Cataloguing in Publication Data
A CIP catalogue record for this book is available from the British Library

ISBN-13: 978 1 84310 136 9
ISBN-10: 1 84310 136 X

Contents

PART TWO: *Thinking Through Practice*

Acknowledgements

Every reasonable effort has been made to contact the copyright holders of material reproduced in this book, and the publisher, editor and contributors would like to thank the following:

Extract on p.41 from 'Dagen svelnar'/ 'The day cools' by Edit Södergran (trans. Allwood 1980) in *Samlade Dikter*. Copyright © Wahlström and Widstrand 1997. Reprinted with permission of Wahlström and Widstrand, Stockholm. Extract on p.41 from 'Inte ens –' / 'Not Even –' by Nils Ferlin (trans. Fredenholm and Allwood 1986) in N. Ferlin *Dikter*. Copyright © Albert Bonniers Förlag 1984. Reprinted with permission of Albert Bonniers Förlag, Stockholm. Extract on p.42 from 'Höstvista'/ 'A song by autumn' by Tove Jansson (trans. Eriksson 2004) in *Sardinen på tunnelbanan och 199 andra dikter*. Copyright © Alfabeta 1996. Taken from the song 'Höstvista' by Erna and Tove Jansson. Printed by permission of Universal Music Publishing AB, Stockholm, and Alfabeta, Stockholm. 'Önskan' / 'Wish' on pp.43–4 by Karin Boye (trans. McDuff 1994) in K. Boye *Dikter*. Copyright © Albert Bonniers Förlag 1996. Reprinted with permission of Albert Bonniers Förlag, Stockholm. 'Romanska bågar' / 'Romanesque Arches' on p.44 by Toman Tranströmer (trans. Fulton 1997) in *Dikter 1954–1989*. Copyright © Albert Bonniers Förlag 1998. Reprinted with permission of Albert Bonniers Förlag, Stockholm. Untitled on p.53 and 'Going Down' on pp.55–6 from *Creativity in Dementia Calendar 2004*, edited by S. Benson and J. Killick. Copyright © S. Benson and J. Killick 2003. 'Up and Away' on pp.57–8, 'The Spider's Eyes' on pp.60–1 and 'Song' on p.64 from *Creativity in Dementia Calendar 2003* edited by S. Benson and J.Killick. Copyright © S. Benson and J. Killick 2002. Untitled on p.63 and Untitled on p.64 from *You Are Words* by J. Killick. Copyright © J. Killick 1997. Untitled on pp.62–3 from *inner→out: a journey with dementia* by A. McKinlay. Copyright © Charcoal Press 1998. Reprinted with permission of Charcoal Press, Rothsay. Untitled on p.66 from *Openings* by J. Killick and C. Cordonnier. Copyright © J. Killick and C. Cordonnier 2000. Extract by Duncan Tolmie on p.67 is first published in this text with permission from Duncan Tolmie. 'Poetry' on p.98 is first published in this text. Copyright © Sally Wallace 2004. 'A Grandmother's Hobbies'

Foreword

A few years ago, there was a bit of a fashion for promoting the benefits of poetry in every area of life. Poetry would, it was claimed, improve your health, your sex appeal, your social skills and your employability. Much of this coincided with the Poetry Society's Poetry Places scheme, a two-year programme of poetry residencies and placements. Poets were 'placed' in a wide range of environments, from law firms to supermarkets, hospitals and even a zoo. The scheme caught the imagination of the press – of the tabloids in particular – and led to a wince-making range of punning headlines.

I was brought in to co-ordinate this scheme and I found that, behind the publicity, a lot of wonderful stuff was going on. People who hadn't encountered writing or literature for years did find great pleasure in reading, hearing and sometimes writing poems. Poetry brought people together in new and interesting ways, cutting across hierarchies at work and encouraging people to open up to each other. A finance manager at Marks and Spencer even claimed that, after one session, he was able to go away and solve an economic problem which had been eluding him for days.

The reports we had back from the various projects sometimes made us laugh and sometimes brought tears to our eyes. There was no doubt in my mind that this was a significant and worthwhile project. Funded by the Arts Council's Lottery Programme, it was a fantastic opportunity to explore a way of working with words on a grand scale and to see a huge range of benefits. Much of this pioneering work has since been consolidated and developed in the Regional Arts Lottery Programme and by various funding bodies.[1]

Poetry and literature in general enrich our lives. Like all art, they are an attempt to impose order on chaos, to find meaning in the everyday and, with the right words in the right order, to capture what it's like to be alive. Poetry may be paradigmatic of these writerly processes: 'Poetry', said the late Alan Ross, 'is an attempt to rescue what matters of one's life.' The Australian poet Les Murray described it as 'a zoo in which you keep demons and angels', while Mick Imlah, Poetry Editor of the *Times Literary Supplement*, sees it as 'a way of talking about things that frighten you.' Poetry can be all of these things. What it isn't, though, is a system for the all-round improvement of human beings. I've sat in meetings, hosted by funding bodies, in which arts workers have gone on and on about the social benefits of their community writing projects; and I've come out feeling like Attila the Hun. Art is art. It doesn't exist to improve people's employability or social skills or to fill the holes in our social and educational systems that governments can't or won't address. If you knew as many poets as me, you'd certainly hesitate to say that poetry improves communication skills: or indeed mental health!

The trouble with funding of any kind is that it often demands firmer outcomes than we can or should deliver. It is also often linked to non-arts outcomes. All arts projects need money to happen but very few funders are willing to pay for projects that are purely exploratory, that are about playing around with language and the imagination and with seeing what happens. They tend, instead, to want monitoring, measuring and those damn statistics. They want to see upward trends, graphs and an overall picture that says 'success'. The ideal arts project would, perhaps, start off with a group of highly depressed people and end, three months later, with a group at the peak of drug-free human happiness. These paragons would also, presumably, be producing best-selling works of genius, feeding back into the economy the benefits of bounty they were lucky enough to receive.

The Poetry Society, of which I was then Director, was involved in a number of projects in a healthcare setting as part of the Poetry Places scheme: these included the Kingfisher Project (see Chapter Two),[2] which led to the Strange Baggage national conference on writing in health and social care, and a book on the subject, *The Healing Word* (Sampson 1999); Rose Flint's wonderful residency at a GP's surgery in Bristol (see Chapter Seven);[3] and Debjani Chatterjee's six-month poetry residency at Sheffield Children's Hospital.[4]

It seems to me that the most successful projects have been ones, like these, where participants have been treated as human beings whose imaginative engagement with the world is worth exploring. Projects which have taken a more scientific approach to these explorations – with questionnaires and monitoring – have been markedly less successful. Of course it's fine to ask people how they are feeling, before, during and after a project, and such questions may offer some interesting insight; but poetry is not a pill and it isn't an anti-depressant. Its benefits are – poetic. If poetry itself countered misery then I should be ecstatically happy all the time: which, sadly, isn't the case. There is no panacea for life's problems and challenges and any attempts to make poetry that panacea are doomed to fail.

After hearing about a range of projects, some of which the Poetry Society funded, some of which they didn't, I'm convinced that poetry can play an important part in the healing and therapeutic process. But poetry itself is not a magic medium. Much of the value of such projects lies in the skills and sensitivity of the poet-facilitator who leads the process of opening up and of creative engagement. If this is not done with due sensitivity and care, then it may be of no value at all. It's a process of trust. If the trust is not there, then it may be better to watch telly. Poetry as therapy, like any kind of therapy, is as good as the person doing it.

I'll end on a personal note. My sister, who had schizophrenia, died of heart failure eighteen months ago. When we went through her things, we found an exercise book of pieces of writing she had done, including some poems. They were not masterpieces, but they weren't bad at all. I cried, of course. I didn't know that she'd ever written any poems, but it made me very happy that poetry had featured in her life and I could just sense the pleasure that the poems had given her.

Christina Patterson, The Poetry Society

Notes

1   Sue Stewart's introduction to Part Two, 'A Provider's Experience', indicates the scope of this work as well as looking at the importance of underpinning range with good practice.

2   It is a testament to the individuals involved and to the value of the work that this project is still continuing today. I visited the project on the day I heard I

had been appointed Director of the Poetry Society, and sat in on the sessions. I was extremely impressed by the work, not just by the quality of poetry produced but by the atmosphere and the commitment of those in the group. It was a very moving experience.

3   In a way, this was the most exploratory project that we did. It wasn't connected with an arts centre or administered by an arts worker, but was simply a creative collaboration between a doctor and a poet. There was no pre-existing structure. Rose Flint initially sat in on consultations between doctor and patients as a kind of witness. 'Is that a poet's job?', she asks in the wonderful report she wrote on the project. 'I think so', she replies to her own question. 'Testifying to a truth', she adds, 'is what we have always done.' Both she and the doctor, Gillian Rice, came to the conclusion that one of the challenges involved in the healing process was the language barrier between patients and doctors, with patients often not expressing their real needs. 'We are supposed to be healing them', said Dr Rice. 'But how can we if we do not know what is wrong?'

4   Chatterjee spoke in quite different terms of her work with patients. Her aim, through a series of games and exercises, including the creation of a poetry gallery in the hospital, was to bring a bright ray of poetry and fun into the lives of children who were having a hard time, to offer a little distraction and make them smile. This she did very successfully.

References

Sampson, F. (1999) *The Healing Word: A Practical Guide to Poetry and Personal Development Activities.* London: The Poetry Society.

Editor's Introduction

Fiona Sampson

In the past fifteen years writing in health and social care activities has expanded enormously in Britain. The national organisation supporting the field, Lapidus,[1] started by a working group of half-a-dozen committed individuals including representatives of the Poetry Society and Survivors' Poetry, now has more than 200 members. Activities in the field are developing in every region of the UK and are an explicit part of Arts Council policy on literature provision in England (discussed further in the introduction to Part Two). Writing in health and social care – or its sister field, writing for personal development[2] – have been the objects of doctoral research,[3] the subject of theoretical and practical studies,[4] and have led to a number of publications, from text books to self-help guides.[5] There have also been a large number of publications, exhibitions, performances and broadcasts of the creative writing produced in health and social care settings.[6] Finally, as anthologies such as Ken Smith and Matthew Sweeney's *Beyond Bedlam* (Smith and Sweeney 1997) remind us, individuals have always written – whether or not for publication – out of their own experiences of illness, distress, care or institutionalisation.[7]

This writing individual seems to be the point at which any survey of the field of creative writing in health and social care will sooner or later arrive. On the one hand, there are the institutional roles associated with a *form of provision* (albeit provision of access to, we might argue, freedom of individual expression): provider,[8] practitioner, clinician, service user, researcher. On the other hand, there is writing as *the repository of an individual's way of going on* in one or more of the following ways:

13

- a celebration of individual voice, character and identity;

- a record of memory or experience;

- an opportunity to communicate or witness;

- a chance to develop skills, thoughts and feelings *through* writing (writing as a form of thinking);

- a way of resisting the tendency for (care) provision for any group to erode the individuality of each member of that group.

It might be argued that there is a tension between these two models of writing in health and social care, between formal provision and the development of individual experience. At its most polarised, this might even read as a debate between provider-led and user-led accounts of the work. (In Chapter Five, for example, it is Sam Moran, the project member, who writes about the poetry itself.) I suggest that there is no such tension. Formal administrative models are simply means to the end which is the writing itself and whatever rewards it brings. Therefore, though this book, which is about the formal provision of writing in health and social care, does not directly address the experiences of individuals who – whether professionally or privately – write *independently* out of experiences of distress, illness or care, it is informed by and acknowledges a continuum with those experiences.[9]

In her Foreword, Christina Patterson discusses the importance of remembering to think about *writing itself* as the goal of writing activities: about 'art for art's sake'. Another way to say this is to remember that the rewards of writing in health and social care settings are the same ones which reward *all* writing, although they may be peculiarly relevant to these settings. At its simplest, for example, accomplishing a poem might make someone feel happy; while they are receiving health or social care, such happiness might be at a premium.

These possible rewards of creative writing in health and social care figure strongly in discussions about what the field consists of: for two reasons, one intrinsic and one extrinsic. The intrinsic reason has to do with the field's *identity*. Only if we know what we are trying to achieve can we know what to do in order to achieve it. In other words, what is the field for (Sampson 1997)? Is it to develop an oeuvre of commercial new writing? In that case literary agents could be called in to meet project members over a glass of day room Chardonnay in the style of MA Creative Writing courses, and certain project members might be 'creamed off' for intensive coaching. Or is it a diversional activity for boring afternoons? In that case it probably doesn't matter if no writing happens so long as the facilitator is personable and everybody has 'a good chat and a bit of a laugh'?

The extrinsic reason for rewards having become so significant in discussions about writing in health and social care has to do with *justifications* of the practice. Because of its hyphenated identity, as an *arts* practice in a *care* context, the work has to speak to both arts and care discourses; and about each discourse to the other. A busy clinician may not automatically agree that an arts practice is a good thing, nor that it is relevant to the care context. An arts professional may be wary of an arts practice which seems to talk about itself in any terms except the artistic. These problems of communication and articulation are immediate and daily for practitioners, since they can generate or limit the very funding and management structures which enable writing in health and social care activities to take place.

Speaking of 'rewards' allows us to think of a range of effects and outcomes associated with writing *qua* writing. There is the suggestion that some of these rewards might be, for example, entirely subjective or even frivolous: such as the scope for personal conceit. By contrast the term 'benefits', which is sometimes used in this context, carries with it a much more thorough-going sense of objectively quantifiable gain: that is to say, of *undeniable goods*. Some of the research activity associated with the field has attempted to quantify such beneficial outcomes. A major problem with this approach is that artistic merit[10] – in other words, the writing practice itself – cannot be quantified, although it may well differ in merit as well as form from other examples in ways which can be *qualitatively* recorded. Quantitative research therefore measures certain *outcomes* – such as reductions in stated anxiety levels, or the need for medication – divorced from their intrinsic relation to other aspects of the writing experience. Not only does this generate the risk of measuring something irrelevant (should a comparative study set poems with 'relaxing' pastoral themes against texts with 'demanding' contemporary language, or are perceived symptoms down to the unforeseeable range of the discussion about death which ensued from one poem?), it fails to take into account a number of essential characteristics of the field:

1.   the *ways in which* writing generates benefits;

2.   other outcomes which are not described as beneficial but which are perceived as positive – '*rewards*';

3.   most fundamental of all, the very *individuality* of each participant's experience which writing serves to record and celebrate.

If we are not to rely on a quantifiable survey of benefits associated with writing in health and social care, how are we to make the case for the practice? The recent rapid development of the field suggests that practitioners and providers, at least, are finding something with which they believe they can work. There is lively debate about whether and how the experiences of participants can be examined for evidence that they, too, find involvement rewarding.[11](Chapter Eleven offers a fuller discussion of the role of evaluation.)

Debate continues, too, about whether creative writing in health and social care is a *proto-therapy*, a primarily 'healing' activity (whatever that is taken to mean), or a form of *arts* work. And what forms can it take? For example, *provider* thinking may be that the writing workshop is somehow 'more' participative than related activities of reading, performance, or the commissioning of a poem for a waiting room. Partner *clinicians* may make assumptions about which groups of people receiving care can benefit from writing. *Service users* may have come to suspect any form of provision which doesn't originate from their own support networks.

In short, it is a complex field; and the roots of that complexity are not merely historical but have to do with the very nature of the practice itself, as Christina Patterson's Foreword makes clear. Writing as a former Director of the Poetry Society, she shows us, through the concentrating prism of poetry, three facets of creative writing in health and social care: the special qualities of language used in certain ways; good practice by publicly accountable professionals; and the human dimension of feeling and experience. In other words, as she demonstrates, the field is built out of the three-way pull between what we could summarise as:

1.   *art* – by which we mean, let us say for now, a certain kind of man-made experience and way of going on which avoids what is reductive and which often exhibits an urge towards transcendence of particular circumstance and individual experience;

2.   *systems of provision*, from the bureaucratic to the clinical;

3.   the *vulnerability* of the human *individual*, who in this case is receiving care.

One of the most obvious things about these three ingredients is the lack of a language common to all. Human experience is individual and disorganised, a chaos of emotion and sensation which cannot speak in the systematic, technical terms of clinical textbook or public accountancy. Creative writing, which may evoke some of the pain and excitement of human experience, cannot be paraphrased successfully by management report or care plan. Clinicians and arts managers understand little of each other's approaches; full-time writers may not 'speak the same language as' either psychotherapists or social workers.

There is, however, another way to think about this complexity. Creative writing in health and social care has sometimes been character- ised by competition between different ways of working; a sense that only one of the many practices which make up the field can be 'correct'. It is possible to turn this on its head, and point out that diversity and range can be a strength; that perhaps the field is developing – not like a method, school, or other orthodoxy but in many directions at once – so that it is equipped to offer 'something for everybody'. Individuals are not inter- changeable: this, I would argue, is one of the very lessons creative writing in health and social care teaches as it enables participants to 'find a voice'. The many skills which practitioners, in particular, bring to the field are characteristic of its multi-faceted character, I suggest, rather than indica- tions of some kind of failure. Instead of thinking of more and more precise – and perhaps narrow – definitions of creative writing in health and social care, it may be more useful to map the range of good practice which makes up the field.

That is what this volume aims to do. However, 'mapping' means more than merely listing sites of good practice without locating them in relation to each other. Mapping is joined up: it does not concentrate on sites of personal interest but tries to present an objective guide for the traveller. Here that hopeful 'traveller' is the reader; and this volume aims to be a guide through the field whether you are new to it, in search of further encouragement and information, or an old hand coming back to see what has changed. You, the reader, join the book's other protagonists: providers, practitioners, partner professionals and participants. The contributors include representatives from all four of these groups: and, although they are writing in depth and addressing key principles and issues, they are doing so with the clarity which comes from experience of working, and having to explain that work, *across* disciplines.

The contexts in which these contributors work fit together to represent the range of health and social care: from hospice to long-stay dementia care to District Health Authority to user-led group to integrated day centre to clinical training to Higher Education. Their practices also represent the whole field of activities. They look at creative reading, writing, and related activities[12] in the following areas:

- in pastoral care, conflict resolution, clinical provision and clinical training;

- in relation to Art Therapy, specialist health care arts and conventional community arts provision;

- as part of professional writers' engagement with their own writing process and in the teaching of creative writing.

For a variety of practical reasons, some chapters view the field through the concentrating paradigm of poetry practice but, since poetry cannot be said to lack any of the attributes of creative writing in other genres, what they have to say is also of general significance. The contributors also represent the best of contemporary research practice in the UK. Finally, because the field of creative writing in health and social care – in the 'open' sense of doing writing as well as reading without being limited purely to the 'therapeutic' model – has so far developed primarily in the UK,[13] this volume indicates its geographic spread within Britain and its influence in two widely contrasted parts of Europe: to the north, in Sweden and the south, in the former Yugoslavia.

For clarity, the book is divided into two parts: 'The Range of Creative Writing in Health and Social Care', which looks at the spread of good practice; and 'Thinking Through Practice' in which practitioners and researchers articulate a range of ways of thinking about practice. Each section has a relevant Introduction outlining some of the principles and ground it covers. Some recent debate has suggested that the field of creative writing in health and social care is divided into practice and research, and that these lack common language and aims with to address each other's concerns. However, all the researchers contributing to the second part of this volume are writing – whatever research approach or theoretical framework they have adopted – out of their own practice in the field, and all the practitioners writing in the first part have extensive experience of reflecting on their practice.

In his Introduction to Part One, where the range of good practice is modelled, Paul Munden, Director of the National Association of Writers in Education (NAWE), looks at the field from the practitioner's perspective. This is in a sense the 'view from the ground' of practice itself. Munden introduces the linked ideas of quality provision and of professional development for writers involved in this work, stressing the importance of training and of opportunities for practitioners to share knowledge and skills. As he demonstrates, NAWE has been closely involved in the historical development of the field as a whole through its provision of just these opportunities, in particular through its journal, *Writing in Education*, its website and national conferences.

The first individual example of practice comes from a specific care area. Inger Eriksson, a Hospital Chaplain from Lund, writes about a long-term poetry reading project in a Swedish hospice. To work in hospice means to work within a specific set of care practices as well as with a group of people who, because they are terminally ill, have special needs; Eriksson is interested in their particular spiritual needs. Her practice responds to these specific terms, using the reading and discussion of poetry to explore the existential issues facing dying patients and their relatives.

By contrast, the practitioner and researcher John Killick discusses work with a group of individuals who may be receiving health or social care or may still live at home. His chapter looks at oral written work with people with dementia. Using examples largely gathered from his own practice in the north of England and Scotland, Killick establishes the idea of a consenting although not independent author, with whom the transcribing practitioner collaborates in an editorial role. Killick is particularly interested in the unusual quality of the language of dementia, seeing in its non-linearity a transgressive creativity which echoes the word-play of childhood and which has often been lost from other adult speech-acts. As a result, he sometimes transcribes the speech of people with dementia as poetry; a methodology he outlines and which leads to a discussion of the need for and significance of interventions by a professional practitioner.

Moving away altogether from health to social care, the book's other international contributor, Macedonian writer Aleksandar Prokopiev, describes a model project using writing and story-telling with disabled and able-bodied young people from a range of ethnic groups attending integrated clubs in post-war Macedonia. An NGO-led initiative in social services accommodation, it is one of a number working to rebuild civil society by encouraging racial integration; and is part of an extensive programme of health education. Prokopiev outlines methods of working including animated graphics, costumed actors and interaction by pre-literate children; and discusses the interest this new initiative has aroused among professional artists in the country.

If the Macedonian model uses high-profile professional artists to work with young people, user-led projects represent a radical break with the structures of authority in care and other social settings. Alison Combes, the Director of Survivors' Poetry, was an early contributor to this project and the experiences of service users are perhaps most strongly summarised here by Sam Moran's contribution to the practical survey outlined by Chapter Five. However, the voices of project participants are to be heard throughout this book in quotations from written work in particular.

Written from a set of roles – as professional writer and lecturer in creative writing in Higher Education – Maureen Freely's examination of writing as a therapeutic practice nevertheless rephrases the idea that there is no absolute division, but rather a continuum, between writers, facilitators of writing in health and social care activities and project participants. Using the idea of 'writing as thinking', Freely identifies a series of parallels: first, between professional writers', students' and new writers' experiences of the writing process; and, second, between the writer's own experience of writing through illness and distress and those of people receiving health care. Freely develops these to suggest some principles for supporting writing participants, whether of university courses or hospital projects. Her personal, writerly approach is completed by an example of her own writing on the topic.

In the case study which ends Part One, a range of protagonists take a closer look at a three-year writing in health and social care project in the South of England. The aims and objectives, history, structure and activities of the project, which took place in a range of usual and unusual settings, are outlined. Perhaps unusually, in order to give as full an account of the project as possible, it is discussed from a range of points of view: those of arts and health care managers, a Sister working in Palliative Care, a peer practitioner-evaluator, the writer-in-residence/researcher and a member of a writing group supporting people with continuing mental health problems living in the community. Even within one project, the chapter concludes, writing in health and social care can display a diversity of approaches and fulfil a series of aims.

Part Two, 'Thinking Through Practice', opens with an Introduction by poet and literature consultant Sue Stewart. Writing in part from her experience as an Arts Council Literature Officer, Stewart stresses the importance of *principled* work: these ethical and artistic principles are the standard of good work. Like Munden, she emphasises the importance of quality provision and its link to giving writers professional opportunities to develop as practitioners. Like Prokopiev, she acknowledges that strong professional writers often develop real interests in this field. Looking at the planning and delivery of provision as *active reflection*, she draws together the viewpoints of both providers and (drawing on her own work across the UK) practitioners to introduce a range of practical thinking in the chapters which follow.

Like Part One, Part Two starts at the heart of the health care context. Robin Downie's chapter on the training of clinicians examines some aims which might justify the inclusion of creative writing and reading in the health care curriculum. He argues for several groups of 'transferable skills': these include 'humanistic perspective' and 'self awareness'. Downie is Professor of Moral Philosophy at the University of Glasgow and his involvement in the medical humanities resulted from using some of the concrete, universal examples which the arts provide in order to help students address abstract principles of medical ethics. His chapter goes on to examine a possible connection between the aims of the educator and those of the therapist – Downie suggests both aim at 'wholeness' – and engages with the question of whether creative writing in health and social care is a means or an end by proposing that a humanistic perspective is part of that 'whole person' therapists and educators alike aim for. To reach this conclusion, Downie has to decide that, while writing in health and social care is an arts rather than a therapeutic activity, it takes the form of arts *education*. This bold idea proves to be the starting point for McLoughlin's chapter (see below).

Also working from within the framework of clinical thought, poet and Art Therapist Rose Flint works to locate the field in another way by drawing the line, but suggesting analogies, between her formal therapeutic work and that in health care arts projects she facilitates. Flint's chapter, based on her practice in the West and South of England, uses theories borrowed from the arts and occupational therapies to look at the way creative writing in health and social care settings can create a space for transformation, trust and imagination, in which different ways of thinking can be experienced.

Flint's chapter demarks the differences between the arts therapies, with their in-depth training, formal clinical model and diagnostic responsibilities, and the much more fluid practices of creative writing in health and social care. Although this book maps diversity, it also makes the case for best practice. The MA in Creative Writing and Personal Development at the University of Sussex is the only postgraduate programme in Britain to offer training in the use of creative writing in healthcare, therapy and education. The founder of Lapidus, academic Celia Hunt, who leads the Sussex course, explores students' experience of engaging in their own self-reflective creative writing and the changes and developments they report in their sense of self. She looks in particular at the role of fictional autobiography in enhancing their reflexivity; and explores what students learn from this experience for their work with others.

Hunt's discussion is underpinned by literary, critical and psycho-dynamic theory and recent work in neurobiology. Lapidus, with its proessional information exchange, is another of the field's emergent structures which is equipped to enable excellence. Dominic McLoughlin, a practitioner writing as a former Chair of Lapidus, uses a range of dis-courses, including psychoanalytic and phenomenological theories of art and ideas from his counselling background, to make an appeal for the use of creative writing as a form of access to personal development. McLoughlin, like Downie, sees this access as a form of educational provision: the task he sets himself is therefore to make the case for teaching poetry in health and social care contexts, arguing, rather like Downie, that poetry develops a range of – primarily cognitive – skills; and, with Eriksson, that it affords opportunities for a range of personal, spiritual and emotional investigations. McLoughlin continually re-establishes the link with creative writing as an arts practice by suggesting that these are attributes of poetry *itself*, rather than of its *delivery*. Con-tinuing this distinction, he argues that although poetry is in itself 'safe', poor-quality delivery of writing in health and social care may not be.

From his experience as a Senior Occupational Therapist, Nick Pollard elaborates on some of the principles McLoughlin's chapter introduces. Writing activities are widely used in mental health occupational therapy settings but too often the writing process is seen as having a purely thera-peutic meaning. Using the analogy of worker writing, he explores the potential for writing in facilitating engagement and participation in the wider community, and considers the move from therapy-directed creativ-ity to producing a literature of disadvantage which does not repeat its authors' experiences of marginalisation.

This book aims to map an introduction to creative writing in health and social care as a whole field of practices spoken for by models of good practice. However, the field is still developing fast and needs to continue to look to the future. A key area of increasing debate which, if not well managed, has the potential to divide and limit the field, is the need for evaluation and research – in order for good practice to be able to represent and advocate itself – which this Introduction touched on at the outset. The book's final chapter draws on practitioner experience as well as discourse theory, ideas from moral philosophy and the writing of participants, to argue that genuine evaluation must be appropriate to the practice, and carried out in that practice's own terms. 'Evaluation' which *paraphrases* or *tabulates* participants' particular experiences misses, for example, the very locus of individuality (if not of individuation) which seems central to creative writing in health and social care.

Both parts of this book end on a note suggestive of future development. For the reader of this book, the bibliographical resources and the short list of addresses at the end of the volume are designed to be an opportunity to further develop individual interest in the field. Any survey of creative writing in health and social care, such as this one, which aims to map diversity rather than try to force that diversity into a single totalising narrative, will also map omissions, initiatives and discordances. It will indicate, in other words, the potential for future development as well as the distance the field and its participants have already travelled. That space of opportunity – which can be traced round each project, each piece of research and each practitioner represented here – is always already a force for change. It should, I suggest, be celebrated as writing in health and social care enters the next phase of its development.

Notes

1 www.lapidus.org.uk

2 We might say that 'writing in personal development' *prioritises the individual's process or experience.* Although such individual experience may take place within the context established by 'writing in health and social care', this field *emphasises that context.* It is a context which may, however, be defined in one or more of several terms: the symptoms of illness, the individual's experience of and reactions to illness and treatment, treatment defined as care, intervention or some form of institutionalisation.

3 Celia Hunt (1999); Fiona Sampson (2001); Inger Eriksson's current doctoral research brings a phenomenological-hermeneutic approach to bear on the use of poetry to discuss existential issues in hospices.

4   Fi Frances (1999) offers context-dependent arguments for work with older people receiving health and social care. Fiona Sampson detailed writing activities across the range of District Health Authority provision (1989) and extended a quantitative approach from responses to writing in health and social care to the actual content of poems (1996). In Australia, Fiona Place has written about writing in mental health care (1990) and published a fictionalised account of anorexic experience (1989). Her compatriot, Mary Hutchinson, 'connects the liberatory discourse of…feminism with the post-constructionalist view that the subject is constituted by language' (Hutchinson 1998, unpaginated). R.S. Ulrich (1984) studied the effect of environment on recovery rates of surgical patients.

5   Including, for example, Jackowska 1997, Killick and Schneider 1997, Hunt and Sampson 1998, Bolton 1999, Sampson 1999, Hunt 2000.

6   Although Lynne Alexander's (1990) collection of voices from Lancaster Hospice 'crossed over' to mainstream publication, in the UK work with a high literary profile has been dominated by writers' *responses to* the institutional setting – for example 'prison poetry' collections (Liardet 2005, forthcoming; Smith 1987) and *professional* writers' experiences of political oppression (Kaplinski 1996), prison (Mapanje 1993, Elfyn 1996) distress or bereavement (Grant 1999, Morrison 1993, Sebald 1999) and illness (Carver 1990, Gunn 1992, Gross 1999, Kay 1998, MacSweeney 1997, Wicks 1994). This is not so strongly the case in countries such as Finland where, for example, the poet and novelist Eira Stenberg produced a TV play with people living in a long-stay psychiatric hospital as long ago as 1971. For a sense of the 'paper-trail' of facilitated and edited work a practitioner may generate, see for example John Killick in Chapter Two.

7   Well-known examples include John Clare (2001), Robert Lowell (1965) and Anne Sexton (1991). See Al Alvarez's *The Savage God* (Alvarez 1972). Some psychoanalytic treatments of this field suggest a tradition of self-destructive women poets whose writing represents the repetition rather than reparation of original harm (Kavaler-Adler 1993). For a more literary exploration of poetry and mental distress, see Dunn, Morrison and Roberts 1996. The recent publication of a number of anthologies of poetry chosen to be 'helpful' in dealing with experience inverts this relationship between poetry and mental distress, suggesting that some texts may have, not a pathological, but instead a supportive role (for example Astley 2001, Paterson and Shapcott 1999, Shapcott and Sweeney 1996).

8   The term 'provider' is used in this book to mean the funding and/or administrative body behind a project. For example, a hospital's Arts Project, such as Artscare at Salisbury District NHS Trust, may have a full-time team of arts

administrators who chose to fundraise for and co-ordinate a particular writing project which they appoint a professional writer to deliver. Or a Literature Officer employed by one of the national Arts Councils may decide to set up and fund a residency for a writer in a particular health or social care setting. Most, but not all, providers in the field are at present arts organisations. For further discussion of the implications of this pattern of provision, see Sampson 2001, pp.254–293.

9   The question of what existing individual practice might gain from formal writing in health and social care provision is touched on in practical terms in Sampson 1999.

10   By 'merit' I mean the quality of an arts experience *as* an arts experience, not the publishability or otherwise of individual workshop outcomes.

11   Such as story-telling, using hospital radio, making tapes, performances by participants, poem posters: cf. Sampson 1999.

12   According to Anne Hudson Jones,

> Literature and medicine as a contemporary academic subspeciality is usually said to have begun in 1972, with the appointment of Joanne Trautmann (Banks) to the faculty of The Pennsylvania State Univeristy College of Medicine at Hershey. She was the first person with a PhD in literature to hold a full-time faculty position in a medical school in this country (and probably the world). (Hudson Jones 1990)

> In the US Poetry Therapy and Bibliotherapy are emerging therapeutic practices which treat reading texts as a therapeutic tool with definable outcomes such that a particular poem can be prescribed by a trained therapist, for someone experiencing a particular difficulty (Leedy 1969, Lerner 1978, Mazza 1999). In this picture, poems and other literary works have identifiable meanings and resulting effects on the reader. Something of the open-endedness and personal nature of the individual's relationship to poetry and literature, on which the practice of many of the contributors to this volume is partly based, seems to have been lost in this therapeutic practice.

13   See the opening paragraph of Chapter Eight for more information.

References

Alexander, L. (ed.) (1990) *Now I Can Tell: Poems from St John's Hospice.* London: Papermac.

Alvarez, A. (1972) *The Savage God: A Study of Suicide.* New York: Random House.

Astley, N. (ed.) (2001) *Poems for Hard Times.* Newcastle upon Tyne: Bloodaxe Books.

Bolton, G. (1999) *The Therapeutic Potential of Creative Writing: Writing Myself.* London: Jessica Kingsley Publishers.

Carver, R. (1990) *A New Path to the Waterfall*. London: Harvill Press.

Clare, J. (2001) *Flower Poems: Selection of Clare's Poetry*, edited by Simon Kövesi. Bangkok: M & C Services.

Dunn, S., Morrison, B. and Roberts, M. (eds) (1996) *Mindreadings: Writers' Journeys Through Mental States*. London: Minerva.

Elfyn, M. (1996) *Cell Angel*. Newcastle upon Tyne: Bloodaxe Books.

Frances, F. (1999) *The Arts and Older People: A Practical Introduction*. London: Age Concern England.

Grant, L. (1999) *Remind Me Who I Am Again?* London: Granta.

Gross, P. (1999) *The Wasting Game*. Newcastle upon Tyne: Bloodaxe Books.

Gunn, T. (1992) *The Man with Night Sweats*. London: Faber and Faber.

Hudson Jones, A. (1990) 'Literature and medicine: Traditions and innovations.' In B. Clarke and W. Aycook (eds) *The Body and the Text: Comparative Essays in Literature and Medicine*. Lubbock, Texas: Texas Tech University Press.

Hunt, C. and Sampson, F. (eds) (1998) *The Self on the Page: Creative Writing and Personal Development*. London: Jessica Kingsley Publishers.

Hunt, C. (1999) *Personal Fictions: The Use of Fictional Autobiography in Personal Development*. Brighton: University of Sussex.

Hunt, C. (2000) *Therapeutic Dimensions of Autobiography in Creative Writing*. London: Jessica Kingsley Publishers.

Hutchinson, M. (1998) 'I am the Amazon who dances on the backs of turtles: Becoming the subject of the story in a community writing and publishing project.' *Text 2*, 1, unpaginated. www.gu.edu.au

Jackowska, N. (1997) *Write for Life*. Shaftesbury: Element Books.

Jay, P. (ed.) (1998) *The Spaces of Hope: Poetry for our Times and Places*. London: Anvil Press.

Kaplinski, J. (trans. Hawkins, H.) (1996) *Through the Forest*. London: Harvill.

Kavaler-Adler, S. (1993) *The Compulsion to Create: A Psychoanalytic Study of Women Artists*. London and New York: Routledge.

Kay, J. (1998) *Off Colour*. Newcastle upon Tyne: Bloodaxe.

Killick, J. and Schneider, M. (1997) *Writing for Self-Discovery*. Shaftesbury: Element Books.

Knight, B. (1996) *The Listening Reader: Fiction and Poetry for Counsellors and Psychotherapists*. London: Jessica Kingsley Publishers.

Leedy, J. (ed.) (1969) *Poetry Therapy*. Philadelphia: Lippincott.

Lerner, A. (ed.) (1978) *Poetry in the Therapeutic Experience*. Elmsford, New York: Pergamon Press.

Liardet, T. (2005 forthcoming) *The Uses of Pepper*. Bridgend: Seren Books.

Lowell, R. (1965) *Selected Poems*. London: Faber and Faber.

MacSweeney, B. (1997) *The Book of Demons*. Newcastle upon Tyne: Bloodaxe Books.

Mapanje, J. (1993) *The Chattering Wagtails of Mikuyu Prison*. London: Heinemann.

Mazza, N. (1999) *Poetry Therapy: Interface of the Arts and Psychology*. New York: CRC Press.

Morrison, B. (1993) *And When Did You Last See Your Father?* London: Penguin/Granta.

Paterson, D. and Shapcott, J. (eds) (1999) *Last Words: New Poetry for the New Century*. London: Picador.

Philipp, R. and Robertson, I. (1996) 'Letter: Poetry helps healing.' *The Lancet 347*. 332–333.

Place, F. (1989) *Cardboard: The Strength Thereof and Other Related Matters.* Sydney: Local Consumption Publishers.

Place, F. (1990) 'Left, right or centre? Finding your own voice within psychiatry.' In H. Heseltine (ed.) *Left, Right or Centre? Psychiatry and the Status Quo.* Sydney: University College, ADFA.

Rigler, M. (1997) *Withymoor Village Surgery – A Health Hive.* Withymoor: Withymoor Village Surgery.

Sampson, F. (1989) *Writing in Health Care.* Hampshire and Isle of Wight: Southern Arts and Hospital Arts.

Sampson, F. with Appendices by Hartill, G. (1996) *Report to the Poetry Society Project on Issues of Health, Healing and Personal Development.* London: Poetry Society.

Sampson, F. (1996) *What Poetry Practitioners Do: Fieldwork Outcomes.* Unpublished report. London and Bristol: University of Bristol and the Poetry Society Special Interest Group.

Sampson, F. (1997) 'Some questions of identity: What is writing in health care?' In C. Kaye and T. Blee (eds) *The Arts in Health Care: A Palette of Possibilities.* London: Jessica Kingsley Publishers.

Sampson, F. (1999) *The Healing Word: A Practical Guide to Poetry and Personal Development Activities.* London: The Poetry Society.

Sampson, F. (2001) *Writing in Health Care: Towards a Theoretical Framework.* Nijmegen: University of Nijmegen.

Sebald, W.G. (trans. Hulse, M.) (1999) *Rings of Saturn.* London: Harvill.

Senior, P. and Croall, J. (1993) *Helping to Heal: The Arts in Health Care.* London: Calouste Gulbenkian Foundation.

Sexton, A. (Wood Middlebrook, D. and Hume George, D. (eds)) (1991) *Selected Poems of Anne Sexton.* London: Virago Press.

Shapcott, J. and Sweeney, M. (eds) (1996) *Emergency Kit: Poems for Strange Times.* London: Faber.

Smith, K. (1987) *Wormwood.* Newcastle upon Tyne: Bloodaxe Books.

Smith, K. and Sweeney, M. (1997) *Beyond Bedlam: Poems Written Out of Mental Distress.* London: Anvil Press.

Stenberg, E. (1971) *Hyvää Huomenta (Good Morning).* Helsinki: Finnish TV.

Ulrich, R.S. (1984) 'View through a window may influence recovery from surgery.' *Science 224*, 420–421.

Wicks, S. (1994) *Open Diagnosis.* London: Faber and Faber.

Further Reading

Anderson, W. (1977) *Therapy and the Arts: Tools of Consciousness.* New York: Harper.

Davila, T. and Fréchuret, M. (eds) (2000) *L'Art médicine: Actes du Colloque.* Lyon: Laurence Barbier.

DeSalvo, L. (1999) *Writing as a Way of Healing.* London: Women's Press.

Downie, R. (1994) *The Healing Arts: An Oxford Illustrated Anthology.* Oxford: Oxford University Press.

Dynes, R. (1996) *Creative Writing in Groupwork.* Bicester: Winslow Press.

Gersie, A. (1997) *Reflections on Therapeutic Storymaking: The Use of Stories in Groups.* London: Jessica Kingsley Publishers.

Gersie, A. and King, N. (1990) *Storymaking in Education and Therapy*. London: Jessica Kingsley Publishers.

Lane, B. (1993) *Writing as a Road to Self-Discovery*. New York: Writers Digest.

Morley, D. (1991) *Under the Rainbow: Writers and Artists in School*. Newcastle upon Tyne: Bloodaxe Books.

Part One

The Range of Creative Writing in Health and Social Care

Introduction:
A Writers' Field

Paul Munden

It is over fifteen years now since a group of writers gathered at the Arvon Centre near Hebden Bridge and formed an association called NAWE. That was the *Northern* Association of Writers in Education. Since then, the organisation has grown dramatically into the current *National* Association. But the *Education* tag has also evolved. It stands not only for the formal education sector – schools, colleges and universities – but also for the wider arena of lifelong learning in which writers share their skills with a great variety of people including those suffering or recovering from illness. In 1995 NAWE and the Poetry Society jointly initiated seminars exploring this area, drawing on the pioneering work of some of our members. It was at that same time that Lapidus was born. It is now another vital organisation with which NAWE works in partnership within the *literaturetraining* consortium.

Over the years we have published a range of articles relating to this field in our journal, *Writing in Education*. Notable early contributions came from Pete Morgan, writing about his work at Whittingham Hospital (Morgan 1996); John Killick on his work with Dementia sufferers (Killick 1995); and Dominic McLoughlin on working in a hospice (McLoughlin 1997). Since then there have also been articles from Simon Fletcher, again working in a hospice, this time as a 'Year of the Artist' residency (Fletcher 2002); Gillie Bolton on her work with health care clients (Bolton 1997); Tracy Austin, going so far as to claim that writing is 'a healthier process than psychiatry' (Austin 1998); and Susan Skinner working in a Hospital School with children described as 'out of the running' (Skinner 1998). We have published work by Celia Hunt, who writes on teaching creative writing through autobiography in the second part of this book (Hunt 2000), and by Rose Flint, whose 'Fragile Space: Therapeutic Relationship and the Word' was first published in *Writing in Education 26* and here gains the wider audience it deserves (Flint 2002).

Other articles have related to health care in rather different ways. Writer Liz Holmes reflected on her own experience as a child aged four in Christchurch hospital in Dorset (Holmes 1995). Joan Michelson described how she collaborated with London Radio Network in Whittington Hospital in North London to introduce poetry into the hospital environment (Michelson 2001). This work was funded by the Poetry Society's Poetry Places scheme, as was David Hart's work in Heartlands, in Birmingham, where he – along with Geoffrey Herbert and Charles Johnson – wrote poems in hospital departments. David's work even prompted him to ask whether such new contexts were redefining poetic form (Hart 2000).

However, these are only the obvious examples. So many writers are working in ways which have social significance, or support and 'care' for particular communities – Harriet Kline with adults with learning disabilities (Kline 1996); Leah Thorn in performance poetry workshops on issues relating to the Holocaust (Thorn 1998); Aileen La Tourette with the *Big Issue's* project to help people on the street (La Tourette 1998); Fiona Sampson in a range of health and social care settings (Sampson 1998) – and on a whole host of 'reminiscence' projects (such as Maggie Freeman's in Brentwood (Freeman 1995)). Articles about their work by all these writers (along with several hundred others) are accessible on the NAWE website.

I think it is fair to say that many of these writers have focused as much on difficulties as rewards. The 'pioneering' label means, effectively, that they first went into such work relatively unprepared and unsupported. Writers are naturally resourceful but there is no doubt that working in any educational or community setting requires specific skills over and above literary talent. That was a driving force behind the founding of NAWE.

Without the proper support, writers can fall into the trap of improvising skills as they go along and may take on inappropriate work because, although not adequately prepared, they are keen. Informal peer learning, which we have used effectively for some time through NAWE conferences, is invaluable but not always enough, particularly in such a sensitive area as health care, where the 'art and craft' of writing may sometimes even play a subsidiary role. There are of course general arts therapy courses but it is only very recently that we have started to provide training specifically for writers.

There – I've used both T words: Therapy and Training. Writers are divided in their reactions to both.[1] It is evident that even if we talk about writing *as* therapy, we are describing a huge spectrum of activity and experience. There are those who write because they feel better after doing it: just like getting out to play football. That is a very different matter from writing in order to help cope with recent grief, or with a particular illness. Neither is it always to do with writing about self, a common assumption which sometimes leads to disapproval. People may write as a distressed response to things going on elsewhere in the world. Even if stress – the problem – is within the self, the solution may not be: thinking and writing outwards can be helpful. However, knowing which approach to adopt in particular circumstances requires considerable judgement. That is where things suddenly get difficult, and where the unskilled writer is potentially out of his or her depth.

As a result of those early seminars and the many reflective accounts of writers' first-hand experiences, we now know more about the challenges of working in this field. Equally, we know (as a result of research within our membership) that there is a tremendous amount of interest – both from writers and those who might work with them – in progressing this area. The aim of NAWE's *literaturetraining* consortium is to cater for professional development needs of just these kinds, helping writers to extend the arenas in which they are genuinely well-equipped to work. This tallies with our founding principle: *to promote and develop the educational ideals of writers and to make the benefits of their work available to a wider cross-section of people.* Happily, Professional Development is a new priority within the arts funding system.

'Professional Development' (itself a maligned and misunderstood term) has tended to replace the term 'Training', not least because it is suggestive of a more flexible range of approaches. The personal angle is all-important – just as it is in health-care and with writing itself, but in all three cases I believe the emphasis is on 'selves' rather than 'self'. It is all about letting other people into one's thinking: learning from other experts; working with other people; working with other characters or viewpoints in fiction or poetry.

When he was appointed as writer-in-residence at Whittingham Hospital, Pete Morgan registered an understandable amusement that funding opportunities for writers so often lured them away from their main creative task – writing. Increasingly, however, writers do their own creative work within these social contexts, and are quick to agree that the situations – and the people involved – are inspirational. Pete Morgan himself admits that, prior to his work at Whittingham, he was 'playing safe'. That writers such as Pete and others ever came together to form NAWE is itself a testament to the fact that writers are interested in social ideals as well as in personal gain.

I suspect that writers and their collaborators in Britain are further advanced than those elsewhere. The contributors in this section, therefore – and they include two who are writing on model projects in countries other than Britain – represent in some ways not only the best of what is going on nationally but internationally. For the past few years I have attended the Associated Writing Programs Annual conference in America. It is an astonishing event, offering hundreds of panels, workshops and discussions. Nonetheless, although it does address 'writing in the community', I have not found that the same level of attention to writing in health and social care as exists in Britain. For example, in a session on 'Writing about Disease', the emphasis was interestingly on the poem as diagnostic aid, not therapy. One panellist explained how she points students to work which addresses a particular trauma, rather than encouraging them to write about it themselves. It is always good to encourage reading as much as writing, but that strikes me as the attitude of the 'writer who happens to teach literature' rather than the 'writer in education' as we understand that phrase within NAWE.

Writers are naturally and uniquely equipped to enable people to enter into other stories, other lives, either through their reading or their own writing. Their own professional lives are all to do with creating stories, characters and images through which they reflect on the world; and they are able to help other individuals to use similar skills in reflecting on their own stories and experiences, and perhaps inventing others. Contrary to its image as a solitary, even self-obsessed occupation, writing is a remarkably social art. As David Hart comments, "writing for health" is not just about healing ourselves… If we can think of writing for the health of all of us, then outward gift poems are as important as self-giving ones, publicly shared ones as significant as secret ones' (Hart 2000, p.10).

Note

1   Mark Robinson tackles the first of them in a survey article (Robinson 2000).

References

Austin, T. (1998) 'Creative writing and mental health: A positive partnership.' *Writing in Education 15*, 19–21.

Bolton, G. (1997) 'Buttoned.' *Writing in Education 11*, 10–14.

Fletcher, S. (2002) 'The hospice residency.' *Writing in Education 25*, 12–13.

Flint, R. (2002) 'Fragile space: Therapeutic relationship and the Word.' *Writing in Education 26*, i–viii.

Freeman, M. (1995) 'Writing reminiscences in Brentwood.' *Writing in Education 6*, 6–8.

Hart, D. (2000) 'Public poetry: New forms for new purposes.' *Writing in Education 19*, 10–12.

Holmes, L. (1995) 'Hospital days remembered.' *Writing in Education 7*, 8–9.

Hunt, C. (2000) 'Creative writing and personal development.' *Writing in Education 19*, 7.

Killick, J. (1995) 'Never so near nature: Writing work with dementia sufferers.' *Writing in Education 6*, 4–6.

Kline, H. (1996) 'Mistakes and successes: Writing with adults with learning disabilities.' *Writing in Education 9*, 28–31.

La Tourette, A. (1998) 'Home is where the art is.' *Writing in Education 15*, 21–22.

McLoughlin, D. (1997) 'Teaching writing in a hospice day centre.' *Writing in Education 11*, 7–9.

Michelson, J. (2001) 'The poetry pause: A hospital radio project.' *Writing in Education 22*, 30–31.

Morgan, P. (1996) 'Whittingham hospital: Writer-in-residence.' *Writing in Education 9*, 25–28.

Robinson, M. (2000) 'Conflicting views of writing as therapy.' *Writing in Education 19*, 13–16.

Sampson, F. (1998) 'Transferable skills?' *Writing in Education 16*, 23–28.

Skinner, S. (1998) 'Poetry in the hospital school.' *Writing in Education 15*, 17–19.

Thorn, L. (1998) 'I place my stones.' *Writing in Education 15*, 13–17.

CHAPTER 1

Communicating Existential Issues Through Reading Poetry

A Project in a Swedish Hospice

Inger Eriksson

Introduction

In my country it is rather unusual to use creative writing or creative reading in health care. I began to work with poetry groups because of a woman I once met – I will call her Anna. This happened several years ago when I was working as a deacon and Hospital Chaplain in a town in the south of Sweden. I met Anna at a nursing home. She was 70 years old, suffering from a stroke and unable to find any meaning in life. She asked me to do something for her. I did: we did it together. She, some other patients and I started to meet regularly to share our experiences. Later on we started to read poetry together.

In an interview with the group members and other patients I discovered how common it was for patients at a nursing home not to show such feelings as sadness, anger, fright and even joy.[1] That gave me the idea that we could read poetry together, to express and share our feelings and thoughts. It turned out well. Since then I have been working with poetry groups in nursing homes and at a hospice.[2] In these groups we mostly read and listened to poems and shared experiences. It was just on a few happy occasions that we wrote poems ourselves. I use the word 'happy' because these occasions were indeed joyful; and recently my colleagues and I have started to introduce creative writing to our sessions.

The body of our work, though – as I will discuss in this chapter – has been *reading* poetry with people who are receiving care. Unlike in other models such as Bibliotherapy,[3] however, we did not read poetry as *therapy* but – as part of a pastoral role – in order to find ways to discuss existential issues of life and death.[4]

The project at Lund Hospice

Over the course of more than two years I led a poetry group at the hospice in Lund. This was a research project, part of my PhD thesis in Ethics at the Centre for Theology and Religious Studies at Lund University, and was sponsored by *Cancerfonden*.[5] As it was a research project I had a student taking part as an observer, making records of what was said and what she noticed.

Lund Hospice is small, and beautifully situated outside the hospital. It has the capacity to care for eight in-patients. The staff have been involved in the poetry project and have supported it. Mostly it was they who invited patients[6] to join the poetry group. The group was held in the day care area, on one evening per week between 6.30pm and 7.15pm, sometimes earlier. Sometimes we moved to a patient's bedside when someone wanted to join but could not leave her/his room. It was extremely rare that the group consisted of the same people more than once. Sometimes only one person attended a meeting, but on average three and at times five or six people participated. Occasionally we had to cancel the meeting because all the patients were too ill to take part. Altogether there were 41 meetings.

An information pamphlet gave patients and their relatives a little knowledge about the group, and invited them to participate in a poetry group where it also would be possible to talk about life and death. They were informed that it was a research project as well. I led the group, and the Hospice Chaplain, Anna Karin Lundgren, joined and supported me and the group. She was able to follow up what happened in the sessions.

Existential issues are important when one is confronted with dying but can be difficult to engage with (Rasmussen 1999, Rinell-

Hermansson 1990). One aim of the hospice study is to develop models
for poetry reading and communication on existential issues, for patients
in palliative care and their relatives. In this article I will focus on one particular model that we used in the groups: in fact a model where we read
and listened to poems more than talked. One reason that we developed
this model was that quite often patients told us they wanted to come to
the poetry group but that, because they were so tired, they preferred to
listen not to talk.

One of my guiding principles, or in other words intentions, was to try
to read poems that were *in tune with* the participants. Because of this I did
not decide in advance what to read. Anna Karin and I brought several
poetry books, mainly anthologies which we knew well, into the sessions.
Sometimes I began by asking the group whether they wanted to listen to
a joyful poem or a sad one. I might also suggest an angry poem. In the rest
of this chapter I would like to describe how one particular session of the
poetry group worked and then to reflect upon it. I am particularly interested in the participants' choices and I will ask: What did the participants
express and share through the poems they chose and how did they do this?
How might they have *benefited* from these poems and the poetry group?

The participants

Let me present some of the participants to you. First, a man whom I will
refer to as Frank. He was about 65 years old. He attended five meetings in
the month of March. His wife, Filippa, took part in three of these and his
three brothers came to one, the one I will describe, and his daughter to
one. You will also meet three other patients: Fred, who was in his sixties,
and Febe and Fanny who were both about 80 years old. These patients all
had some form of cancer in the terminal stage.

Some background

Two other sessions when Frank, Filippa, Fred and Febe attended the
group are significant. The first evening Frank came to the group, he and
his wife Filippa were the only participants. They told us at once that they
used to read poems to each other, and started looking in the anthologies
lying on the table. The themes which compelled them became evident
during this first session. Frank favoured love poems. On this occasion he

asked his wife to read a love poem written by Edit Södergran, 'Dagen svalnar' / 'The day cools'. Listening to Filippa reading this beautiful poem made a deep impression on all of us. This is the first stanza:

The day cools towards evening...
Drink warmth from my hand,
my hand has the same blood as the spring.
Take my hand, my white arm,
and take the longing of my slender shoulders...
It would be strange indeed to feel
one single night, one night like this
your heavy head against my breast.

(Södergran 1997, trans. Allwood 1980, p.17)

Filippa wanted to hear 'En visa' / 'A song' by Alf Henrikson (Wallensteen 1996, p.53), a poem written in a humorous style about the shortness of time, a theme to which she would return. Frank did not himself read the poems he chose; he asked either his wife, Anna Karin or me to read them, while Filippa read several of the poems she wanted to hear and to share. In the group Frank never spoke directly about death but indirectly through poems as he did at this occasion. Suddenly he said that he had been thinking of a poem by Nils Ferlin but could not remember the title. After a while he recalled it: 'Inte ens –' / 'Not Even –' and asked Anna Karin to read it:

Not even a little, gray bird that
sings in a flowering tree,
will be found on the other side, and
that seems quite boring to me.

Not even a little, gray bird, and
no white birch with leafy lace –
but it's happened on summer's most beautiful day,
that I've longed to go to that place.

(Ferlin 1984, trans. Fredenholm and Allwood 1986, p.35)

On the second occasion, Frank came without any relatives. Four other patients joined the group, among them Fred and Febe. When I asked whether they wanted to hear a joyful, sad or angry poem, Febe asked for a joyful poem and Fred for an angry one. I read 'När jag är arg' / 'When I am angry', a poem for children by Brita af Geijerstam (Widerberg and Widerberg 1997, p.13). I also read poems by Tage Danielsson, a much loved entertainer and a special poet of humorous and deep poems, who himself died of cancer.

The participants expressed and moved between different feelings. For example, Fred talked about being angry, laughed, and also wept upon hearing 'Höstvisa'/ 'A song by autumn' by Tove Jansson (Schildt 1996, p.94). This beautiful, sad song says: 'Come and comfort me a little, for now I am rather tired and by now so terribly alone.' The refrain, as I have translated it, reads:

Hurry my love, hurry to love,
The days are darkening, minute by minute,
Turn on our lights, it is close to the night,
The flowering summer is soon gone.

(Jansson 1996, trans. Eriksson, p.94)

Febe said, in reference to this poem, that it is important to have memories to think of and live by. In response I read a well-known love poem by Birger Sjöberg 'Den första gång jag såg dig'/ 'The first time I saw you' (Wallensteen 1996, p.91). And Frank said that it was a fine poem.

A description of a Poetry Group

Frank, his wife and his three brothers came to the particular session from which I want to give some glimpses. Febe and Fred came as well. Filippa had brought some poems and Frank's brothers chose poems from our books. We read many poems that evening and it was obvious that we communicated through the poems. The atmosphere was both joyful and serious. The participants seemed eager to share poems that touched them. Many poems were love poems, some were about nature, and some about death.

Frank's eldest brother asked directly for 'Complaint upon the cold weather', an old Swedish poem by Olof von Dalin (Wallensteen 1996, p.24). When I remarked that Frank had asked for this poem as the last one of another session, Frank said that his brother knew him very well. Frank chose a poem about joy and sharing and I got the impression that he was happy to share this moment with his family.

Fred, who had been sitting aside, looking through an anthology of poetry, told us he had found a poem that was about death. He hesitated, as though not sure he could read it. We encouraged him and solemnly he read 'Avsked'/ 'Parting' by Karl Vennberg. In the first stanza there is the line 'Now time is loneliness,' and in the last, 'Now time is wonder' (Vennberg 1993, pp.136–137). Listening to this we fell silent. Then Fred was answered by Febe, who read 'Önskan' / 'Wish' by Karin Boye:

Oh let me live aright,
and rightly die some day,
so that I touch reality
in evil as in good.
And let me be still
and what I see revere.
so that this may be this
and nothing more.

If of all life's long course
a single day were left,
then I would seek the fairest
that lives on earth possess.
The fairest thing there is on earth
is only honesty,
but it alone makes life to life
and to reality.

So is the wide world
a dew-cup's petal here.
and in the bowl there rests
a drop of water clear.
That single still drop

is life's eye-apple, sure.
Oh, make me worthy to look in it!
Oh, make me pure!

                            (Boye 1924, trans. McDuff 1994, pp.76–77)

This was the only time Febe herself read a poem in the group. At Fred's request we read a poem by another Swedish poet about the death of Karin Boye – who committed suicide at the age of 40 – a poem about her disappearance. Later on, after Filippa had read a poem about believing in and caring for oneself, Anna Karin, remembering that Fred had asked for a poem by the very well-known Swedish poet Tomas Tranströmer, read 'Romanska bågar' / 'Romanesque Arches', a poem often read in Sweden:

Inside the huge Romanesque church the tourists jostled in the
                                                        half darkness.

Vault gaped behind vault, no complete view.
A few candle-flames flickered.
An angel with no face embraced me
and whispered through my whole body:

'Don't be ashamed of being human, be proud!
Inside you vault opens behind vault endlessly.
You will never be complete, that's how it's meant to be.'
Blind with tears
I was pushed out on the sun-seething piazza
together with Mr and Mrs Jones, Mr Tanaka and Signora Sabatini
and inside them all vault opened behind vault endlessly.

                            (Tranströmer 1989, trans. Fulton 1997, p.158)

After hearing 'Romanesque Arches' Filippa remembered a song her grandmother sang for her as a child, a song about heaven, and at our request she sang it to us. This was a moment of tenderness. Later on, I again asked whether they wanted to listen to a sad or joyful poem. Febe at once requested a sad one as this was her mood. Anna Karin read 'Det är vackrast när det skymmer' / 'At twilight is the most beautiful' by Pär Lagerkvist. The first line in the second stanza, as I have translated it, reads: 'Everything is tenderness, everything is gently touched by hands.' The last stanza begins, 'Everything is mine, and everything will be taken away from me.' The poem ends, 'I will walk – / alone, without any trace' (Lagerkvist 1996, p.28). The group had become grave. Filippa said that she remembered that at another time we had read a poem by Tage Danielsson. Frank then asked for 'Dumtummen' / 'The Dumbthumb' but said that he did not want to break the atmosphere. He compared this poem and his wish to hear it to a well-known and often requested Swedish song. It was obvious that for him 'The Dumbthumb' had become a special poem.

'The Dumbthumb' by Tage Danielsson (1998, p.499) is impossible to translate into English. No translation can to do justice to the subtle humour, the tenderness, the rhyme and the rhythm. This poem about the thumb says that among the fingers the thumb is the especially dumb one, even foolish. A lot of things that this fat finger cannot do are mentioned – such as pick your nose, dial a number – as is happens when he tries. For example, he points backwards. We are told the thumb can't do anything, not even such a simple task as scratching the writer's own bum. Still he's so pompous. He is fat, short and stuck-up and because of that he prefers to sit by himself away from his mates. The poem ends with the conclusion that we shouldn't lean upon him but we can always suck him.

I read 'The Dumbthumb' and there was a hearty laugh. After one more poem by Tage Danielsson, I asked if anyone wanted to choose the closing poem and Frank chose 'A sad song in spring' by Bo Setterlind, a poem that his wife had brought.

Some other occasions

Before I continue by reflecting on this session I would like to say something more about the other occasions when Frank, Filippa and Febe took part. The next time Frank came to the group it was just him and another patient, Fanny. On this occasion we spoke more. Fanny read a poem about eternity, 'Tidlöst', by Alf Henrikson (Alfons and Henrikson 1991, p.5). She told us a memory from her life and said that she did not like the thought of eternity as a very stagnant place. I said that eternity might be like the first day of a summer holiday and Fanny agreed that it should be a surprise. Frank said nothing about eternity but he turned to

Anna Karin and asked her to read the love poem he had wished his wife to read that first evening they came to the group.

On this occasion Frank and Fanny shared happy memories, such as swimming. They also talked about being ill, of making plans for the summer despite their prognosis. Frank found 'En sommardag'/ 'A summer day', a poem by Erik Lindorm and asked me to read it. Two lines read, as I have translated them: 'It is so great that I am able to walk upon the earth / one more summer, a summer of smell and shine.' (Lindorm 1957, p.17). Fanny told us that this poem expressed exactly what she felt. Another in the same strain, about being allowed to live one more day, was read. Frank said it was a fine poem and Fanny said she looked upon her life like this. At Frank's request, the closing poem this evening was a love poem.

The last time Frank was in the group, shortly before he died, his wife and daughter were with him. Fanny was there as well. Filippa read 'A song', the poem she had asked for on the first occasion, and said that she liked it because it speaks about how everything passes too quickly. Fanny spoke again about her visions of eternity.

Frank suggested just one poem and it was about playing football, 'Dragningen' by Cidden Anderson (Schildt 1996, p.22), a poem he found in one of my anthologies and asked if I would read. We talked for a while – he and Fanny got very involved – about playing football and well--known games. I asked what it was like to score a goal. Frank exclaimed: 'Wow, wow!' His daughter said: 'This is happiness!' She then read 'Lingonben' – a humorous poem – that seemed to be of special significance for her and her father. She asked us – but not the father as he knew – to guess who was the author. Because I recognised the poem I was able to answer Povel Ramel (Widerberg and Widerberg 1997, p.36), who is a Swedish entertainer and poet.

After that, when Fanny asked for a poem by Tage Danielsson, Frank said that his daughter had not heard 'The Dumbthumb'. I read it and the poem raised another hearty laugh. Fanny said it was a pity that Tage Danielsson had died so young, he was only about 55. I asked whether they wanted to hear a joyful or sad poem. Filippa responded that we usually read both. So I read a sad poem by Harriet Löwenhjelm (1988, p.150) 'Am I until deadly tired', a poem that Fanny had asked for once before. She said: 'Sometimes one can feel like that.' Frank felt tired and left with his daughter while Filippa stayed. At the end she read a beautiful poem for us about hands and touching.

After we closed, Filippa told me that she had not thought Frank would have come to the poetry group that evening as he was so tired, but she said: 'He likes it so very much.' She asked for a copy of the poem about playing football for herself and Frank's brothers, as they had once been a football team together.

Febe continued to come to the group. Once, when Anna Karin asked in what mood she wanted us to close, she asked for a hopeful poem. On this occasion we were in her room. Febe was lying in her bed as were two other women. One of them mentioned a very well-known poem by Karin Boye, 'Yes, of course it hurts when buds are breaking.' Yet I choose to read a prayer that our group had received from the wife of a man that had died that week. I still remember this as 'my hesitating moment'.

The last time Febe came, the group consisted of her and Fanny. They had never been in the group together before and this was the last time either of them came. When they arrived they were prepared. They had chosen two poems together, poems in tune with their mood. First was 'Äktenskap', 'The marriage', by Gustaf Hildebrand (Wallensteen 1996, p.55), a poem about sharing everyday life. Fanny read it and said that this was what life was about. At Febe's request, we later read it once more. The other poem was 'Jordevandring' / 'Our walk on earth' by Alf Henrikson. The poem, which Fanny read, begins with 'The first step is difficult to take, / the last one is heavy to walk.' (Henrikson 1997, p.152). They told us that they had chosen 'heavy' poems because life was heavy for them now, and they were very aware of the fact that they would soon die. But Fanny also said: 'One feels joyful about little things.'

Fanny also asked for the football poem Frank had suggested. We mentioned that he was now dead and that was a little unexpected for Fanny. At the end, as I asked for a closing poem, Fanny answered that the poem she had in mind, 'Am I until deadly tired', was not a poem to close with. So I suggested and together we read 'A letter from Lillan', a well-known Swedish song by Evert Taube (Palm, Lundquist and Kleberg 2000, p.484), about a little daughter's longing for her father to come home. It was all very solemn. We could feel that this was the last time that we would all meet.

Reflection

I have said that I will comment briefly on two questions – how did the participants benefit from the poetry group and what did they express and share through the poems? – but these questions are intertwined and it is not self-evident which to look at first.

The fact that participants returned to the group tells us that they did benefit, as do their spontaneously positive but rather general remarks, such as that it was 'fine', 'restful', that they had 'enjoyed themselves' or that it gave 'more than they expected'. It was obvious how many of the participants left the group in a good and happy mood. The staff also often noticed this. To give just one example, as Frank was leaving his first session in his wheelchair, he sang a little tune to himself.

Another outcome of the poetry group was that staff communicated about Fred. Fred came to the group on the two occasions I have mentioned. Soon afterward he died. At a meeting with the staff where Anna Karin and I talked about the groups, we discovered that after the first meeting he had attended, Fred had started to eat in the dining room which he did not want to do before. The staff also expressed relief when they heard that he had asked for an angry poem, as they had felt that he was angry. Our conclusion was that in the poetry group the patients and their relatives experienced a feeling of *solidarity and communion* and that this was one of its benefits.

In the poetry group we expressed and shared existential issues like love, death, time and eternity. In the examples I have given it is evident that we communicated mainly through the poems. This worked either in a metaphorical way or because poems were able to directly name an experience. In both cases, participants could express themselves, their feelings and thoughts through the poems. They recognised their own situation in the poems.

Through some poems the participants became aware of forgotten memories and shared happy memories of things that made life meaning-ful in simple ways, like playing football and swimming. Different feelings such as joy, sadness, loneliness, fatigue and anger – together with the need for comfort and hope – were expressed and shared. This was often done in an indirect way through reading a poem without any comment. Frank's remark that he did not want to break the serious atmosphere, when his wife mentioned the very special humorous poem – coupled with his pledge to read 'The Dumbthumb' – is one such episode with a message. My interpretation of this and similar episodes is that this often requested, humorous poem helped in different ways, not only through arousing laughter but by offering consolation. The poem gives permission to feel the way you do. It tells us about a thumb which, like someone who is very ill, cannot manage ordinary things; and says that it is all right to be angry with him but also to let him comfort you (echoing the way patients may feel towards their relatives).

It was my intention to read poems that were in tune with the participants' moods. I was partly inspired to do this by the isoprinciple (Leedy 1969, 1985; Mazza 1993). According to this principle a patient is helped by a poem that is in tune with his /her own mood and at the end reflects hope. It is an interesting question whether sad and troubled participants wanted to listen to sad or joyful poems. What I found was that this differed from person to person and from time to time. Some people preferred poems which reflected their mood and others wanted to change that mood; but the same person could move between these wishes, as Febe did. Mostly we read a mixture of sad and joyful poems and I found it was important to keep the balance. However, it was obvious that participants preferred the last poem to be joyful, hopeful or uplifting.

When I described how Febe, having listened to Fred reading 'Parting', read 'Wish', I used the word *answered*. Her action was in line with our own intention of reading poems in tune with the participants' feelings. Another example is that, when I read 'The first time I saw you', Febe said that it is important to have, and live by, memories.

If I try to reflect more deeply about these acts and how the poetry group worked in this particular session, one possible interpretation is that it can be compared to a ritual or even a rite. By a rite I mean an act through which the members of a fellowship express and communicate in a symbolic way the emotions and thoughts raised by their existential situation. This formulation is close to Emile Durkheim's theory of the rite developed in his work on the religious life, where he looks at what happens in a group suffering from death and canalising mourning through rites. The essence of the rite is that people come together and express and share feelings in an act (Durkheim 1995). My formulation is also inspired by an approach to ritual discussed by Jörgen Straarup. His description of an alternative interpretation of rite is: 'The experiences are the cause and the rite the effect' (1994, p.21).

To read in turns, to read a poem to each other to express what you might have no words for or a special feeling, is one way to communicate existential issues which experience is generating. A poem gives shelter to and can contain what it evokes, such as strong emotions. The poem can be a place of safety.

To conclude, then: this ritual of reading poems is a good model to use in a group which may include people who are too tired to talk and discuss: for example patients in hospice. But even then, to be touched by a poem tells you that you are still alive. It is a form to rest in. And it gives rest.

Notes

1   This was a pilot interview to test questions about life and meaning. One question was: If at the nursing home, you feel joy, sadess, fright or anger, do you show that? I have written about this interview in an essay in ethics: *Kom närmare se mej- sjukhemspatienter samtalar om livsfrågor och delar existentiella erfarenheter utifrån poesi* (1995), at the Centre for Theology and Religious Studies at Lund University. This essay looks at the first poetry groups I worked with.

2   Some of the poetry groups were part of the research programme 'Arts in Hospital and Care as Culture', sponsored by Stockholm County Council, who published my report *Poesigrupper och livskvalitet på sjukhem* (2000) about poetry groups and quality of life for patients at nursing homes.

3   According to a definition by McCarty Hynes and Hynes-Berry, bibliotherapy has a therapeutic goal: 'Bibliotherapy uses literature to bring about a therapeutic interaction between the participant and facilator' (1986, p.17).

4   Therefore, I have used qualitative rather than quantitative methods for the collection and interpretation of data (Taylor and Bogdan 1998).

5   *Cancerfonden*, SE-101 55 Stockholm. *Cancerfonden* is a Swedish foundation, a non-profit organisation with three important tasks: to promote and co-ordinate cancer research, to inform about cancer and to develop new methods for the care of persons suffering from cancer. The chapter is part of

my disertation, in Swedish, to be published in *Lund Studies in Ethics and Theology.*

6   In Sweden the term 'patient' (it is the same word in the Swedish language), is still widely used and so is unchanged here [Ed].

References

Alfons, H. and Henrikson, M. (eds) (1991) *Glädjen kalender i dikt och bild.* Stockholm: Eva Bonnier.

Allwood, M. (trans.) (1980) 'The day cools.' In *The Collected Poems of Edit Södergran.* Mullsjö, Sweden: Anglo-American Center.

Boye, K. (1994) 'Wish.' In *K. Boye Complete Poems* (trans. D. McDuff). Newcastle upon Tyne: Bloodaxe Books.

Boye, K. (1996) 'Önskan.' From 'Gömda land' (1924) in K. Boye *Dikter.* Stockholm: Albert Bonniers Förlag. (Original work published 1942.)

Danielsson. T. (1998) 'Dumtummen.' From 'Samlade dikter 1967–1967' in *Tage Danielssons Paket.* Stockholm: Wahlström and Widstrand. (Original work published 1984.)

Durkheim, E. (1995) *The Elementary Forms of Religious Life.* New York: The Free Press. (Original work published 1912.)

Eriksson, I. (1995) *Kom närmare se mej – Sjukhemspatienter samtalar om livsfrågor och delar existentiella erfarenheter utifrån poesi.* Lund: Centre for Theology and Religious Studies at Lund University.

Eriksson, I. (2000) *Poesigrupper och livskvalitet på sjukhem – En interventionstudie.* Stockholm: Stockholms Läns Landsting.

Ferlin, N. (1984) 'Inte ens – .' From 'Goggles' (1938) in N. Ferlin *Dikter.* Stockholm: Albert Bonniers Förlag.

Fredenholm, T. and Allwood, M. (trans.) (1986) 'Not even – .' In *With Plenty of Colored Lanterns – Selected poems by N. Ferlin.* Mullsjö, Sweden: Persona Press.

Henrikson, A. (1997) 'Jordevandring.' From 'Aftonkvist' (1966) in *Samlade dikter.* Stockholm: Atlantis.

Hermansson. A.R. (1990) *Det sista året: Omsorg och vård vid livets slut* (Caring in the last year of life). Doctoral dissertation at Uppsala University. Uppsala: Department of Social Medicine and the Centre for Caring Sciences.

Lagerkvist, P. (1996) 'Det är vackrast när det skymmer.' From 'Kaos' (1919) in P. Lagerkvist *Dikter.* Stockholm: Albert Bonniers Förlag. (Original work published 1965.)

Leedy, J.J. (1969) 'Principles of poetry therapy.' In J.J. Leedy (ed.) *Poetry Therapy.* Philadelphia: PA: Lippincott.

Leedy, J.J. (1985) (ed.) *Poetry as Healer: Mending the Troubled Mind.* New York: Vanguard.

Lindorm, E. (1957) 'Sommardag.' From 'Tal till mitt hjärta' (1912) in E. Lindorm *Dikter.* Stockholm: Albert Bonniers Förlag.

Löwenhjelm, H. (1988) 'Är jag intill döden trött.' In *Dikter.* Stockholm: Norstedts. (Original work published 1949.)

Mazza, N. (1993) 'Poetry therapy: Toward a research agenda for the 1990s.' *The Arts in Psychotherapy 20,* 51–59.

McCarty Hynes, A. and Hynes-Berry, M. (1986) *Bibliotherapy: The Interactive Process: A Handbook.* CO and London: Westview Press.

Palm, G., Lundquist, M. and Kleberg, C-J. (eds) (2000) *Den Svenska Högtidsboken.* Stockholm: En bok för alla.

Rasmussen, B.H. (1999) *In Pursuit of a Meaningful Living amidst Dying: Nursing Practice in a Hospice.* (Medical dissertations, New series No 592.) Umeå: Umeå University.

Schildt, M. (ed.) (1996) *Sardinen på tunnelbanan och 199 andra dikter.* Stockholm: Alfabeta.

Straarup, J. (1994) 'Ritens sociala sammanhang.' In O. Wikström (ed.) *Rit, symbol och verklighet. Sex studier om ritens funktion.Tro tanke 1994:6.* Uppsala: Svenska kyrkans forskningsråd.

Södergran, E. (1997) 'Dagen svalnar.' From 'Dikter' (1916) in *Samlade dikter.* Stockholm: Wahlström and Widstrand. (Original work published 1949.)

Taylor, S.J. and Bogdan, R. (1998) *Introduction to Qualitative Research Methods. A Guidebook and Resource.* New York: John Wiley and Sons, Inc. (Original work published 1975.)

Tranströmer, T. (1997) 'Romanesque Arches.' In *New Collected Poems* (trans. R. Fulton). Newcastle upon Tyne: Bloodaxe Books.

Tranströmer, T. (1998) 'Romanska bågar.' From 'För levande och döda' (1989) in *Dikter 1954–1989.* Stockholm: Albert Bonniers Förlag. (Original work published 1989.)

Vennberg, K. (1993) 'Avsked.' From 'Fiskefärd' in *Karl Vennberg dikter 1944–1960.* Stockholm: Albert Bonniers Förlag. (Original work published 1949).

Wallensteen, I. (ed.) (1996) *Dikter att minnas.* Västerås: ICA bokförlag.

Widerberg, G. and Widerberg, S. (eds) (1997) *Barnens versbok.* Stockholm: En bok för alla. (Original work published 1986.)

Further Reading

Ruin, H. (1960) *Poesiens mystik.* Lund: Gleerups. (Original work published 1935.)

Tafdrup, P. (2002) *Över vattnet går jag.* Lund: Ellerströms. (Original work published 1991.)

CHAPTER TWO

'It is Mine! It is Mine!'
Writing and Dementia

John Killick

'How are you?' is a common question when we meet someone. Answers frequently fall into one of two categories: the cryptic – 'alright', 'fine' – or the long-winded, where the respondent embarks upon a catalogue of real (and imaginary?) ailments. One day on a dementia unit I asked this question of someone who replied:

> How am I today?
> Well, generally speaking
> Standing up
> In a sitting-down situation.
> In short, I'm ok. Nobody's
> Kicking my behind.
> Of course, if it's too hard
> It's a matter for the police.
> But if it's
> Only tickle-wickle
> It's alright.
>
> I thought a lot of things
> Would have gone by now.
> But they haven't,
> They cling on.
> I go out and
> I make do, but
> It's difficult to make do.[1]

This brought me up short. One rarely receives such a full and frank answer. But I should have known better. One does not often encounter reticence or dissimulation in people with dementia. If there is a lack of verbal response it may be caused by communication difficulties (Killick and Allan 2001). My interlocutor is giving what may be a fair evaluation of his state of mental health: he is managing better than he expected, but it isn't easy. The degree of insight displayed seems most remarkable.

Over the past ten years I have worked as a writer with hundreds of people with dementia: listening to what they have to say, writing it down, or tape-recording and later transcribing it, sharing the text with the author him- or herself, sometimes with family carers and staff and, with permission, on occasion with the wider world in the form of poems. Predominantly, my experience confirms the psychosocial approach to dementia (Kitwood 1997): that, whatever difficulties they may face, the 'person' is still recognisably present; that communication is a fundamental and rewarding activity; and that how we treat the person is a strong contributing factor in how the dementia presents through them.

I suggest my work appears to confirm that many of the things people with dementia say are not nonsense. They are actually subtle and profound: and we ignore them at our peril if we take diagnosis and treatment seriously. One problem faced by relatives, carers and the wider society is that we are often too blinkered by the medical model of dementia (e.g. World Health Organisation 1992) – indeed of illness in general – to be able to see people as other than a parcel of symptoms to be categorised and prescribed for without any real consultation or consideration.[2] Another is that the language with which we are presented by people with dementia is not necessarily susceptible to logical analysis, being often more emotional and symbolic than rational.

Unusual features of this language have been investigated and described as part of a predominantly biomedical approach to understanding dementia (Miller and Morris 1993). Such a 'deficit approach' assumes that what the person has to communicate is unworthy of consideration (for example that is merely a manifestation of word-finding difficulties or problem with comprehension). But to a writer it is immediately fascinating, for two reasons. First, it often seems 'poetic', in that it frequently makes seamless use of metaphor and simile. There seems to be less inhibition about using language's more imaginative characteristics than adults characteristically display. Second, there is an apparent emotional truthfulness. Many of the statements people with dementia make have an astonishing force and honesty. The two come together in examples like these:

> I can't place the breakdown. I can't place the pickup either.

> The brilliance of my brain has slipped away when I wasn't looking.

> I've been playing in the House of Ages.

> I don't understand a word here that shows the face of the people.

> Is it opening or seizing? The view – it has the ring of expand.[3]

Such statements exhibit economy and directness. At times it is as if the language is being reborn in the crucible of experience, as in this complete poem which combines certainty of content with a halting quality of expression:

Going Down

Do you know,
       I'm going down?
       Yes, really.
              Nothing to ask for now.
One year,
       and a half-year,
              at the most.
My mother's down...
       down that street...
you know,
       whatever they call it.
              But I'll not be going there.
I'll be going
       down there...

down the long…

you know,

into the ground.[4]

Some poems have a more complex structure. In poems transcribed by the professional but made entirely from the words of the person with dementia there may be a temptation to simplify or to complicate. When I start to interact with someone, unless there has been a prior agreement with the person that it will be a transcribed session (in which case I will remind them and check that this arrangement is still acceptable), I will spend the first part (maybe the whole) of a first session getting to know the person, and explaining what would be involved in transcribing if this seems appropriate. We will be comfortably seated in as private a place as is available if transcribing is to occur, although the interaction may begin in a public area.

I will first of all say who I am, what I do, and ask if the person would welcome a conversation. I will obviously ask their name, and how they wish to be addressed, but will then ask as few questions as possible, both not to appear inquisitive, and also so as to avoid as much as possible putting a person challenged by memory loss 'on the spot'. Also, I want as much as possible to encourage the person to feel at ease and to talk naturally. The object of the exercise is for the individual to express what is on his or her mind, whether it is a memory of the past, a concern about the present, or a speculation about the future. When I have written down or taped and later transcribed everything that someone has said – and they clearly lack the capacity to discriminate about what is now on the page – I am faced with that task of revision which is part of any creative process. But here the words are not my own. An unscrupulous writer might be tempted to go for the sensational effect. What is necessary, however, is an attitude of humility in the face of an individual's struggle to communicate what is happening to them during complex and profound changes in their lives. My own practice is, whilst paring away what seems to me to be inessential, to leave what I perceive to be the underlying preoccupation intact; and I often find that the overall shape of the text is dictated by that sense of urgency and emotional logic. I read through the whole transcript two or three times, seeing if any themes pre-dominate. I also look at passages where the language may be particularly charged or vivid. I am also on the lookout for underlying rhythms: on the basis of these I will make a decision as to whether the finished piece is prose or verse. The majority of edited passages (80–90%) will be prose, though many pieces will contain the occasional phrase or sentence of a metaphorical nature. Having once decided a theme and a form for a passage I will be editing to maximise the potential of the transcript in accordance with these criteria. A rule I have set myself and never broken is not to add a word to the original but only to make use of exactly what is given by the person.

In the following poem the author makes three attempts to break away from his meditations, only to keep returning to them. He is poised between stasis and movement, and so is the poem:

Up and Away

Sometimes you can see where
The smoke blows right across
From the factories. Beautiful trees.
Apple blossom. It's a favourite place
Of mine – wouldn't it be of yours?

Well I'll have to be off now –
Temporary circumstances.

When it's stormy there
We used to nip over.
All the apples got blown off.
That's where most of them lie.
Over the terrace and over the garden.

Well I'll be on my road
Or they'll be getting the guns out.

Sometimes I think about running away.
Right up through the meadow
To the cliff. It's reasonably steep.
Always keep myself trim.
There's no change in this place.

Well I'm still on a tether
So I'll have to be getting back.[5]

The question why some people with dementia show a propensity, in their language use, to express themselves creatively is not easy to answer. Perhaps not enough is yet known about brain functions when normal patterns of activity are disturbed. The neurologist Oliver Sacks makes a general point about human creativity in these circumstances:

> In Korsakov's, or dementia, or other such catastrophes, however great the organic damage and Humean dissolution, there remains the undiminished possibility of reintegration by art, by communion, by touching the human spirit: and this can be preserved in what seems at first a hopeless state of neurological devastation. (Sacks 1984, pp.37–38)

This suggests certain aspects of language may be susceptible to exploitation even where its more logical uses have been impeded. In this context it may be useful to draw an analogy between children and people with dementia (though only in this context, because people with a whole lifetime of experience behind them should not otherwise be compared with those just setting out on their life journeys). A fresh approach to words, their sounds, and the suggestive possibilities offered by them, is being demonstrated. Perhaps creativity is curtailed by the systematic demands imposed on the growing mind; perhaps it is corralled into playground rhymes and classes in literary appreciation, and gradually fades away in most adults (Aitchison 1994). Nonetheless, the potential must still be there, under the conscious mind's lock and key: for dementia seems to disarm the gaoler and let oblique and lateral forms of thought slip out once more.

All the work I have done with people with dementia over the years has been one-to-one. This seems to me to be essential: not only is every person different in terms of personal characteristics and life history; but the illnesses which make up the dementia family affect each one uniquely and they display individual language features which must be respected and embodied in the resulting writing. Very few of those I have worked with have retained the physical ability to write. That may be because my experience has been in nursing homes, to which people usually come after a period of years of coping in their own homes.

However, there is an important job of work to be done with the newly diagnosed, with people coming to terms with what dementia means for them, and its consequences for their memories of their past lives. One rare example of someone in this group is the American Cary Smith Henderson, who has published a remarkable journal entitled *Partial View*. Over a period of some nine months he tape-recorded his thoughts, which were edited by his daughter, wife, and a photographer who also contributed to the book. In this extract he is reflecting on the continuing human meaning of his life with dementia:

> I've been thinking about myself. Some time back, we used to be, I hesitate to say the word 'human beings'. We worked, we made money, we had kids and a lot of things we did not like to do and a lot of things we enjoyed. We were part of the economy. We had clubs that we went to... I was a busy little bee. I was into all sorts of things, things that had to do with charities, or things that had to do with music. Just a lot of things I did back when I was, I was about to say – alive – that may be an exaggeration, but I must say this really is, it's living, it's living halfway.
>
> But one thing is for sure. You never can be, never will be, what you once were, and that's hard to swallow. It certainly was for me. I was very busy in all sorts of things when I was alive, you might say. Then, just gradually, these things became impossible. So we must factor that in, I suppose, something that's going to be with us forever, as long as we live at least. It's either that or die, and dying is something that you have to plan for and want very much. I'm not that much into dying right now – yet. (Henderson 1998, p.35)

It is difficult to overestimate the significance, for the individual coping with all the mysterious and frightening changes that dementia brings, of being able to clarify in this way what is being thrown at them. Only a handful of the hundreds of people I have worked with have been able to act as their own scribes, but I would like to think that a similarly useful process is taking place when I write down (or tape-record and subsequently transcribe) what people say.

Sharing their own words with these authors afterwards is an essential part of the proceedings. There is always a complete text as a record of the transaction that has taken place, which I keep on file. However, where it seems appropriate (and permission has been obtained) I have edited out my own contributions, which are usually confined to word of encouragement, and turned the pieces into monologues or occasionally poems. Only a handful of people have appeared to retain the capacity to see the possibilities inherent in the texts handed back to them. The critical faculty necessary for selection seems to be absent. So I am exercising this on the authors' behalf. This is no different in kind from the shaping process one undertakes with one's own early drafts of a poem, except that one must employ empathy and a sense of responsibility in carrying it out.[6] In one sense it is more challenging than teasing one's own insights into shape, because one is engaging with the sensibility of another person. In another sense one can be more ruthless because objectivity is easier to achieve, and one does not have to combat the demands of the ego. In this respect it is closer to the work of a literary editor. The resulting text can be shared with the author themselves, relatives, staff, even a wider public. The degree of dissemination that goes on depends upon consultations with the person and those closest to them. If there is any serious doubt that permission has been granted, then confidentiality must be respected.

Even those of my subjects who can write down their own words usually seem to lack understanding of how to pare away redundancies until their language serves a common and concise purpose. One woman kept up a constant activity of writing down her thoughts and feelings. When invited to examine her texts, however, she showed little interest, preferring to concentrate on producing new material. I extracted the following poem from a much longer piece:

The Spider's Eyes

Nae baby born has a name.
The midwife can ca' her oniethin'.
Ma claes 'r stitched on wi' tabs 'n red letters.

Ma godfather took a job drivin' a lorry.
It wis fu' o' barrels; they wis empty,
So he threw 'em i' the harbour.

Ma brither, he was troublit.
They sawed aff his feet frae the ankles,
'n ma sister blackleaded the soles.

The parson put his hat on his heid.
The brim 'n the croon separated.
He didna pick it up.

I couldna spin a web.
There's nae hairm in me.
But the spider's eyes see everythin'.[7]

When she received a copy of this poem the author's instructions were precise: 'Publish it!' During a subsequent conversation I ventured the suggestion that I too was a writer. 'No you're not', she snapped. 'You're my editor!' Many comments suggest a similar understanding of what I am about: 'That man who's doing what you're doing could be onto something big', said one man. Another commented, 'This writing it down, it's got a bit of merit. It's tantamount to saying you're speaking from your memory all the while.' A woman said, 'You're snip, snip, snip, picking up the bits that fall from the lips. Don't be leaving them around!' (Killick and Allan 2001, p.201).

For the writer, to have something to write down would seem a reasonable objective. Yet nothing can be guaranteed in work with people with dementia. I have had to learn a new vocabulary of communication in order to interact with individuals, and much of this is non-verbal (Killick and Allan 2001). Establishing contact with someone with dementia, using whatever means, empowers them. It is also extremely satisfying and makes up for all the occasions when one fails. This is a demanding activity, and it is important to build in personal and professional safeguards (Killick 1999). The work takes a high degree of motivation and perseverance. Many people with dementia seem to experience a barrier within themselves that work with writing may help them to overcome. This is a fluctuating condition, however, so the writer may have to wait for the right moment. Then, suddenly an individual may 'open up' and say the most profound things. As Michael Ignatieff states in his novel *Scar*

Tissue when we are stripped down to our core by illness, we are still beings of words, who send messages from the depths of sickness.

Here is someone speaking in just such a moment, and using metaphor to deliver her message:

> I have a problem:
> I have a house on either side of the road,
> But I only have a room in one of them.
> How do I cross the busy road?
> And what happens if I break down in the middle?[8]

She is surely articulating more than a literal truth, and when she goes on to speak of a further problem as a 'stain' on her skirt (one that no-one else can see), we shouldn't take that literally either. The woman in a nursing home who speaks of 'the monkey puzzle' helps us to interpret her metaphor by identifying the puzzle as 'this place' and a major part of her problem as being with the staff, when she wonders 'how to cope with the monkeys'.

In the following short transcript of a conversation between a woman with dementia and her daughter (italicised), the mother speaks first:

> I was looking at the wall for ages
> Then I realised
> That there was an encyclopaedia hanging on it.
> *An encyclopaedia? Hanging on the wall?*
> Yes.
> *The huge book? Hanging on the wall?*
> Yes.
> So I said to myself
> 'Well – that's doing no good hanging up there' –
> So I went over and took it down,
> And hung it up inside my head
> And you've no idea the difference it's made.
> *What kind of difference?*
> Well, I'm learning all kinds of things that I didn't know before.
> *Like what? Can you tell me something?*
> The acid and passive.

Do you mean the active and passive?
Well, you could say active but I don't want to.
Why?
Acid is stronger – it takes the surface off.
Is that important?
Yes, very.
Why?
Because then you can see what lies beneath.[9]

The concepts 'encyclopaedia' and 'acid' are clearly being used here in a symbolic sense, and the mother is exploring the nature of the dementia she is trying to come to terms with in the only way she is able: by bypassing logical processes in favour of her experiential truth. The daughter gives her own perspective on this conversation as follows:

My mother encouraged me to look beyond the surface of things, and to live from my deepest self. My questions in [the conversation] are to draw out of her what she was meaning to communicate to me. In terms of her dementia, it was often my experience that without such questions she would 'stop' as if losing momentum and then would 'start up' again immediately following on from a question – when she could hear in my voice that what she was saying was very important to me and I wanted to understand. I was learning so much from her about how to listen and how to live. (Killick and Allan 2001, p.136)

The idea of 'learning from' a person with dementia is unfortunately rarely encountered. Unless staff in institutions are sensitive to the unusual language processes adopted by their clients they may completely miss the meaning of what they see and hear.

One woman was singing quietly to herself from morning to night and staff pronounced her 'happy' and 'contented'. When I transcribed the words she sang, however, this is what I found:

Song

I don't know what to do
I want to go home
I can sit here but
I don't seem happy any more
I don't know what to do
I want to but
I can't any more
I want to lay
I don't know when it'll be
I want it so let me have it
Don't make it so hard for me
O World, I don't know what to do
I want to see my sunset
I want it as it was promised
I'm waiting for the hour
I want to see my sunset good.[10]

This woman was communicating with herself, confronting death in her lyric, and her anguish had gone unnoticed. On another occasion I heard a mother haranguing her son for regaling her with an endless recital of the trivia of her life. She sent him packing with the shouted words: 'The truth is mine not yours!' and 'All I'm interested in is my life's going!'

Many people with dementia are close to the end of their lives. It is natural for people approaching death to try and make sense of all their experience up to the present. Why should it be any different for this group of individuals?

I would like to suggest that the process of interiorisation many people with dementia practice is worthy of greater recognition. It seems that the condition can drive individuals inwards, causing them to put more emphasis on their present memories and the continuity of the inner self. One woman I met was extremely forthcoming on the first occasion. The resulting poem is a resumé of her life in terms of meaningful relationships and occasions:

There have been other loves
But none like that of my mother.
She had birds that came onto her hand,
Pecked and flew away.

What a wonderful time! –
We were brought up that way.
She was very particular
How and where. I shall not forget.
She would make little noises
And then pull it in –
The string of human kindness…

… My father was a man that spent
His life with all that was spread.
He was a beautiful man.
I looked up to him.
He would walk a mile
To rescue one little chick
He thought was on bad legs.

If anyone came to the gates
He would get hold of their head
And shake it from side to side
And tell them not to come again.

But at the end of her monologue she says:

Twice and twice over
What I think is important.
My hiding place now is one
That I can stretch out to
And run away to for a while.[11]

On the second occasion we met I gave her the poem text which she approved, but her mood had clearly changed in relation to a further interaction. She said:

I don't mind you writing it down –
I can always alter it...

Who are you? A gentleman?
No, go and look for one!

I lived on a farm. I still do.
It is higher up than this.
I'd take you there.
But I wouldn't want to take you there
To start with. *It is mine! It is mine!*

Between you and me, you know,
It's a battle of wills.
Why don't you just lose first![12]

That emphasis on her ownership of her own experience seems crucial. It is as if she regrets her expansiveness on the first occasion and wishes to withdraw it. She is asserting herself and the singularity of her own personhood.

We have to remember, in our zeal to go out to meet people with dementia more than halfway and accommodate their interactional difficulties, that we must also avoid trampling on their right to privacy and confidentiality. Communication with such individuals may have the weight of a moral imperative but it carries with it commensurate responsibilities.

I am very conscious that so far in this chapter I have only been considering writing with people with dementia themselves. That is because all my experience has been in that area. However, there is a whole world of potential personal writing relating to the condition which is not covered by this practice, and which, so far as I am aware, has been almost entirely neglected. Writing by carers may also be a form of release, an attempt to make sense of the frequently bewildering and frustrating experiences they are going through. At its least literary this can be an outpouring of little interest to anyone except, perhaps, others in the same situation, who may recognise their own predicament in it. At its best, however, it can be a sharing and transforming instrument, capable of interpreting a condition which is mysterious to us all. Duncan Tolmie is the son of someone with dementia and he is writing a journal/book about how he and the rest of his family are coping. His main emphasis, however, is on his mother's experience. Here is the opening of his chapter on a case conference:

> The table is round, of heavy blonde oak, and feels expansive under my fingertips. There are six of us gathered around it: six relative strangers who share varying degrees of familiarity, and varying degrees of a common goal. Each of us has met, on and off, at different times and in different places; all of us purporting to be in pursuit of 'the best thing for Susan'. Now we have been forced into this: an ugly hour of stark officialdom; all of us together, all at once, about to discuss my mother's long-term future. I regard it as a defining moment. Because, today, as we sit round the heavy, blonde oak table, three lives will be changed forever, with far-reaching consequences.
>
> Only, there is no table; nowhere to lay our pads, our pens. Our cards. That table exists only in my mind, solid and steadfast like memories of my mother before dementia took its toll. There should have been a table; a table to add dignity to the proceedings, a table to stamp them with formality, with respect. My mother deserves no less. Because, sitting outside the Social Work Department in my rain-battered car, putting our lives in perspective, putting off the inevitable, that's how I imagined it would be.[13]

In conclusion, I would like to predict that we are likely to see more accounts of dementia of literary quality by carers. A recent non-fiction account of her father's Alzheimer's by Susan Miller (Miller 2003) is a case in point. The author brings all the skills of a professional novelist to the task and the result is highly readable.

We are also likely to see ambitious projects by people with dementia themselves, particularly those in a younger age group and with an early diagnosis. *Losing My Mind: An Intimate Look at Life with Alzheimer's* by Thomas deBaggio is far and away the most sophisticated attempt so far to 'tell it like it is'. The author keeps three narratives going: early childhood memories, the course of his diagnosis and treatment, and the results of his medical reading, and he interweaves them regularly and dramatically 'to illustrate the memory's many faults and strengths' (deBaggio 2002, p.xi).

This could only have been brought off by someone largely in possession of his cognitive abilities.

Nevertheless, the challenge for writers who would help to unlock those with the condition to enable them to express their hopes, fears and confusions is to work with those at a later stage of dementia than deBaggio's. This is difficult and stressful work, but immensely rewarding. Dementia is one of the most baffling conditions known to humankind, and to be a part, however small, of pushing the boundaries of knowledge forward, and assisting individuals to a greater clarity of perception in the process, is a calling and a privilege.

Notes

1   Previously published in Benson and Killick (2003), pages unnumbered.

2   An example is given by Julie Goyder (Goyder 2002). The author, who is working as a care assistant, bathes a man who is protesting that he has already been bathed, only to find afterwards that his story is true. Her colleagues, however, dismiss the incident claiming that anyway 'he doesn't know what day it is'.

3   Examples from my own work with individuals with dementia.

4   Previously published in Benson and Killick (2003), pages unnumbered.

5   Previously published in Benson and Killick (2002), pages unnumbered.

6   See the chapter 'Developing pieces of work' in Schneider and Killick (2002) for examples of redrafting.

7   Previously published in Benson and Killick (2002).

8   Previously published in Killick (1997).

9   Previously published in McKinlay (1998), pages unnumbered.

10   Previously published in Benson and Killick (2002).

11   Previously published in Killick (1997).

12   Previously published in Killick and Cordonnier (2000).

13   Unpublished manuscript.

References

Aitchison, J. (1994) *Words in the Mind.* Oxford: Blackwell.

Benson, S. and Killick, J. (eds) (2002) *Creativity in Dementia Calendar 2003.* London: Hawker Publications.

Benson, S. and Killick, J. (eds) (2003) *Creativity in Dementia Calendar 2004.* London: Hawker Publications.

deBaggio, T. (2002) *Losing My Mind: An Intimate Look at Life with Alzheimer's.* New York: Touchstone Books.

Goyder, J. (2002) *We'll be Married in Fremantle.* Fremantle: Fremantle Arts Press.

Henderson, C.S. (1998) *Partial View: An Alzheimer's Journal.* Dallas, TX: Southern Methodist University Press.

Ignatieff, M. (1993) *Scar Tissue.* London: Vintage.

Killick, J. (1997) *You Are Words.* London: Hawker Publications.

Killick, J. (1999) 'Pathways through pain: A cautionary tale.' *Journal of Dementia Care 17*, 1, 22–24.

Killick, J. and Allan, K. (2001) *Communication and the Care of People with Dementia.* Buckingham: Open University Press.

Killick, J. and Cordonnier, C. (2000) *Openings.* London: Hawker Publications.

Kitwood, T. (1997) *Dementia Reconsidered: The Person Comes First.* Buckingham: Open University Press.

McKinlay, A. (1998) *inner→out: a journey with dementia.* Rothesay: Charcoal Press. (Pages unnumbered.)

Miller, S. (2003) *The Story of My Father.* New York: Knopf.

Miller, E. and Morris, R. (1993) *The Psychology of Dementia.* New York: John Wiley.

Sacks, O. (1984) *The Man Who Mistook His Wife For a Hat.* London: Picador.

Schneider, M. and Killick, J. (2002) *Writing for Self-Discovery.* London: Vega.

World Health Organisation (2002) *The ICD-10 Classification of Mental and Behavioural Disorders: Clinical Description and Diagnostic Guidelines.* Geneva: World Health Organisation.

CHAPTER THREE

Mission Impossible

Storymaking with Young People Attending Integrated Clubs in Macedonia

Aleksandar Prokopiev

This chapter will look at some uses of storymaking and writing in conflict resolution, ethnic integration and integrated work with disabled and able-bodied young people. It will look in particular at a project called Mission Impossible, which provided integrated activities for young people from a range of ethnic groups, both with and without disabilities, as well as offering education and outreach youth work on these issues. Mission Impossible formed part of a project, called Alternatives for Children in Public Institutions in the Republic of Macedonia, funded by the Humanitarian Aid Office of the European Commission (ECHO) and implemented by UNICEF with the Macedonian Ministry of Labour and Social Policy.

Contemporary Macedonia is a small country with a population of 1.5 million, which shares its borders with Albania, Kosovo, Serbia, Bulgaria and Greece. It is the southernmost country of the former Yugoslavia and is ethnically mixed, as were all the Balkan countries. The main population groups are ethnic Albanians and the Slav ethnic Macedonians; there are also Armenian and Jewish communities. The main religions are Eastern Orthodox Christianity and Islam. Along with the rest of former Yugoslavia, of which it was then a part, Macedonia shed its communist regime in

1990. It became an independent Republic in 1992 and continued to experience ethnic conflict until 2002.

Health and social care in the country has consequently undergone rapid transition and radical upheaval in just over a dozen years. However, Macedonia is a country with strong literary traditions. Contemporary literary writing has sell-out print runs and achieves a high media profile; writers are public figures who contribute to contemporary debate about social issues. Although creative writing workshops do not flourish to the extent that they do in Britain, there are a large number of aspiring and published writers in Macedonia and writing is therefore an attractive choice for public-access health and social care projects and for work with young people.

It will be a difficult and long-term project to encourage integration in Macedonian society, because the war which came to an effective end in 2002 became in practice a conflict between two ethnic groups, Albanian and ethnic Macedonian. Only a small section of each of these populations was involved in the war itself, but the entire situation was a scenario well known throughout the world: you have two sides and each creates an extraordinary range of propaganda about the other. All opportunities for actual knowledge or communication are closed down. Luckily the war in Macedonia was quite short: but even in this time there were many victims of this propaganda as well as in the conflict itself. Perhaps the most significant victim was that ethnic diversity which is very characteristic of my country: mixed-race families, friendship and love between young people. The integration process which we must undertake as a legacy of this conflict is now much more painful than it has been even in Bosnia or Serbia. At its most intense and certainly at a local level it still includes conflict-resolution work.[1] This requires a lot of commitment and effort, and the initiative is mainly being taken by young adults and young people of school age. For example, young people have been involved in large-scale projects using creative activities – including video work, creative writing, cartoons and billboards – to work together and explore these issues.

Many of these difficult initiatives have been led by international organisations – including UNICEF, UNESCO and ECHO – but most of the work itself is now being carried out by Macedonian citizens, especially younger people. One initiative which has proved very successful has been the foundation of the Babylon Centres for young people in all the main cities of Macedonia, starting with Veles, Delcevo, Manasitrec, Prilep and Tetovo.[2] There are more than ten of these ethnically integrated centres and they are open daily, providing education and other opportunities full time to young people with and without learning difficulties. Initially they were helped by international organisations,[3] but now they are independent and self-financing. They have been such a sigificant and positive development in part because many of our best-known artists – writers, photographers, painters and so on – are happy to be part of the teams working there. They develop scripts, model scenarios and other projects with the young people using the centres; these project outcomes in turn serve as a form of social and health education for the wider community.

This way of working is new to writers and artists in Macedonia, but the professional community has shown itself very interested in the work. A number of other high-profile writers, for example, have become involved in collaborative community work in health and social care and there is no evidence to suggest this is merely the result of curiosity rather than genuine interest and commitment. Perhaps Macedonia's relatively small size and recent history make it more likely that the best of our arts professionals will want to get involved in all sorts of ways in the reconstruction of a modern civil society in our country.

There are also some projects which are not at first sight specifically ethnically integrated but which help with the process of integration because every young person, from whatever ethnic group, takes his or her own part in them. They work *together* on a particular issue. These are youth and health education projects working to combat drug and alcohol abuse, smoking and, in one especially successful project, AIDS. AIDS has become widespread in the Balkans in the past ten years but, because of this preventative work, in Macedonia we have a proportionately small number of patients compared to other countries in the region, including Greece. These health prevention initiatives worked so well because they were presented across the range of media and because they involved the young people in their production.

The Babylon Centres were set up jointly by non-governmental organisations (NGOs) in partnership with the Macedonian Ministry of

Labour and Social Policy. They provide integrated care and activities for young people with and without learning difficulties. They also support the ethnic integration of young people, because those attending these centres are from the range of ethnic groups. Although there can be no positive *selection* of young people from these different groups for what is, after all, essential health and social care provision, attendance by members of all groups is positively *encouraged*. For example, Mission Impossible was one of the Babylon Centres projects which enabled and promoted this work of integration.

Mission Impossible got its name because it had at its heart the idea of encouraging young people to explore the *strange world* of difference. Young people were encouraged not to think of differences in motor ability or cultural and linguistic differences as marks of inferiority, but instead to imaginatively 'visit' the worlds of each others' experiences. One way to do this was to imagine a world so different from earth that the visiting child would experience physical and cultural challenges which illustrated how any particular way of being is not automatically 'better': for example, a soundless world in which speech is rendered useless, or one whose inhabitants live like flies on sheer vertical surfaces. Difference, in this project, was pictured as something to be explored; and diversity as an adventure. The title, Mission Impossible, also suggested the team-work of a group of astronauts exploring the universe *together*; and it was a lively, contemporary name – without regional cultural references – which could equally be culturally welcoming to all the young people taking part in the project.

One of the key elements of Mission Impossible was Bate.[4] Bate, whose name means 'older brother', is primarily an animated figure. He is a baggy, oversize, yellow character, a little like an amorphous bear. As well as sessions in the centres themselves, there were a large number of live public events where Bate gestured, moved about and spoke with the young people watching him on a full-size screen. He was 'driven' from a remote 'cabin' where I was manipulating him in real time to interact with the audience. At these events the children speak to Bate; and at the same time another Bate – an actor in a Bate costume – works elsewhere – for example, in another part of the city, with improvised street performances and interventions. The screen is usually set up in the city centre and many children are attracted to these performances. It is very good publicity for the Babylon Centres; it also provides wider knowledge and education about the principles of integration. Bate's key message is that: 'Children are the same, even when they're different.'

Although the Bate animations also take place in the Babylon Centres themselves – where they may be working with pre-lingual children and young people so that the interactions between audience and screen are non-verbal though vivid: they include gesture and sound, working with imitation and repetition, for example – these public performances in the cities were a kind of open invitation to all young people. The project's objective was to bring children together in the clubs: disabled and able-bodied alike. In this the Bate animations were particularly successful.

Integration initiatives become necessary where groups are being excluded from mainstream society, or have established parallel but isolated communities within that society. I would argue that the position of disabled people in Macedonian society has only begun to change substantially in the last ten years. It is a development which has come about for three main reasons: first of all, because of the work of NGOs, who bring new cultures as well as resources into the Macedonian context;[5] second, because the parents of disabled children have begun to join together and form support and lobbying organisations; and, third, because of improved communications between local communities, local government and NGOs working together. Now the Babylon Clubs are open it is easier for children with disabilities to integrate with their peers and not be isolated, as they were before, in special schools or institutes often far from home. For a traditional society like Macedonia – and maybe this is true of all the Balkan states – this is a very big step, because having a disabled child had always been something to be kept very secret.

Aldo Biondi, the Head of Office of ECHO, Skopje, writes that the Mission Impossible initiative 'is a reminder of the duties of every local community to provide persons with disability with the possibility of accessing all services, helping them enjoy their lives, as all citizens in all communities should be able to do' (Prokopiev 2002, p.5). A social mobilisation campaign was promoted in the towns where the first centres opened, with the aim of creating a positive environment around these new initiatives. Thousands of leaflets were distributed to children and adults in the schools and on the streets of the cities where the centres were opening. Debora Comini, Head of Office of UNICEF in Skopje, quotes from Article 23 of the Convention on the Rights of Children when she says that

> We would like to enter all schools and homes, and remind everyone that all children should enjoy a full and happy life, in conditions which ensure dignity, promote self-reliance and facilitate the child's active participation in the community, regardless of their individual abilities. (Prokopiev 2002, p.5)

Disabled children now have access to good occupational clubs staffed by trained specialists – including child psychoanalysts, paediatricians and care workers – as well as many volunteers. In other words, they receive both health and social care at the Babylon Centres. This is another way in which this provision is integrated. It allows the whole of the young person, with the whole range of their potentials and special needs, to be addressed. There are no longer 'gaps' in provision through which the young person and their individual contribution can fall; nor are there parts of this provision which still force them, as before, to travel long distances or be isolated from friends and neighbours.

This provision continues to develop. There is now much better inter-action with the schoolchildren who also come and participate in the work of these clubs. There have also been many small but very important supplementary improvements in provision, such as the provision of special buses for children attending the clubs. It is a shame, however, that, although social care is much better than before, because Macedonia is very poor and has so little money for any activity which is not an immediate national economic or existential necessity, such centres do not receive much government finance for this important social provision. They are forced to turn to other sources of funding, looking for support through international organisations. The Macedonian branch of the International Red Cross do very good work in this area, as do UNICEF. However, local councils are also beginning to realise the need to make a real contribution to these initiatives, which are necessities for a modern civil society.

The disabled young people do not only attend the Babylon Centres for training, but also for day care. They communicate, they interact socially and they spend leisure time there. There are also other clubs which are not Babylon Centres, but are run on the same model. For example in Bitolj, a city in the south of Macedonia, there is an integrated club which is run in an exceptionally beautiful house. There are also numerous initiatives in other cities which are further away from the capital Skopje: attractive buildings sympathetically and appropriately converted, they provide day care in a warm human-scale environment. Care provision is usually eight or ten hours a day, at the end of which the young people return home. There are now clubs for primary-aged children, for teenagers and for adults too; and provision is not only for young people with learning difficulties but for those with other special needs including physical disability.

The public Bate performances took place over a couple of months in 2001. They were held in more than ten cities, and generated wide media coverage. One of the outcomes of this work was a book of stories and pictures by young people. Called *Alone in Space*, it collected together the best 64 out of a total of 600 pieces entered into a competition for primary-aged children (Prokopiev 2002). The participants were asked to imagine themselves being alone in space and to describe their feelings and experiences. Their starting point was a story I wrote with the team's animateur.

When children step onto their path in life some face more constraints than others. They discover and research the new path using the skills and the means available to them. Some walk faster, some more slowly, some find it difficult to walk at all: and all walk with a different style. We searched for an interesting approach in presenting the diversity of life's paths to the young people taking part in this competition. We wrote a story about a child's journey to a faraway planet, named Calon, which presents an unfamiliar environment where the young earthling faces physical and emotional challenges with such familiar and fundamental tasks as walking, communicating and understanding. The story ends where the child arrives and meets the friendly inhabitants of Calon: at which point the children are asked to continue the story. What does it feel like to be in a completely new and alien environment? What is behind the imaginary journey to a mysterious planet where the body and the spirit of the traveller do not perform well while adapting to changes in circumstance?

Dreamy and imaginative works from the young people reflect how they were truly able to relax and enjoy the creative and reflective process without linking it to any immediate social problem faced in their daily lives. With kings and queens, demons and machines, through towering cities and wild countryside, innumerable paths were followed, but they all shared one common notion: the fragility of the human being when facing new and unexplored terrain.

The most common problem that the traveller faced in the stories was communication. All the stories discovered ways to overcome the communication gap between the newly arrived child and the Calons. As one child stated, 'good will can overcome differences'. Some of the inspired solutions children offered include a machine that translates all languages immediately, picture-messages drawn in the sand, a new sign language or even quick lessons in the language of the Calon. Another common theme was the amount of time it would take the traveller to adapt to and understand the new world. His or her senses are overwhelmed and confused. In some stories it takes just two days to adjust but in others the time required is 50 years. Although analogies with the experiences of people with physical disabilities were mentioned in a few stories, the effort that children made to find a solution to establish contact with someone who is different was accomplished in a spirit of a fantasy about a faraway planet.

With the publication of this book, the young authors and artists as well as other members of their communities were able to discover that their stories were actually about accepting the children right next to them in all their diversity. In *Alone in Space* it is in fact the Calons who are the norm in their environment; and the traveller-explorer of the unknown is the child who attempts to communicate and be with others despite challenges and differences. We hope that the young people who took part in this project left the distant planet of Calon enriched with a new understanding of something that can be used in the here and now: the importance of reaching out to other children and transcending barriers using creative bridges built with compassion.

Notes

1   As I write this, in late 2003, Skopje and other parts of Macedonia still experience occasional acts of terrorism.

2   Tetovo, for example, was the scene of the fierce fighting of the Tetovo Offensive.

3   As well as the Macedonian Ministry of Health, ECHO and UNICEF were involved in setting up the centres.

4   Pronounced 'Batu'.

5   I have explored the mixed impact of NGO culture on Macedonian society elsewhere (Prokopiev 2001).

References

Prokopiev, A. (2001) 'Close strangers *contra* strangers to each other.' In J. Sujecka (ed.) *The National Idea as a Research Problem*. Warsaw: SOW.

Prokopiev, A. (ed.) (2002) *Alone in Space*. Skopje: ECHO, UNICEF, Republic of Macedonia Ministry of Labour and Social Policy.

Further reading

Farhi, M. (2002) *Children of the Rainbow*. London: Saqi Books.

Prokopiev, A. (2003) *The Man With Four Watches*. Belgrade: Geopoetika.

CHAPTER FOUR

Writing as Therapeutic Practice

Students, Teachers, Writers

Maureen Freely

I teach on a writing programme at the University of Warwick that is expanding rapidly. My colleagues and I combine our work there with many other jobs and commitments, and in Spring every year we decide that we haven't got the balance right. So we sit down to work out how to make our lives run more smoothly in the year to come. After we've spelled out all the demands on our time, we draw up a new list of priorities. This year, because we've all been working to the point of exhaustion, health was at the top of the list. But so was writing. We all had books we were desperate to finish. Books we *had* to finish. In the end, one of my colleagues suggested that it was impossible to put one of them first and the other second. Writing and health were one and the same thing.

For my colleague, I think they are. At least they are at this stage in his life. They are for me right now, too. But this hasn't always been the case. Writing has often restored me to health and kept me sane. But it can and it has driven me to distraction. Once I almost wrote myself to death. As a teacher I've watched a number of students write in the same direction. So far I've managed to see them through the danger, or pull them back. But it's always a worry. The pen is mighty: it can heal and redeem and transform. It can also maim and kill.

I thought about this paradox a lot over a period of some months in 2002: partly because I was invited to speak at *Strange Baggage*, a conference on writing in health care,[1] and also because I'd been peripherally involved with a project initiated by David Morley, the colleague I just mentioned. This project was a book called *The Gift* (Morley 2002).[2] It's a collection of prose and poetry donated by writers and NHS workers which was distributed free to at least 30,000 NHS employees in the Midlands, in gratitude for all the thankless work they do every working day. The brief was open-ended. Write about illness, David said, or health, or recovery, or birth, or death, or hospitals, or doctors. What drew me was the uncertain relationship between health and writing. Rather than waft about in safe clouds of generalisation, I chose to be personal, to look at my own health, my own writing, and the paradox that binds them together. An extract from this piece, 'The Mighty Pen', concludes this chapter.

I wanted to ask why, when I live to write and write to live, the act of writing has not always been a life-force. I found myself thinking a lot about a ten-year period during which I was very ill. I had pneumonia and bronchitis more times than I can count. I had three operations. I was seriously depressed and I couldn't sleep. It was in the middle of all this that I almost wrote myself to death. I eventually managed to pull myself out of it. To a large degree, I wrote myself out of it. But the turning point was not an insight that jumped off the page. It was watching a nurse who was keeping a wordless vigil next to a disabled woman who had no family and no friends and who had only hours to live. It is a memory that still makes me feel very humble and very small.

Ten years have passed since I 'returned to myself', as they say. But I've never been able to look back and understand why I went into that downspin, why I got ill, how I got better, how writing helped and where it hindered. I probably won't ever understand it fully, but the small piece I wrote for *The Gift* did illuminate a few things (Morley 2002, pp.218–225). I am beginning to understand the event that triggered it, or rather, the original illness. In 1983, when I was seven months pregnant with my second child, I came down with pneumonia. I spent the next two months in bed, but I kept on working on a novel I was desperate to finish.

I did finish it, but within the same week I went into labour. There were complications and the baby almost died.

I had always known this was the beginning of my decline. What I had never seen was what a deep effect the almost-death had on me and on the baby's father: how much it affected not just our relationship, but also the things we did to that relationship in our writing. I had not realised how much I blamed myself for what had almost happened to my daughter, how I saw the near-disaster as having been caused by my drive to write, and how much I came to fear that my drive to write had turned me into a death-force. It was only when I finished this small piece in 2002 that I realised for the first time that it wasn't really like that, that the almost-disaster wasn't my fault, that my desire to write was not a murderous impulse.

Knowing this was like being released from prison. I was able to forgive myself and even more miraculous, I was able to forgive my ex-husband. But this took 18 years. And writing about this time of my life even so many years later was still like going back into a whirlpool from which I was not sure I would ever emerge. I did, but this was using every safety device and every balancing trick I know.

I am talking here about a very particular kind of writing. You could call it *salvage writing*: when you go over the walls you built yourself to shield yourself from the past, to re-immerse yourself in it, to relive it, to try to understand what happened. It's dangerous work, but when you go about it the right way it can release you from stories that are doing you nothing but harm. If you write about it openly and honestly, you can also help release others from those same stories.

If writing is a form of thinking, then it is a form of thinking that lets other people into your mind. Even when it's something you begin alone it is a conversation, a way of conveying your thoughts to others.

Writing-to-think has two great advantages. First, it allows you to *fix* your thoughts on a page, so that you and others can reflect on them. Second, it lets you *change* your thoughts. When you write something down, your feelings about whatever it is you're writing don't stay fixed. The next thing you write will begin at that new point. You can build on what you've done. You can move on.

But there are as many ways of writing as there are ways of thinking and talking. Not all of them are therapeutic, or honest, or vehicles for free expression. We all know the contracts and the unspoken rules that bind writing in the everyday world. As intricate as these rules are, we know them almost instinctively, even though we rarely spell them out. Most adults don't need to be told what sort of language you should use in a letter to a great aunt; or what's the right tone for a funding bid and what sort of adjective would dash your chances; or what is appropriate to say in a postcard to a child and what would be a breach of trust.

And there are rules not just about language, but also about plots. If you're writing to the trustees who have given you a grant for a project, you can talk about the downside of that project, but you must shape your narrative so that the trustee is reassured that it was a rewarding venture overall and the money well spent. Likewise, you are a failure at writing thank you notes if you always say exactly what you thought of that dinner party or that useless present. Your main job in most forms of everyday writing is to honour the contract, confirm the power relation, keep the connection, tell people at least part of what they want to hear.

It's true in fiction, too. People buy the books that tell them the stories they want to live by, stories about rags that turn to riches, about dangers faced, lies exposed, truths uncovered, illnesses overcome. As with fiction, so it is with autobiography. The story a writer tells about her life can be factually true – or emotionally true – and still dissemble. A story is not a story unless it is a selection and a patterning of facts. There is always something left out and sometimes it is the thing left out of the story that is most important.

Consider, for example, a mature student I worked with many years ago. She was in her seventies when we met. She had had seven different careers in her life and along the way she'd picked up three PhDs. But every chapter in her autobiography told the story of a disillusionment, with each disillusionment ending a career. One day I handed back a chapter with a question. After you gave up on politics, I asked, what did you do the next day? I came up with a wonderful new plan, she said. I decided to get a degree in psychology. It turned out that she'd always come up with a wonderful new plan within hours of giving up on an old one. Once she had putting in these missing links, it wasn't just the shape of the story that changed. The story itself said something new to her.

I like what the poet Gwyneth Lewis said in *Sunbathing in the Rain*, her account of her struggles with depression (Lewis 2002). She has come to the idea that her many and serious bouts of depression offer her the opportunity to look again at the stories she has been telling about herself, in her life and in their writing, and see how they are forgeries. She makes herself better, she thinks, by going back, and looking again, and finding the truth.

I think this is what all writers try to do in one way or another. It's also what I am trying to do when I teach writing. The aim is to move beyond the forgeries and to find out what's beneath them. When I look at my students' writing, I tend to see the words on the page as clues. My job, as *editor*, is to sift through the received ideas, cover stories and conventions to find out how a student really sees things, what he or she is trying to say. If their main character won't speak, if their style is flat, if the story peters out at the end of the first page, there's usually a reason, and it generally resides not *in* the words on the page but *beneath* them. Admittedly, some reasons are better off staying there. In my early teaching days, I taught a number of very happily married women who could not stop themselves from expressing their every thought in the passive voice. I am deeply suspicious of the passive voice and what it does to people, and I have been known to lecture on this subject at length. In my time, I've made many converts. But I soon discovered that converts who were happily married woman often became unhappy when they moved into the active voice and ended up filing for divorce. So these days I think twice before proselytising.

I'm hard on my students. But I try not to be negative. I'm always looking ahead, always focusing on what's most interesting in their work, and suggesting that they cut out what no longer interests or convinces so that they can spend more time on the things that still do. I try to put them in charge. The final decision should always be theirs. I'm there to put out the choices they have and to outline the consequences. I urge them to listen to their own gut feelings. When they seem to be writing to please, I try and remind them that their opinion is more important than mine, that

I'll be pleased only if they stop trying to write to please me and write their stories in their own words.

My job is to guide this process through honest *writerly* responses. This is one of the reasons I am wary of anyone who comes to me hoping for therapy. What I worry about is not just that I'm untrained. I also worry about their often unspoken but still very powerful assumptions about ideas what writing should do for them, and about the power I hold over them just by virtue of being their teacher.

I am particularly worried if I'm working with students who are very troubled. Over 18 years of teaching, I have worked with many. My most troubled students have often been very gifted writers. But I can't help but worry about pushing them as hard as I might do if they were going through a happier time. Whenever I have a student who is seriously distressed, I try and make sure they are getting appropriate help.

If they are very very troubled and I think I am out of my depth, I act accordingly. Everyone has limits, and sometimes a student will write about things that exceed mine. My limits include poem cycles about hacking families to pieces, racist fantasies, and violent or sexual fantasies in which I have been assigned a part. When I draw the line, the students always say the same thing. 'But you said we should take risks! And now you're changing the rules.' They're right. There are times when I'm the one who's curbing free expression. But there are limits to what I'm prepared to take on, and there are limits to what the other students in a class should have to hear.

But inside these extremes, I have worked very fruitfully with students who are profoundly troubled. I have two ways of limiting the risks. First, I use the text as evidence in the way I described earlier. I try to give the student a chance to stand outside her stories by asking her to look at technique. I can think, for example, of a young woman who self-harmed, and whose every story ended in a mutilation. Instead of talking about the *content* of her stories, I asked her to look at their *shape*: in particular what happened in her stories just before they ended. In every story, just before the end, the heroine would flip out of herself to consider herself from a corner of the ceiling. When my student saw this was happening in every story, she was intrigued. Not long afterwards, she wrote a new story in which the heroine did not flip out of herself. This story did not end the way all the others did. My student still writes some pieces that end in mutilation, but she is not stuck inside the one story anymore. She writes in many other ways, too. It was by looking at her *narrative technique* that she was able to see she had choices.

Another thing I do is to give students exercises specifically designed to counter the patterns of their thoughts. I can think of one young woman whose heroines all longed to return to some sort of foetal state. Once we had noted this together, we decided that she should try writing a story in which the heroine was 'already there'. The result was a sublime story about a little girl sitting inside a yellow tent. I'm not quite sure how or why but it seemed to break a spell. It freed this writer to write (or think) about adults who longed for more than a return to childhood. Often all you have to do to get a writer to break out of a pattern is to design an exercise that breaks it for them.

Individually tailored teaching can lead to breakthroughs: break-throughs that take great weights away, give power and dignity, illuminate, educate, heal, cure, transform. It can get people to express the things that are most important to *them*, in their *own* words. It can get them to challenge the masterplots that define them: as Fiona Shaw did when she decided that the textbook definition of post-natal depression was dehumanising and sat down to write *Out of Me* (Shaw 1998).

Her account of post-natal depression is personal in the best sense. Like Gwyneth Lewis, she is coming to terms with forgeries: in this case, not just the story that plunged her into depression but also the story the doctors imposed on her afterwards. It is by ridding her story of outside voices, by putting it back into her own words, that she is able to heal herself. Her story is the best advertisement I can imagine for writing-as-therapy. Writing like this can release you from the position of a patient who is healed by others. No longer are you the object of study, with observable symptoms but no inner life worth mentioning. You can take charge of your life. Not only can you come to an understanding of your own history: you can let others understand what you've been through, what you learned along the way. You even stand a chance of correcting expert opinion.

Even if you are not suffering from an illness at the moment of writing, the process can help you live with your past. You can discover things that release you from old curses. It helps you explore what Martin Amis calls the 'terrain' of fiction: not what was, but what could have been, should have been, might have been. Sometimes, you can even find out what you believe in. The bursts of energy I get when fiction is going right for me are huge and, although I can never prove it, I believe healing.

But when fiction goes wrong it's a very different story. In my experience, it goes wrong if you're lying, settling scores, avoiding responsibility. It doesn't happen. It goes wrong if you take on more than you can handle, or if you don't give yourself limits and safety valves and escape routes. It goes wrong if you're trying to please someone. And this is why it can go wrong so fast and so easily in a classroom or therapy setting. All teachers have preferences, agendas, power and influence. All teachers have to set limits. They have responsibilities to the group, not just the individual.

Many teachers don't want to hurt feelings, especially when their students are doing personal writing, and this is particularly the case when the student is already hurting. But dishonest responses are very harmful. In my view they're also unnecessary, as there are many ways of giving an honest response. When you put mental balance first, you don't just impose an agenda, you censor yourself as a teacher. By urging the student to find a 'healing plot' you risk suggesting that they avoid all unpleasant subjects: even those that are essential to the healing process. You stop students from exploring the very things they need to explore most, from saying the things they most long to say. You keep them writing as students and patients, instead of as fully-fledged, dignified human beings.

The important thing is respect for the thing on the page: respect for the person who has written it, for the thing they'll write the next day that will be even better. It's essential to take every piece of writing seriously, even if you have reservations about it. You can show that respect by giving your honest response to it, and then by urging the writer to do more, to the degree that seems right and appropriate. You can let the student know that what they think is important, and that what they write counts. Most important, you can make it clear to them that their accounts of what they've been through matter just as much or more than what the experts say about them. Working honestly with the written word means conducting a dialogue, so that the teacher and the student, the therapist and the client, the doctor and the patient, become equal and cooperating partners, with shared values and agreed goals. When this happens, the patient-student-writer is no longer passive, no longer just a case for treatment, but recognised as fully human.

I am sure most of us would agree that this is or ought to be the definition of mental well-being. And if it is then there's no problem. Health and honest writing become one and the same thing. But our models of health delivery don't always recognise the full dignity of the person marked 'patient'. And neither do our models of education. Patients and students are often confined to scripts that suit their 'superiors'. These superiors are still the ones who write the scripts. There is still an asymmetry of power between expert and subject, teacher and writer, therapist and client.

My hope is that writing by people who are suffering great challenges will help redress that imbalance. The main reason we should encourage them to write and write courageously is that we have a lot to learn from them. So, the plea I'd like to make to writers teaching and working in health and social care, just as much as with keen apprentice writers on university creative writing courses, is: let them tell the truth.

Telling the truth
An extract from 'The Mighty Pen'

All I wanted was a temporary separation. Paul was trying to talk me out of it, usually by trying to convince me that I had lost my mind. Night after night, we'd argue about my mind and whether or not 1 had lost it, and my fear of being turned into a vegetable, and what this signified. If I went to bed without giving in to his version, if he asked me if 1 still loved him and I said no, he'd wake me up in the middle of the night to ask me again. I got more and more run down. 1 came down with more colds that turned into bronchitis or pneumonia. And then one night I found a lump in my breast.

It was a cyst, not a tumour, but they weren't sure it wasn't calcifying. So in January 1986 I checked into the John Radcliffe Hospital for a biopsy. I went in the afternoon before my operation. Paul came in to keep me company and stayed at my side into the night. His eyes were like lights in an interrogation room. He began by telling me he had been into my computer and read everything I had written. He asked me why I was so angry, what he had done, how he could change. He told me I had to get better. He couldn't bear to see me so weak, couldn't bear watching me turn my anger against myself. He told me I had strengths I didn't know about, while I had nil by mouth.

In the morning they gave me my pre-op. When my operation was delayed, they gave me another. I spent the day floating in a morphine haze, listening to music. It does not seem plausible that the controllers of Radio 3 had decided to give over the entire day to multiple performances of Mozart's Don Giovanni. But that is what I remember hearing. The music got mixed up with all the other sounds. I kept hearing footsteps coming down the hallway. It must have been the heart patients, clattering to the smoking room at the end of the hallway. I thought it was the devil, coming for my soul.

Late in the afternoon, the orderlies came for me. They wheeled me off and parked me in front of a set of green swinging doors. A doctor dressed in green put me under, and next thing I was waking up to the chill of the recovery room. I could remember my name when they asked for it but only just.

They wheeled me back to my ward. I tried to help them help me onto my bed but I couldn't. They propped me up in my pillows, because I couldn't do that either. In the morning, when the consultant did his rounds, he explained that I had lost an unusual amount of blood. They had decided not to give me a transfusion because of the recent scare about blood supplies contaminated with the HIV virus. I was going to feel unusually weak for some time he said, and it was also going to be some time before my test results came back. 'I'm sorry to leave you in limbo, but there you are.'

There was one thing I could take comfort in. Things could be worse. All I had to do was look around the room. Begin with Mrs Miller, the woman next to the window. She was suffering from a wasting disease. Then there was Mrs Flynn across the aisle and Mrs Swallow, right next to me. Both had just had double mastectomies, probably too late.

You would not know to look at them though. They were dressed in chirpy pink nighties and aquamarine slippers and sky-blue padded robes. They commented often on the loveliness of the floral arrangements and Hallmark cards that surrounded them. They kept themselves busy with knitting and magazines and thank you letters, and when a nurse wheeled in the pay phone trolley, they spoke to their husbands, sons and grandchildren in terms that they would have used if they were phoning from Marbella. They said things like, 'Oh, I'm having a whale of a time,' and 'Oh you shouldn't have!' and 'What a perfectly lovely thing to say!' They talked about clouds and silver linings, and everything being for the best at the end of the day. Even when the heart patients clattered down the hall for their smoking break, gaunt and grey and gasping, even when the smoke in the smoking room got so thick it rolled into our ward, the most they did was purse their lips. 'Oh dear, it's so sad, isn't it!' Mrs Flynn would say. And Mrs Swallow would say, 'But some things can't be helped, can they.' If there was a nurse in the room checking pulses, she would sigh and allow a dark thought to cross her face and then she would brighten as she thought of yet another way to revive the charade.

The charade got more difficult after lunch, when we were joined by Mrs Meadows, an elderly woman with a thick white beard and a serious incontinence problem who kept falling out of bed. At tea time we were joined by a woman with restricted growth named Miss Mendoza. They put her into the bed right across from mine. She was conscious but only just. She lay flat on her back, her hay-like hair splayed on the pillow, her glassy eyes fixed on the ceiling, her little chest heaving and rattling under the sheets.

I had never heard this sound before. I had stupidly assumed that it was just a figure of speech. The rattle got louder in the night. Every time it woke me up, I'd look over at her bed. I'd see a nurse there, whispering to her, patting her hand. She had no family, they explained in the morning. That's why they were filling in. Around lunchtime, when the rattle grew fainter, the nurse who was holding her hand called in two orderlies and had them wheel her away. Mrs Flynn put down her magazine to watch her go and then turned sharply towards the window. Mrs Miller said 'Oh dear,' and Mrs Swallow said, 'It's so sad, isn't it?' The nurse who came in to change the sheets said not to worry, they had only taken her off to a private room.

Miss Mendoza died that afternoon, just before smoking break. It was just as well, a nurse told us. She had so enjoyed the quiet of the private room. She had slipped away so peacefully. It was sad, but some things couldn't be helped, could they? Nods all around. And sighs. And here and there a pursed lip. Then the tea lady wheeled her trolley in, and that was that.

But that night I couldn't stop looking at the blank sheets on her bed. I looked at them until they were there again: Miss Mendoza in her bed, the nurse in her chair. Miss Mendoza rattling louder with every breath she took, the nurse holding her hand.

I didn't want to die.

I couldn't stop myself.

I closed my eyes.

I woke up to the clatter of a trolley. 'Milk?' said the tea lady.

I tried to nod.

'Feeling a little low this morning, are we?' I nodded again. 'Let's prop you up then,' she said. 'There now. That's better then, isn't it?'

'Got some sleep, did you?' Now it was the nurse to check my pulse. 'Tell you what,' she said. 'I'm going to get you on your feet today.'

'You can't,' I said.

She shook the thermometer. 'We'll see about that.'

After she had finished her rounds she came back for me. She lifted me to a sitting position and told me to use her arm as a prop. 'Now put one foot down, very gently,' she said.

'I can't,' I said.

'Just try.'

So I put one foot on the floor, and then I put the other foot on the floor. 'Now walk,' she said. I did. I made it all the way to the end of the hall.

'Well done,' said Mrs Flynn when I had made it all the way back.

Mrs Swallow said, 'Now that wasn't so hard, was it?'

I sat down on my bed. I was short of breath and my stitches hurt.

'You did have us worried, you know,' said Mrs Miller.

'But everything works out in the end, doesn't it?' said Mrs Flynn.

'Sometimes you can worry yourself sick just by thinking too much,' said Mrs Swallow.

'My thoughts exactly,' said Mrs. Flynn. 'It does make you think, though, doesn't it?'

I'm sure I didn't cry, but I still ache when I think about it, even all these years later. I can't get it out of my head. I can't decide what I feel worst about – their dignity or my lack of it, my histrionics or their kindly acceptance of it or my sudden change of heart. No, now that I thought about it, now that I had seen it, I didn't want to die after all. No, from that moment on, I knew I wanted to live, no matter how much it hurt. I can't explain why. And perhaps I shouldn't. This is what I see when I try to find the words: the little woman rattling in her bed, and the nurse holding her hand, saying nothing, saying everything.

Notes

1   Strange Baggage, a national conference on creative writing in health and social care, Salisbury Arts Centre, April 2002, was held as part of the Kingfisher writing in health care project, managed by Artcare and Salisbury Arts Centre. For further details, see Chapter Five. The conference was funded by PPP Health Care Charitable Trust.

2   David Morley's project in association with Birmingham Health Authority was published by the poetry small press Stride, who are based in Devon. Thirty thousand copies were given away free to NHS staff in the Midlands in an initiative funded by The Nuffield Trust.

References

Lewis, G. (2002) *Sunbathing in the Rain: A Cheerful Book about Depression.* London: Flamingo.

Morley, D. (ed.) (2002) *The Gift: New Writing for the NHS.* Exeter: Stride in association with Birmingham Health Authority.

Shaw, F. (1998) *Out of Me: The History of a Postnatal Breakdown.* London: Penguin.

Further reading

Freely, M. (1996) *The Other Rebecca.* London: Bloomsbury.

CHAPTER FIVE

A Case Study
The Kingfisher Project

Graham Hartill, Jill Low, Sam Moran,
Maria Purse, Emma Ryder Richardson, Fiona
Sampson, Catherine Sandbrook

So far, this book has looked at the work of key individual practitioners and particular care areas. This chapter will offer a more detailed case-study of a four-year – and continuing – writing project conducted in a range of health and social care areas in Salisbury, Wiltshire.

Every writing in health and social care project is the result of a number of successful collaborations between participants and writer, but also between institutions, clinicians, carers and arts providers. In this chapter the key local providers, a clinician, a participant and two writers experienced in the field – one leading the project and one evaluating it – each offer an account of how the project worked from their point of view.

The Kingfisher Project in Salisbury is a writing in health and social care project which was set up in response to local need and as a national model for good practice. Jill Low, Director of Salisbury Arts Centre, and Catherine Sandbrook, Centre Manager, outline the background, origins and aims and objectives of the project:

The Kingfisher Project was set up in 1999 as a collaborative Literature in Health project between Salisbury Arts Centre and ArtCare, the arts service for Salisbury Health Care NHS Trust. The main funding for the project was provided by Southern Arts, though the first year's work was also funded under the Poetry Society's Poetry Places scheme. A highly qualified and experienced researcher and practitioner in the field was appointed as lead writer. The overall management of the project was shared by the two partner organisations via a steering group, which also had user representation, meeting four times a year.

ArtCare and Salisbury Arts Centre merged their experience and skills in developing arts opportunities for users and former users of the health and mental health services, and in the management of community arts projects in a wide range of settings. Their joint mission was based on the fundamental belief that the arts, in this case literature, have a far-reaching potential to enhance the quality of people's lives and to contribute towards maintaining and/or regaining health and well-being.

The core of the project has been a programme of poetry and creative writing workshops based in Salisbury District Hospital and other health-related organisations within the Salisbury community. The workshops were led with inspiration by Fiona Sampson, initially fortnightly and then weekly, in a variety of groups based on hospital wards and in the community. These included patients on a Spinal Injuries Unit, Salisbury Hospice, a secure psychiatric ward, an acute orthopaedic ward, a stroke unit, a surgery and a group of day centre attendees meeting in Salisbury Arts Centre.

The format for these workshops was kept open because the nature of health and social care settings dictates a variable approach: sometimes group-sessions, at other times one-to-one meetings. From the beginning the quality of the literary encounter was given as much value as the quantity of people involved. Extreme care was taken to guarantee good practice in terms of confidentiality, permission-giving and the obvious sensitivity of working in these settings; and whenever appropriate and possible the involvement of staff in the workshops was encouraged.

Through the run of this programme during the period 1999–2002 a large number of health care users were able to benefit from the workshops. We believe that the sessions have contributed considerably to the process of dealing with and/or recovering from illness in many people's lives.

Mission statements

ArtCare's mission

To bring colour and inspiration to SHC NHS Trust and contribute to healing and well-being through the provision of participatory literary, writing and reading activities.

Salisbury Arts Centre's mission

To surprise, challenge and include the people of the District of Salisbury and the wider region in a range of innovative, high-quality, diverse and stimulating arts experiences.

The Kingfisher Project's mission

To provide a platform for sharing and celebrating literature in health and social care settings in Salisbury community and Salisbury District Hospital as part of that community.

With these mission statements in mind a number the project's aims and objectives can be articulated as follows:

1.   For reasons of inclusion both organisations have an interest in extending the field for this project from 'health and social care settings' to 'well-being in the community'. By 'well-being' we mean physical and emotional well-being.

2.   The use of creative writing as a means of contributing to healing could be expanded to literary activities as 'preventative care' and a means of well-being. This concept could be further promoted amongst primary care providers.

3.   As creative literature is by nature a means of communication it is important to incorporate presentations and performance of the project outcomes within the core structure.

Aims

1.   To continue to encourage, enable and advocate the use of literature in a health-care and personal development context.

2. To offer a model of good practice of literature in health care based on the best of previous and existing work.

3. To provide a high-quality experience for all participants whether health-care users, clients, staff, carers, workers or the general public.

4. To continue to manage the project collaboratively, and develop wider partnerships where appropriate.

5. To continue to develop new strands for the project which might include elements specific to, and led by, one of the managing organisations.

Objectives

1. To provide workshops in a variety of health-care and social settings.

2. To continue a flexible approach which is sensitive to the different settings worked in, so that sessions may range from one-to-one, to group sessions, and participants will range from one-off to long term.

3. To enable participants to develop their own literary and personal development skills.

4. To develop other opportunities to promote creative writing activities including publications, performance, broadcasting, and creative reading, both formally and informally.

5. To involve other art forms where appropriate.

6. To plan for a series of outcomes / special projects, appropriate to the differing groups and settings, to punctuate and give focus to the core workshop work and to render the work more visible / benefit a wider public: at least two 'special projects' per year.

7. To incorporate into the project a training element / guide for care staff / workers.

8. To encourage participants to take an active role in the development of the project and to support individual, and, where appropriate, group independence.

9. To identify and initiate new ways of working.

10. To work collaboratively and mutually benefit from each organisation's specific expertise.

11. To develop resources for work in the field.

12. To *continue* to evaluate the project on an ongoing basis, in order to inform future work and disseminate codes of good practice.

13. To maximise the links between the core project and other projects being undertaken separately or together by the two managing organisations.

From the outset, as Jill Low makes clear, Kingfisher was jointly managed by Salisbury Arts Centre and ArtCare, the arts provider in Salisbury Health Care NHS Trust:

> I believe that the strong commitments made by partners in the partnerships involved in this sort of project and the ownership felt and commitment given by them are an essential element of the mix. Sometimes the growing of this partnership was painful: we all have our own reasons, missions and strategies underlying the reasons for doing the work and they are not always a perfect fit. The Arts Centre joined in because the Kingfisher Project fitted with its mission; it stayed in the partnership because the project had an energy, creativity and a body of work it could be proud of being a part of. The creativity, ownership and teamwork gifted to the project by the individuals within the groups: that is the thing that sends a shiver of excitement down my spine.

Emma Ryder Richardson, then Director of ArtCare, explains how this partnership came about:

ArtCare, the arts service at Salisbury District Hospital, was founded in 1991 in response to a desire by hospital building planners to provide artwork in a new hospital building. After a year of commissioning visual artworks it was very apparent that the arts provision in the healing environment was having a considerable effect and that there was a need to build on work in the visual arts to include participatory arts, music, even cinema – in fact the whole range of arts/environment-related activities.

In 1998/9, ArtCare was keen to expand its service into the community – encouraging people to enjoy arts activities before they come into hospital may well prevent them from coming in at all. It also needed to bring outside expertise in to its service and to afford that expertise new opportunities to fulfil its own development needs. Preventative medicine and health education have an important place in the NHS of the twenty-first century together with patient independence and involvement as far as is possible.

Planning was relatively easy from ArtCare's point of view. For a start, here was recognition from external professional arts organisations which gave professional credence to the project and a firm background with which to launch it within the hospital.

In order to give the writer a wide range of bases in which to work, several contrasting areas were selected – hospice, acute/secure mental health unit, a ward for elderly, long-stay patients with Alzheimer's Disease, spinal injuries unit, stroke unit and an acute orthopaedic ward. A designated staff member was identified to head the project and initial briefing meetings were held with the writer and a representative of SAC attending with the ArtCare manager. The response was incredibly positive. In response to the mutual needs to work within the community as well as at the hospital, two other groups were approached – a surgery and day centre for mental health service users.

Sister Maria Purse, of Salisbury Specialist Palliative Care Services, was one of the clinicians who worked closely with the writer to enable the sessions in her unit. Here she reflects on some of the practical challenges this involved, as well as the rewards which, like Inger Eriksson in Chapter One, she sees as having much to do with the chance to engage with existential issues of life and particularly death:

Poetry

It's very relaxing, poetry.
It's like the radio: you
can conjure up the picture
and go into a sort of
free flow of thought.

It's rather like a parachute
– you can go into free fall
can't you –
and different things mean
different things
to everybody else, don't they,
in their imagination.

(Sally Wallace, May 2001)

The creative arts have had a dramatic effect on the care given at Salisbury Specialist Palliative Care Services based at Salisbury Hospice. Palliative Care is the active total care of patients and their families, usually when their disease is no longer responsive to curative treatment. The Millennium Arts Project at the Hospice was designed to ensure that the physical, emotional, psychological and spiritual care of the patients and families was achieved to the highest possible standard. Entitled 'Putting life into their days rather than days into their lives', the project introduced Music and Art Therapy along with Theatre Work-shops to the Hospice patients as an additional way of providing supportive care. The positive evaluation of this project led to the appointment of an Activities Facilitator with a budget to continue this creative/therapeutic aspect of Palliative Care provision funded by Salisbury Hospice Care Trust.

The reputation of the creative aspects of the Millennium Arts Project and its benefits to patient and family care ensured that when the Hospice was offered participation in the Kingfisher Project we agreed without a moment's hesitation. Not only did the project live up to, it managed to exceed all our expectations.

Among comments gathered from staff, patients and relatives who were involved in the Kingfisher Creative Writing Project:

- For both patients and relatives Fiona's face was non-clinical and non-threatening, leading to acceptance into their lives at this time.

- There could be a lack of privacy for those in double rooms who may not have felt comfortable opening painful or intimate discussions with others present, but were too unwell to enable movement to another area.

- 'Sleep': Fiona's allocated time was mid-afternoon, when many patients take a much needed siesta. The dilemma was to balance the benefit they may gain from time spent with Fiona against the benefits gained from an afternoon nap.

- The work allowed patients the time and opportunity to reflect upon the positive aspects of their life, achievements and the legacy they were leaving behind in a safe environment.

A Grandmother's Hobbies

My hobbies are my grandsons really
because we've been looking after them.
The youngest is just going to school.
There's Ben, he's the eldest;
Jakey, Jake, he's the middle one;
and then my pickle, Luke.
They live in Romsey and we live in Salisbury
but before my daughter went back to work
we used to have them;
and she works three mornings a week
and, you know, we try and step in
as needed.
It's been lovely looking after them.
It's given us such a lot of pleasure.
The middle grandson – Jakey –
he was in intensive care at Odstock when he was three weeks
old

and of course we got very involved then
because Susan was visiting – she came to see us –
and luckily it was that night he got ill
and I remember my husband drove with her
and she was driving through traffic lights and everything
in the middle of the night
and of course they were marvellous with him.
Jake is six. Ben is eight and Luke is five.

(Pamela Fitzgeorge, February 2002)

It was necessary to acknowledge that not all patients, relatives or staff would feel the Kingfisher Project was an appropriate use of charitable funds or staff time and that it might be viewed as an intrusion on patients at a vulnerable time of their lives. We had, however, risen to the challenge of humour therapy, winning over the majority; in comparison, Fiona and the Kingfisher Project were a walk in the park! It was also essential that we did not allow our appraisal of the particular patient or relatives to prejudice us against offering them the opportunity to participate in the project. The information leaflet was a valuable tool here. When we were unsure how to introduce the project to individuals, it offered a distraction the patient could browse through as I searched for the words to 'sell' what I knew was a worthwhile aspect of the care we provided.

Fiona was able to spend time with the patients and relatives providing emotional, psychological and spiritual support under the umbrella of creative writing – something the clinical staff were not always able to achieve during a busy shift. Patients would often be discharged or die between Fiona's visits. It was vital that the team provided Fiona with support and supervision when this happened, discussing the situation and reflecting on the impact the project had unmistakably had in the provision of total patient care.

On the few occasions patients declined to participate in the project this was seen by the nursing staff as an opening to discuss gently with the individual their reason for declining involvement. This frequently led to intimate conversations acknowledging feelings at this stage of their cancer journey – an unintentional, yet positive outcome of the project. As a clinical team we gained many new insights into the patients' lives and personalities from the poems they created with Fiona. Details that had not come to light during conversations or whilst providing intimate nursing care. A reflection of how little we truly know our patients sometimes and how the opportunity to express themselves in a different manner is essential and valuable for them:

And This Is How

And this is how I'm going to lead my life:
With every day
a little bit more

and I'm determined
that is what we're going to do;

I'm determined
to prove them wrong!

(Elizabeth Jones, August 2001)

I acknowledge that the introduction of Fiona to the patients and relatives was often carried out in a haphazard and rushed manner. As her arrival time rapidly approached during a hectic shift it required Sister to make a frantic dash around the unit touting for business: not an ideal situation. Yet the Kingfisher Project offered a gateway to opening up painful topics, expressed in a different way. For example, it enabled patients and relatives to discuss with Fiona favourite poems, or one she sought out individually, for use within their funeral services. Later, the presentation of patients' work to bereaved relatives evoked a powerful response, moments I felt privileged to witness and which reinforced the benefits of the project. The quiet reflection, knowing smiles and laughter at phrases contained within poems. Expressions of amazement, unaware of the deceased person's creative ability brought to light during their time with Fiona. A precious memory to be treasured from a traumatic time most wish to forget:

Honesty

I think, really what I think, is
the number of people who've rung me up
told me how special I am...
they tell me I'm brave
they tell me I'm strong
they tell me I'm deep
but to me
that's just me.
And people can tell you,
you can do this
and you can do that
and you make me feel small;
and people say,
but you never give the impression
that you're in pain.
I try not to
because I don't want people to think
she's always whinging and moaning about something.

But I'm just me really.
They seem to think I do something special.
Maybe I do.

And I think the people who have come out
and said these things to me,
I'd probably never ever have expected them
to do things like that.

(Elizabeth Jones, August 2001)

To sum up: the Kingfisher Project allowed patients to express feelings of sadness, experience moments of happiness and create memories within the safe medium of poetry.

From her complementary perspective as an arts in health care manager, Emma Ryder Richardson stresses the role of writing in resisting the depersonalisation and institutionalisation which people receiving health care can experience. She also values

> the long term, permanent results: a project with the hospital's resident artist to brighten up a corridor, a published poetry collection, regularity of provision, working collaborations within individual departments which are now really recognizing the effects that writing can have and a consultant who regularly consults patients' written pieces held in their notes as a vital way of reviewing that person's progress.

Moreover, 'For many people, the quality of life has been improved in a way which may not have seemed possible at the onset of terminal illness.'

Although the main body of Kingfisher's work took place in four-weekly or fortnightly workshops, as the project developed opportunities to share, celebrate and creatively expand on this work emerged. There were exchange visits, performances, commissions for the projects participants making work alongside professional poets, radio programmes and publications. Jill Low identifies some of these discrete activities, public outcomes and highlights:

1. *Radio programmes*. The making of a 30-minute radio programme for Wiltshire Sound, recorded in their Salisbury studio and broadcast on the first weekend of Salisbury Festival's Last Words Festival in October 1999. Also played as part of the Last Words Exhibition at the Arts Centre. This project gave members of the Greencroft Group and Men's Words experience of performing for radio and choosing and editing for the programme. In 2001, BBC Radio 4's *All in the Mind* featured the project, broadcasting participants' work and interviewing them about their involvement.

2. *Performances*. Project members first performed as part of the Feel Good Fair (marking World Mental Health Day) in October 1999. Members of the Greencroft and Men's Words groups performed some of their poems to a public audience at the Arts Centre. A performance by the Greencroft Group and Men's Words (under the stage name *The Upstarts*), at a 'Live Lunch' at the Arts Centre in May 2000, came from a

request from the group and led to further appearances under this name, at the Arts Centre and elsewhere.

3.   *Research, writing and publication* by the Poetry Society, as part of their Poetry Places partnership funding of the first year of the project, of a practical guide to poetry and personal development activities based on the Kingfisher Project (Sampson 1999). During the life of the project, the writer in residence gave a number of conference papers and articles and completed PhD studies and a monograph on work in the field (Sampson 2001).

4.   *Training sessions* for members of Kick Start Poets, a local poetry group meeting at the Arts Centre, wishing to develop skills in this area.

5.   Supported by the Mind Millennium Awards Scheme, a series of *poem posters* were commissioned for distribution in community health settings. The Greencroft Writers, Mens' Words and Greencroft Centre Art Group collaborated to interpret each other's work for these posters which served as both poetry platform and health-education outreach. Editing, redrafting and proofing skills were developed by this public project.

6.   Also as part of the Millennium Scheme, the Greencroft Writers and Men's Words published *Strange Baggage*, an *anthology* of their work (Sampson (ed.) 2002). An exhibition of the posters, the launch of the books, and an exhibition of other writings from the Kingfisher Project, took place in December 2000 at Salisbury Arts Centre.

7.   *Sprung Release.* With support from Southern Arts, the writer in residence and poet Pauline Stainer were commissioned to produce a half-hour radio script to be broadcast on national radio, exploring and reflecting on our experiences of language, its sounds, shapes and textures, how we come to it and what we do with it. This commission, which included taped interviews with and readings from group members, was performed live at Salisbury Arts Centre in July 2000 to an invited audience.

8. *International Exchange*. With support from Southern Arts, an exchange took place between the writer in residence and Finnish writers Leena and Vaino Kirstina in August and December 2000. Fiona appeared at a conference and a festival in Finland and the Kirstinas visited the Kingfisher Project and performed alongside project members at Salisbury Arts Centre. This was a research and development project enabling the writers to explore international practice in community writing.

So what does it feel like to take part in such a project? Sam Moran writes:

It's all about telling practitioners what it is like to be on the other side of the fence and what can be achieved using creative writing not only to improve someone's health but also to help them realise their own capabilities as a writer, perhaps even enabling them to become published.

OK I'll come clean: I have an agenda, but don't most people? I want the people who work in health care, in the mental health system, to recognise the potential in the people they are working with; to understand that they have something to say and will say it given the opportunity. Perhaps when I started going to the Kingfisher writing group I used my writing skills to express my personal feelings about my life and my mental-health problems but it soon became quite obvious that this was not what it was all about: that I had other things to say, other stories to tell, because I am part of society not just part of my mental-health problems. It was like this for the other group members too: we live in the same world as everyone else and we have comments to make on it – observations uniquely ours – just like any other group of writers. This wasn't just about therapy; the therapeutic aspect of creative writing is a by-product. This was about creativity itself. About knowing that we could achieve something, that the work we were producing could stand on its own merits: worth being read, inescapably accessible to everyone. You didn't have to be suffering from a health problem to relate to it or to know that we were writers trying to write, not patients trying to get better. Let's not beat around the bush here; we were something quite different right from the start.

Other writing groups I've been involved in through the health service have all had a quality of Occupational Therapy about them. Not that Occupational Therapy is a bad thing; but these writing groups definitely put therapy first and writing second. At times I found them slightly patronising. They were fun but not very serious; and maybe for the hour I was there they took my mind off things but I don't think any of the participants went away and began to use writing as any kind of tool in their lives. It certainly didn't make them better and I never once found that anyone got any great insight into their problems through what they had written. If they did they never told me. Don't get me wrong: I think writing *can* be a useful tool. My partner certainly believes that her writing helps her to exorcise the demons in her past, but as an artist she would like the work to stand on its own. I suppose it's that terrible cliché – we write about what we know and if that happens to be our health problems then so be it – but writing for me is about creating and connecting with people. It's not just about me but about the world I live in; and any health problem I might suffer from really is secondary. Writing is not therapy for me it is something I want to earn my living by. It is a way of life.

When I first went to the Kingfisher writing group I though it would be the usual run-of-the-mill group for poor little mental-health users who needed something to occupy their time. How wrong I was! So what made this group different? Two things. First, all the members had a genuine interest in writing and, second, Fiona Sampson who led the group took us seriously. I can't emphasise this enough: straightaway she saw that we could write, that we were interested in writing for writing's sake, and that it wasn't beyond our capabilities to actually achieve something for ourselves from within the group. This was a creative writing group, not an exercise in psychobabble.

Of course at first we all drew upon our own experiences. One of the first poems I wrote was 'Goodbye', a poem describing how I felt about the death of my mother:

Goodbye

It was hard
Trying to make you understand
That the journey you'd be taking
Was yours alone.

I held your hand.
I felt helpless
Struck dumb;
Mute with the fear
Of making you frightened.

The machines hummed hypnotic tunes
And the oxygen you sucked on
Stretched the days for you;
Prolonged the moment of departure.

I thought to pack a bag
To be useful
But there was no need
You were travelling light.

I tried to explain
But the words stuck
Like a claw in my throat.

I mumbled that I'll miss you
But you didn't hear me
You were caught between letting go
Or holding on tight.

And so we waited
Like passengers at a bus stop.
Bus pass and ticket in hand
You stood bravely
Trying not to say you didn't want to go.

(Sam Moran, 2000)

It was a good thing to put it down on paper, but it was an even better thing to have it made into a poem poster that might be read by other people. It was a good thing to have it published in the anthology *Strange Baggage*, and it was an amazing thing to have people come up to me after a reading and tell me how much they connected with it. Death is a universal theme: people understood the sentiments of the poem and I achieved my goal, which was to communicate something to other people. Later, as the group progressed, we got to do a programme for local radio, Wiltshire Sound; we were interviewed by Radio 4 for the programme *All in the Mind*; our poetry got on national radio and we began to branch out on our own, stepping out from under the Kingfisher umbrella to do our own poetry readings, 'Live Lunches' at the Salisbury Arts Centre. Now the Poetry Café, where I compere, has been set up there too. This was the turning point, at least for me. I now began to put my writing first; I wanted to learn all I could. I still do.

A few of us went to Ledbury Poetry Festival and there I performed the poem 'Lost for Words' at the Ledbury Poetry Slam! 'Lost for Words' is a poem describing a time in my life when I became incapable of coherent speech as a result of a nervous breakdown. It's a long-drawn-out stutter:

Lost for words

You see I could
I could speak
I could speak a few words
Some strange
Some strange half felt sentiment
I could
I could try
If only I could make the connection
The connection
Connection between thought
Between thought and sound
Sound
That's it
Sound
A collection

A collection of
Of what? Yes, that's it
A collection of vowels
To string
To string
To string a sentence
A sentence together
To connect
To make
To make some sort
Some sort of contact
A statement
A statement to
A statement to the effect
To the effect
To the effect
To say
To say
I AM STILL ALIVE.

(Sam Moran, 2000)

Afterwards a man at the performance came up to me and told me that his brother had just had a stroke and this was exactly how he was speaking; and that the poem helped him a lot. Of course I was delighted by this; but I so wanted to break away from this kind of confessional writing. The support from the group and Fiona at this time was immense. I was learning from the other members, I like to think we were all learning from each other, and with guidance I was beginning to find my own distinctive voice, we all were. One of the greatest assets of our group was that we were able to grow as writers, develop our skills.

With renewed confidence and Fiona's help and support I got myself a place on an Arvon course. Here I got the chance to work with the poets Lawrence Sail and Elizabeth Garrett. I also got the opportunity to meet other writers from all walks of life whose main objective was to get their work published. It was a wonderful experience, I worked hard on my writing every day! At the end of the week we put together an anthology of some of the work we had managed to compile as a result of the course. I contributed two simple poems:

Fragments

The car is polished now
It stands bright red under green trees
Striking in colour sharply defined
A contrast
I see my face in its bonnet
Stretched wide across its surface
I see my whole self in its windscreen
Oval or bell shaped
My smile like a straight thin line
Bending at the edges
I am both small and big
Distance determines my size
I move forward into gianthood
Or backwards into a shrinking violet
I am all expression
Distorted as though in a funfair maze
I flap my large hands
And exercise my disfigured face.

(Sam Moran, 2000)

O

Out in a big way
Making up for the hole in itself
The dark round mouth
Open in permanent surprise
Wide as a tunnel
Louder than a scream
Obviously
Obsessively
Openly mean
In a gaping sort of way
An oracle of open endings
Chasing its own tail
Moaning
O's
Into disappointment.

(Sam Moran, 2000)

By now I was experimenting with blank verse, sestinas and even riddles! And Fiona took the group to new heights by introducing us to various forms of poetry, bringing in books and reading poems and excerpts from books, showing us various uses of form and metre. We had quite heated discussions about what she brought along to read to us and I began to compile a reading list picking up books that Fiona recommended, trying to find out what other writers were writing about and what was going on. I went to Covent Garden and read at the Poetry Café, I went to see other poets perform and I began to attend numerous writing work-shops.

All this experience has meant my writing has changed. I like to think I am achieving one of my aims, which is to write about the things going on around me. I liked seeing my work in print; I would like to have more published one day! The group has opened doors for me, there's no doubt about that. I have a writing mentor now, thanks to funding from Southern Arts; I've been asked to run two creative writing groups; and I hope to get a place on a university writing course if possible in the near future. But I'd like to see more writing projects which take the work itself seriously. The world's our oyster, so to speak, and there are a lot of writers out there who need a platform from which to present their work. Health matters aside, we write because we write because we write.

As the lead writer on the Kingfisher Project at the time of her writing, I agree with the project priorities Sam articulates. Like Sam, I would argue that writing in health and social care, as in all settings, must be about *writing* itself – about the transformative power of language – before it can enable any other kinds of benefit.[1]

Yet, the various benefits the Kingfisher partners have identified – a chance to explore existential issues; the possibility for reflections which might fit under the remit of 'therapy'; the scope for the participant to individuate and become better known to care staff; celebratory and creative work which can impact on the broader health-care environment, on clients' families and even, as a form of health education, the general public; as well as the possibility of developing a real relationship with language and writing – do not contradict each other. Perhaps it is easier to think about the example of *reading*. Just as we cannot 'get involved in' a book which we find is badly written, so it is the *quality of the writing* experience which allows us all that good literature enables: an involvement which is not just aesthetic but imaginative, intellectual, emotional and even spiritual.

My own experience of this project was shaped by issues of quality. The Kingfisher Project was set up as a model of good practice; and I would argue that, insofar as it fulfilled any of these expectations, it did so through the particular quality of its partners. A management team already very experienced in community literature activites and arts in health care saw writing in health and social care as a central, rather than a peripheral, form of provision. Several clinicians and carers with a real commitment to making the project work for their clients had already been identified through their involvement in past projects. There was also the influential support of the project's initial funders – the Poetry Society and Southern Arts – which raised expectations of quality.

Particularly unusual, though, was a commitment to artistic quality and experimentation, and to practitioner development. In this book both Paul Munden[2] and Sue Stewart talk about the importance of this area of literature provision. If writers are not stretched, encouraged and developed, it seems likely that they may become demotivated or 'stale'. They will certainly not be the professionals they might have become, given such opportunities. A project such as Kingfisher, which integrates the writer's own creative and reflective practices (through commissions, performances and support for research) with their workshopping activity, benefits directly from the very 'writerliness' of the lead practitioner which less-well-managed projects exploit but may also suffocate. It also allows the project to benefit more fully from the writer's experience in the field of writing in health and social care. An experienced facilitator who is always forced into the most basic activities by an inexperienced manager is a facilitator whose skills are being wasted.

For those involved in a project such as Kingfisher, certain strengths and weaknesses are all too apparent. But others may go unnoticed. The Kingfisher Project was evaluated in December 2001 by a peer-practitioner, Graham Hartill (Hartill 2001). His report stressed that: 'it is clear to me that the matter of evaluation is itself integral to all aspects of the project and of great importance to the growing field of writing in health care.' And he found that:

I heard the same kind of positive comments again and again regarding the benefits of the project to participants. Other than the purely creative ones (such as the Arts Centre Group's focus on skills, practice and networking) these include:

- increased self-esteem and confidence;
- a sense of achievement;
- entertainment and reduced boredom, providing an 'escape from the ward' (not unimportant, bearing in mind that, say on the spinal unit, some patients may be in therapy for a year);
- humanising influence: 'people treated as people, not just as patients';
- stimulated memories (stroke patients) and mental activity generally;
- a developing sense of companionship on the wards – opening participants up both to each other (helping develop friendships) and, significantly, to staff, sometimes resulting in a clearer understanding of patients' symptoms and experience of life on the ward;
- bringing like-minded people together and developing a sense of solidarity (Arts Centre Group).

Any creative writing workshop demands a wide range of expertise from its facilitator, never more so than in health-care contexts. He or she needs to be not only a good writer who knows the tricks of the trade of each writing genre, but also a good 'presence', capable of holding a group (often comprised of seriously troubled individuals) together, of reading the situation for its possibilities and potential, and of enthusing people about what is going on. Only experience shows how to recognise and acknowledge when poetry is happening, when the discourse has entered a deeper level, when language work is taking place, even when nothing is, or even can be, actually written down. From an ethical point of view, too, there is no reason to consider the work done here as anything other than entirely professional. Fiona's work confronts conflicting demands and less than perfect circumstances. Some of these reflect a cultural difficulty which no one project can rectify; but we can work on improving conditions and debating recurring problems with an eye to change. The following suggestions are based on my own considerations of strongly-felt comments:

- *All staff working on a unit should ideally be given the opportunity for briefings on the work.* On the stroke ward (where many of the benefits mentioned above are particularly marked) the can was carried almost exclusively by a sister with great faith in the project who would like to see a much more holistic input to the care of her patients, but is up against the ignorance and suspicion of fellow staff. Poetry is commonly seen as a 'crackpot idea' (especially by staff engaged in cognitive work), there is no dedicated space for the sessions (an unlikely luxury admittedly), and sessions are continuously interrupted by the unbudgeable routine of medicines, tests and dressings. Patients themselves are too disempowered to protest.

  By contrast, briefing/training of staff was particularly encouraged at the hospice. The introductory leaflets were seen as good – 'informative but not too "in your face"', and any feedback from the project to staff (who were curious about what was going on) was be welcomed. Poems were sometimes passed on to participants' families and even used at their funerals.

  Willingness to set aside time for staff training may or may not be mirrored in other situations, (NB: at another venue the same leaflets were seen as being uninformative and were 'just thrown away' by staff) but the general acknowledgement of its usefulness should, I think, be explored further.

- *Poem-posters were not given the exposure expected by the poets involved.* This provoked strong feeling which bears on the broader matter of the relationship between the management of the project and the participants.

- *What happens to the poems?* is a question worth looking at. There can be no one answer to it nor should there be, but several participants have expressed a desire to put the work to greater 'use'. Public presentation is by no means the only way to put 'finished' work back into the cycle; again, a workable system of discussion with ward staff might produce intriguing possibilities.

The feelings expressed on the wards and by participants regarding the work was overwhelmingly positive. 'More please!' was the common plea. Fiona was congratulated for her skills with the participants and her sensitivity and adaptability to specific situations (which are, after all, extremely varied).

As a practitioner myself, it does seem important to me to get the priorities right. The Kingfisher Project is about people writing; the rest is a way of allowing and encouraging this to happen. Management is about managing, and if a project like this is going well, *the task of management is to actively support the work in a self-effacing way*. It goes without saying though, that the machinery needs to be working smoothly for a job to get done with the minimum of friction. The real work *is* getting done and getting done well. Rather than devoting too much attention to its own processes, the Steering Group should, in my opinion, congratulate itself on an excellent project (based on a constructive partnership) and devote itself to its practical development.

Quality provision, then, continues to develop; and the Kingfisher Project is now led by Rose Flint, who writes on her practice elsewhere in this book.[3] However, arts funding – and so the work it supports – is always uncertain and short term. How, then, might we model an ideal future for projects like Kingfisher? Emma Ryder Richardson argues that:

It was always stressed in the initial planning that this was not simply a one-off project; and this is a significant reason for its success. Having had the project core-funded at its concept, wards and departments are now beginning to make their own financial commitment – admittedly from charitable trust funds – but these are vitally important resources that supply not just add-ons but basic equipment. One day the worth of Kingfisher will, we hope, be reflected by including a budget allowance from revenue funding. Arts provision is not just an added extra to provide a feel-good factor or only to be experienced when hospitalised. In the ancient civilisations the arts, sciences and philosophy formed the bedrock of everyday life: perhaps the time has come in our own society to review the significance of this.

Notes

1   This is a point I return to in my Introduction and Chapter Eleven; see also Sue Stewart's Introduction to Part Two and Dominic McLoughlin in Chapter Nine.

2   In his Introduction to Part One.

3   In Chapter Seven.

References

Hartill, G. (2001) *The Kingfisher Project: Evaluation*. Unpublished report.

Sampson, F. (1999) *The Healing Word: A Practical Guide to Poetry and Personal Development Activities*. London: Poetry Society.

Sampson, F. (ed.) (2000) *Strange Baggage*. Salisbury: Kingfisher Project.

Sampson, F. (2001) *Building a Wall with Words: Creative Writing in Health and Social Care*. Nijmegen: University of Nijmegen Press.

Sampson, F. and Stainer, P. (2001) *Sprung Release*. Unpublished radio script.

Further reading

Hartill, G. *Creative Writing: Towards a Framework for Evaluation*. Occasional Papers No.4, Edinburgh: University of Edinburgh, undated.

Hunt, C. and Sampson, F. (eds) (1998) *The Self on the Page: Theory and Practice of Creative Writing in Personal Development*. London: Jessica Kingsley Publishers.

Sampson, F. (1997) 'Some questions of identity: what is writing in health care?' In C. Kaye and T. Blee (eds) *The Arts in Health Care*. London: Jessica Kingsley Publishers, pp.157–165.

Part Two

Thinking Through Practice

Introduction:
A Provider's Experience

Sue Stewart

Most of us reflect on our working practices from time to time. In the arts this is a fairly commonplace activity, bound up as our work often is with our beliefs, value systems and personal experiences as well as the business of earning a living. It is important that we do reflect on our professional practice in this way so we can refresh and re-energise ourselves, change direction, and take on new challenges: in order to keep growing and to have something to offer beyond our habitual stock-in-trade. For those providing[1] 'literature in the community', such as writing in health and social care settings, this reflection is a pretty basic tenet of daily life. We need to keep asking ourselves certain key questions: What is literature in the community for? Why spend so much of one's working life providing it? What is 'community' anyway? Does it matter, and if so, why?

My working definition of literature in the community – the field of which writing in health and social care is such a significant part – is threefold.

First, there are the *activities*: writing, reading, commissioning, displaying, broadcasting, performing and promoting poetry, prose, plays, etc. For example:

- a poet visits a primary school to work with 100 children on creative writing workshops, culminating in a performance and/or an anthology;[2]

- library authorities work in partnership with youth services to deliver 'reader development' to socially excluded teenagers;[3]

- a virtual literature festival, celebrating a landmark day in the literary calendar, reaches a national and international audience through the net.[4]

Second, my working definition involves commitment to the *quality* of the writing itself: that is what 'literature' is. Writers working in the community should be recognised by their peers and qualified in their field, and should continually strive to maintain their own professional development and practice. This is not a culturally specific view of 'quality' (i.e. 'that which I know'): we should strive to offer the community the best writers and performers available, from a variety of cultural backgrounds. This applies whether we are in the business of 'live literature' (literature events, festivals, residencies, workshops or other activities) or 'reader development' (the promotion of books and reading, primarily through the public library sector and/or the commercial sector). Offering members of the community less than the best only puts them off literature and does nobody any favours in the long term. This is so whether that 'community' is a dedicated local writers' group, experienced on the live literature circuit, or an 'at risk' teenager opening up a book of his own free will for the first time in his life. There are balances to be struck, of course. If an 'at risk' teenager, who may associate reading with formal education and failure, can first be made interested *at all* in reading through, for example, exploring a book on card tricks, or snakes, or Planet Earth – great, that's a 'way in'! But he or she can also be introduced unobtrusively to the best poetry and prose available, from writers of all ages and cultures, and these may – and often do – ignite a spark which, whilst it might appear slight to others, can have life-changing significance for the individual: probably we all remember at least one book we feel indebted to for the way it helped us to define our lives.[5] This is not simply 'entertainment', but something far more powerful, meaningful and rewarding.

Third, literature in the community means thinking about our *definition of 'community'*. Who or what is it? Are we talking about one big community, or many multi-faceted ones? Is it defined by culture, geography, or interests? And who needs enhanced access to arts provision? It seems fairly obvious that, while 'one world' or even 'one nation' may be an appealing proposition, arts or any other service delivery addresses many different communities or target groups, defined in many different ways. Some of these communities will overlap, and one person can belong to several at the same time. Likewise, artists and writers may specialise in working with one particular group (such as people receiving health care), but work in other contexts too.

It is important here to look at what is happening in the arts funding system, as this will impact upon arts practice over the next few years. Any community arts project applying for public funding today will need to address some key questions: Who is the project for? How will it be delivered? Is partnership funding in place? How will it be managed, monitored and evaluated? Is it aiming to be a national model, or is it simply a good local or regional initiative? Is it sustainable?

On the broader strategic level, during 2003 Arts Council England (ACE) has been developing a national Arts and Health Strategy[6] informed by the ACE philosophy that excellence and social inclusion go hand in hand. This type of work is about genuine access, for all, to the best available art and artists, and involves identifying target groups in, for instance, the health care sector, engaging them, and thereby helping to improve the experience of care. It is most definitely not social engineering, or the arts being used solely for therapeutic purposes. Neither is it about the arts doing something *to* disadvantaged members of the community; on the contrary, artists learn and grow creatively from doing this type of work, which impacts as much upon them as it does upon the target groups.

Many writers actively seek out this work as otherwise they feel they are practising in a vacuum; and ACE facilitates this type of activity for the benefit of the community and artists alike. As part of the Arts and Health Strategy, ACE looked at a range of development packages to help artists work in areas such as health and prisons – resources, professional development, training, marketing opportunities, art form development and, for organisations, capacity building. ACE is also working with government departments to look at the impact of the arts upon key government priority areas. This includes looking at the evidence base, including longitudinal studies, to start building the case for using the arts to address these wider social issues. The arts are not a panacea for social ills; however, with a multi-agency approach – for instance, working across housing, the NHS and the criminal justice system – the arts can make a significant contribution to social policy.

One of the most important things about literature in the community is the way it centres on and reminds us of people as individuals. Writing activities in the often dehumanising contexts of health and social care are a paradigm of this. As the other writers in this book make clear, writing in care contexts restores the dimension of subjective meaning to the individual who is passively (think of the Latin root of the word 'patient') receiving care. This brings us back to the issue of quality: this time, not only the quality of the literature on offer, but the underpinning philosophy of the writer/tutor, their sensitivity and responsiveness to individuals, and their integrity.

The medical term 'person-centred care' could easily apply to a good writing workshop, which is based not on traditional educational methodology and practice (though these may help), but on the willingness and ability of the writer to establish a one-to-one relationship with each individual client, student or patient. A relationship that respects autonomy and maintains professional distance, but at the same time fosters a unique kind of intimacy and trust. For the writer in health and social care, developing this type of sensitivity and responsiveness is at least as important as developing their own writing, publishing and performing track record.

So, one mark of quality is reflective practice: learning from and questioning experience. This is what this section of the book addresses, from a variety of perspectives. Quality – in all its different forms – is vital to the success of arts projects delivered in community settings, particularly in the health and social care sector. Only by constant reflection on our own and others' professional practices can we hope to offer the best, or even recognise it when we see it. This section, with contributions from distinguished practitioners in the field of writing in health and social care, shows how real reflection on practice can generate that success.

Notes

1   'Providers' are, in this context, not only the writers and carers involved in any project but the arts and other organisations that 'provide' – initiate, manage and fund – such projects as a whole. I am writing from my perspective as Director of literature consultancy Write2B and former Literature Officer of Arts Council East Midlands, as well as a poet with many years' experience of literature in the community.

2   This is the usual format for poets' visits to schools, such as one I made to Dunchurch Primary School, Northamptonshire, on National Poetry Day 2002. However, some can last much longer: for instance, a residency where the poet visits one or two days per week throughout the term.

3   YouthBOOX, Splash Extra, and Positive Activities for Young People Programmes, The Reading Agency. See www.boox.org.uk, www.readingagency.org.uk and www.Write2B.co.uk

4   The World Book Day Online Festival, funded by Arts Council England, involves a groundbreaking partnership between libraries and booksellers. I was Project Manager on behalf of The Reading Agency and Festival partners in 2003 and now in 2004. See www.worldbookdayfestival.com, www.readingagency.org.uk and www.Write2B.co.uk

5   I will always remember discovering the poetry of Medbh McGuckian (formerly published by Oxford University Press, now by Bloodaxe) when I was a poet in my early thirties. At that particular time, I was fortunate in having mentoring support from an older male poet who believed in the pared-down approach (which was a good grounding for a young poet). However, the lateral thinking and linguistic acrobatics of McGuckian propelled me into another way of appreciating as well as writing poetry.

6   The Arts Council Arts and Health Strategy has been developed by Nikki Crane, Head of Social Inclusion, Arts Council England.

CHAPTER SIX

Writing, Education and Therapy
Literature in the Training of Clinicians

Robin Downie

Introduction

I became involved in the discipline now known as the 'medical
humanities' in the mid-1980s. For some years I had collaborated with
Professor Kenneth C. Calman (at that time the Post-Graduate Medical
Dean at Glasgow University) in the teaching of ethics to medical students.
We found that the students were more interested in the details of cases
than in general principles. Their attention was captured more by the
dramatic narrative of the cases – what the patients said or felt and how the
professionals reacted – than by our efforts to slot the cases into the
quasi-legal framework of medical ethics. As a result of this response we
decided to offer the students the opportunity to discuss stories, plays or
poems, works actually created as dramatic narratives, or as meditations on
human interactions. To begin with this was more an after-hours club than
a class, but it was enthusiastically received by the students and some
doctors who came along to join the discussion.

These activities developed in the early 1990s and I was able to
organise four one-day conferences in Glasgow on medicine and the arts.
The conferences attracted audiences of around a hundred participants,
mainly medical. For each of them I prepared a small anthology of poetry
and prose which was discussed in groups. One of the anthologies – 'A

Poet's Cure' – was compiled by the present editor, Fiona Sampson. Finally, the anthologies were published by Oxford University Press as *The Healing Arts: an Illustrated Oxford Anthology* (1994; 2000). The impetus in Scotland continued when the Royal College of Physicians and Surgeons of Glasgow celebrated their 500th anniversary with a two-day conference on medicine and literature.[1]

Meanwhile my collaborator, now Sir Kenneth Calman, had become the Chief Medical Officer of the UK and threw his considerable authority behind the medical humanities movement. He is now Vice-Chancellor and Warden of the University of Durham where he has created a Centre for the Arts and Humanities in Health and Medicine (CAHHM) under the direction of Dr Jane Macnaughton (who is a graduate in literature as well as medicine). The function of this Centre is not only to introduce the arts and humanities to the Durham Medical School but also to encourage community arts in the North of England, and to carry out research on ways of evaluating such movements.[2]

Evaluation is of course of the first importance because anyone who wishes to mount a course in creative writing, or the arts generally, for medical or nursing students, undergraduate or postgraduate, is going to be faced with a demand from deans or the like for the aims and evaluations of the courses. With a new subject this is not an unreasonable request. This chapter, therefore, will be concerned with making some suggestions about what can be said to sceptical deans, and then with the connections between education and healing. Although I have worked with the wider field of medical arts or humanities, I will concentrate on creative writing and reading.

One preliminary point must be made. Enthusiasts for creative writing often say that the aim is to produce doctors who are more compassionate or who have empathy. However, it is not at all clear that such aims can be achieved through creative writing or a study of the arts, and certainly they cannot be evaluated. To be versed in the humanities or to be a creative writer is not the same as being humane, a point often illustrated by referring to Nazi officers. It might be more tellingly illustrated by inviting those of us who profess the humanities or creative writing to consider ourselves and our colleagues and to ask whether we are really more compassionate and humane than our medical colleagues. Some humility is required from those who claim from the safety of the study that doctors lack compassion: and then seek to remedy this alleged defect by recommending the practice of what they happen to be good at. I shall therefore suggest more concrete and realistic aims which writers might be in a position to help students and doctors achieve.

In general terms, the hope would be to introduce students and doctors to a *range of concepts and methods,* other than narrowly scientific ones, which can *assist with the understanding of human beings and their interactions and with doctor–patient communication.* These aims can be placed into groups for convenience of discussion.

Aims

Group A: Transferable skills

1. TO DEVELOP THE ABILITY TO WRITE CLEAR ENGLISH

Medical English often has one or other or both of two faults. Either it is turgid and larded with professional terms or it is written in bullet points. However, when it comes to presenting a case to a wider audience, some attention to brevity and clarity and to what people might want to know is important. Perhaps such skills can be developed from courses on, say, journalism or creative writing. For example, practice in letter writing can be an unpretentious but useful aspect of creative writing. The General Medical Council, the official disciplinary body of UK medicine, reports that many complaints against doctors refer to the harsh, even arrogant, tone of some letters received by patients. Yet, when they are taxed with this the doctors concerned are genuinely surprised that their letters had such an unfortunate effect. What was lacking was not compassionate feeling, but a grasp of appropriate prose style. Style could be improved through a study of the letters in some of the many available anthologies of letters and then by writing practice.

2. TO DEVELOP SENSITIVITY TO NUANCES, AMBIGUITIES AND HIDDEN MEANINGS IN ORDINARY CONVERSATION

Some humanities, especially literature, involve concentration on language, and a study of such disciplines will develop sensitivity to what patients may be saying. It is worth noting here that doctors and others who wish to promote the employment of the arts in medical education are currently making the idea of 'narrative' a central concept. Like the use of the term 'evidence' by their scientifically minded colleagues, this wide use of the term obscures as much as it illuminates. In the brief time a doctor spends in consultation with a patient that individual might be able to relate a short anecdote, but there is not likely to be much time for anything that would justify the grand term 'narrative', unless perhaps in psychotherapy. Doctors who wish to learn from the humanities might do well to become aware of the range of conceptual tools which are available – from hermeneutics, rhetoric, linguistics, and so on – rather than march behind generalised slogans such as 'the patient's narrative'. There are many other concepts which might more precisely direct the doctor's attention to the nature and implications of the language used by the patient (Culler 1997).

Perhaps it might be helpful by way of example to mention two, from literary interpretation, which can be helpful in a medical context: 'voice' and 'iteration'. 'Voice' can be explained initially in simple grammatical terms. It is the difference between an account of what *I* feel/think/experience and what *he/she* feels/thinks/experiences. But the voices become intermingled when the patient says: 'I had a touch of pain last week and I wouldn't have bothered about it, but my husband – he's a great worrier – said, "Jean, you must go to the doctor". So here I am'. The wife is here putting the blame on the husband, and this is of significance. It means that she is worried but does not wish to admit to the worries. Some practice in using this kind of distinction in works of literature will enable a medical student or doctor to develop a sensitivity to certain types of nuance within a patient's narrative or account of their problems.

Another helpful concept is that of iteration. If a problem is especially worrying to us we tend to return to it in different ways. This is a device used to great effect in poetry. For example, in the following short poem by John Davies of Hereford (1565–1618) the lines themselves are not striking – banal even – but the iteration makes them together very effective in conveying the state of mind of the poet.

> Death has deprived me of my dearest friend,
> My dearest friend is dead and laid in grave,
> In grave he rests until the world shall end,
> The world shall end as end must all things have.
> All things must have an end that nature wrought,
> That nature wrought must unto dust be brought.[3]

Sensitivity to a certain sort of repetition is a quality which a doctor might find worth developing.

Nevertheless, the term 'narrative' does have the merit of identifying a general type of explanation of behaviour which can be as revealing of a medical condition as an X-ray. It depicts a slice of life-story, a way of understanding patients through their own language rather than through that of science. Skills of this kind can be developed through reading and writing narrative. Indeed, it cannot be overemphasised at the moment that the evidence from randomised clinical trials is only one sort of evidence relevant to clinical judgment. A biographer, say, or a detective, will look for a different sort of evidence: one related to *specific* incidents or events. Their sort of evidence may be logically closer to the kind which influences a clinician, who is dealing with the particular patient, than the evidence of trials, which is generalised. In general, science works mainly with inductive evidence, but the arts can introduce doctors to a range of other ways of thinking which are equally relevant to the practice of medicine (Downie and Macnaughton 2000). Familiarity with these alternative sources of evidence comes from creative writing and reading.

3. TO DEVELOP THE ABILITY TO SEE CONNECTIONS BETWEEN APPARENTLY DISPARATE SITUATIONS

E.M. Forster's novel *Howard's End* states its overriding theme before the book starts: 'Only connect…' (Forster 1946, p.1): and the story illustrates the tragic consequences when the characters fail to do this. The ability to see connections is one which can be developed by creative writing. For example, a good plot will be one in which clues are given in such a way that, as the story develops, the reader is led to feel the inevitability of certain sorts of development. Developing skill in plotting will assist medical students in noting the diverse clues to meaning which we all scatter around in our everyday encounters.

Group B: The humanistic perspective

1. TO ENABLE STUDENTS TO DEVELOP BROAD PERSPECTIVES ON HUMAN BEINGS AND SOCIETY

These will place medical practice into a wider context or into a social framework. There are many different ways of seeing human beings, of which the scientific is only one; and there are many different ways of seeing society, of which the Western Liberal view is only one. For example, I was involved in teaching a Special Study Module (SSM) on Plato's *Republic* to medical students. (Downie and Macnaughton 1999; Plato 1955). It so happened that the medical students had just finished their Family Project, a piece of work which presupposed the importance of the family unit. They were then faced with Plato's arguments *against* the family. It was salutary for them to appreciate that not everyone thinks that the family and family values are good, and to be obliged to make explicit and defend the values which their project presupposed.

The development of broad perspectives may be especially important in medicine because, like the military and the police, medicine has its own ethos and bonding is encouraged. There is therefore a tendency to develop narrow perspectives and to close ranks. In the present age this can be undesirable.

2. TO DEVELOP MORAL SENSITIVITY

The teaching of medical ethics has tended to fall into the hands of philosophers. Philosophers, however, are interested in general principles and theories which have a limited appeal to medical students because of their abstract and generalised nature. On the other hand, literature or film can make a much more powerful impact on moral awareness because of their immediacy. Like medicine itself, literature deals with the detail of individual cases. Indeed, there is a danger that philosophy actually blunts moral awareness, because students become caught up with abstract terms – such as 'deontology' or 'patient autonomy' – or with the technicalities of moral argument which blind them to the reality of the situations they will be dealing with. I have discussed this elsewhere (Downie 1999).

Group C: Coping with the particular situation

TO DEVELOP THE ABILITY TO UNDERSTAND AND TO COPE WITH
PARTICULAR SITUATIONS WHERE RULES AND GUIDELINES DO NOT
EXACTLY APPLY

In this context it is helpful to refer to Plato's discussion in Book X of the *Republic* of an 'ancient quarrel' between philosophers on the one hand and poets and dramatists on the other (Plato 1955, pp.370–386). The quarrel concerns the qualifications of each to make recommendations about the nature of the good life. Plato has no doubt that poets and dramatists are trying to do the same sort of thing as the philosophers (otherwise there would be no quarrel) but he holds that they lack proper understanding for the job. Plato's view is that real understanding comes from having insight into the blueprints, the timeless patterns, which make things as they are. In our day the task of discovering such patterns has been taken up by scientists, and of course doctors are keen to follow the lead of scientists.

Plato's arguments against poets and dramatists as a source of knowledge or understanding are limited because they depend on his assumption that the arts are essentially imitative, an assumption which would not nowadays be accepted. However, even those who do not make that assumption may agree with Plato that the arts are not a source of real understanding. According to this point of view, the arts are merely decorative or entertaining or expressive of emotion. However, it is possible to challenge this position by maintaining that the arts and humanities can provide a distinctive sort of understanding: an understanding of the particular situation and the qualitative distinctions involved. Let us examine this sort of understanding.

Literature, drama and film are concerned above all with qualitative distinctions. There is no one measure or scale in terms of which the interaction of the characters can be measured. One event or action is not just of a different quantity from another; rather, novels, plays and poetry are concerned with the qualitative richness of human interaction and the possibilities for tragedy involved. Moreover, literature shows us that in order to understand any particular action or character it is necessary to see the interrelatedness of them all. This kind of understanding is quite different from the understanding generated by science. Science enables us to understand by demonstrating the patterns or laws which cover individual events or changes. Social science tries to do the same, perhaps less certainly, for human actions. However, such understanding is achieved only if we abstract from the complexity of human motivation and interaction. For example, 'rational economic man' is not any single man of flesh and blood, but an abstraction. But he is an explanatory concept in economics, just as 'the role of the patient' and its associated behaviours is thought to be explanatory in medical sociology. Yet, although 'the role of the patient' may *help* to explain the behaviour of Hamish MacTavish who has just been admitted to hospital, it may also mislead, since it is abstracted from the complex motivation and interrelatedness of this specific individual. It is in literature, drama or film that we find this distinctive sort of understanding pre-eminently illustrated. It is a genuine kind of understanding, but quite distinct from that provided by science or social science. Through imaginative identification with the characters in a story or play we can develop the capacity for insights into the human condition with which medicine is concerned.

Group D: Self-awareness
TO DEVELOP SELF-AWARENESS, INCLUDING AWARENESS OF ONE'S OWN EMOTIONS

One criticism sometimes made of doctors is that they are not always aware of how they are coming across to patients; and one problem of some doctors is emotional burn-out, which is not only self-destructive but also has a bad effect on patients. What we call a person's inner life is the inside story of his own history: the way living in the world feels to him. This kind of experience is usually only vaguely known, because most of its components are nameless; and it is hard to form an idea of anything which has no name. This easily leads to the conclusion that feeling is entirely formless, that it has causes which may be determined and effects which must be dealt with (sometimes by drugs) but that it itself is irrational: a disturbance of the organism with no structure of its own.

Yet, subjective experience has a structure which can be reflected on and symbolically expressed. It cannot be expressed through the discursive – everyday or scientific – use of language, but it can be articulated through reading and creative writing. Works of art are expressive forms; and what they express is the nature of human feeling. The arts make our inner subjective life visible, audible or in some other way perceivable, through symbolic form (Langer 1953). What is artistically good is what articulates and presents this inner life to our understanding. Note that while an artist expresses feeling it is not as a baby might. The artist objectifies subjective life. What the artist expresses is not his or her own feelings but what he or she *knows about* feeling. A work of art expresses a conception of life, emotion and inward reality. That is why the arts can help to create the self-understanding which is important for any doctor dealing with vulnerable human beings. As J.S. Mill puts it: 'It really is of importance, not only what men do, but also what manner of men they are that do it' (Mill 1962, p.188).

Group E: Joint investigation
TO EXPERIENCE THE PROCESS OF JOINT INVESTIGATION

All the aims so far discussed have been constructed in terms of the *outcomes* of studying the arts or of practising creative writing. Nonetheless, it is arguable that for some subjects these outcomes, in terms of new knowledge or skills, are less important than the process by which they are approached. In the arts, or some of them, it is possible for the student to challenge the teacher's point of view to an extent that would not be possible in a subject such as biochemistry. This is not the same as learning to work in a team (which, though important, is learned elsewhere). The study of the arts can involve a joint exploration in which the student can put forward points of view which can then be modified in the light of what his peers say. The result might be that all members of the study group, including the teacher or facilitator, reach a more considered understanding than they had before. The point here is the nature of what is learned in the *process* of discussion rather than the outcome. Process-led approaches to higher education have been proposed by Stenhouse (1975) and more recently by Laurillard (1993).

Education and healing

It is a familiar idea that education is of the whole person. In this paper I have been arguing that the use of creative writing and reading brings to medical education a broadening which is an essential supplement to its basically scientific core. The practice of creative writing can produce this rounding or wholeness which is characteristic of the educated person. Is there any connection here with healing? Some in the 'arts and health' movement claim that creative writing can also be a healing activity. In what sense, or in what respects, can literature be said to heal?

The verb *to heal* comes from an Old English verb *haelan* meaning *to make whole*. It is only derivatively that it comes to mean *to cure a disease*. It is in this older sense that we can see the arts as healing, although healing in this older sense may well have some impact on the curing of disease.

Before we can develop the idea of making a person whole or sound we must have some general view of the nature of a person, and why a person might *not* be 'whole' or 'sound'. Certain characteristics are widely regarded as constitutive of the human person and the human situation. Persons have physical bodies which are in many respects vulnerable to, and also dependent on, the environment and other persons. They have varying degrees of rationality and consciousness of themselves and their surroundings. The combination of their bodies, reason and self-consciousness creates human feeling and emotions, many of which are caused by and directed towards other human beings and the environment. The complex interplay of all these factors creates many possibilities for disorder in the relationships among persons, and for the fragmentation of human personalities. One device which has evolved to minimise this kind of disorder and to enhance harmony, cooperation and wholeness is morality or ethics; another is education; a third is art. Great art always has in the background (sometimes in the foreground) some vision of an ordered society or of what a human being should be like. In this sense art does heal by making whole. This point is made by M. Therese Southgate (1997, p.201), a physician and former deputy editor of the *Journal of the American Medical Association*, a medical journal which publishes reproductions of paintings on its cover:

> Medicine and art have a common goal: to complete what nature cannot bring to a finish...to reach the ideal...to heal creation. This

is done by *paying attention*. The physician attends the patient; the artist attends nature… If we are attentive in looking, in listening and in waiting, then sooner or later something in the depths of ourselves will respond. Art, like medicine, is not an arrival; it is a search. This is why, perhaps, we call medicine itself an art.

My conclusion here then is that medicine, art, and education can all be seen as related and mutually interdependent processes of attempting to make persons whole through a creative enterprise.

Means and ends

One aspect of all this which can disturb creative writers is the thought that their creative work is being seen as a means to an end: education or therapy. The point can be put even more bluntly. Deans of Medicine may not be willing to give time in an already crowded curriculum to creative writing unless it can be shown to be of direct instrumental value in producing a good doctor, whereas a writer may regard this emphasis on instrumentality as a kind of prostitution. Again, a funding body may not be willing to fund a creative writing project unless it has demonstrable therapeutic value, whereas to approach writing in this way may destroy creativity at the very start. How are we to respond to this kind of dilemma?

One line would be to argue that creative writing and other arts can be *both* instrumental for educational or therapeutic ends *and* also worthwhile for their own sake. This line is plausible only if we grant two assumptions: that we can stretch the meaning of 'instrumental' until it is really very thin; and that something can be at one and the same time instrumentally good and an intrinsic good or 'final end'. If we take the first assumption, we can see what I am calling the 'thinness' of this use of the concept of instrumentality. For example, this 'thinness' is apparent if we say that creative writing is 'instrumental', if it conduces to human flourishing or to a better understanding of the outside world or to personal develop-ment. This application of 'instrumental' is far removed from base-line applications of that concept: as when we say that a hacksaw was instru-mental in the prisoner's escape, or that the headmaster was instrumental in influencing the pupil's choice of career. The base-line use of 'instrumental' has two features: it implies that there is a causal connection between the instrument and what its use leads to, and it implies that the instrument has no place in the end brought about by its use. Neither of these conditions hold when we say, for example, that creative writing or the appreciation of the arts conduce to human development. The term 'conduce' does not here indicate a causal connection, for a causal connection would imply that the appreciation of the arts was one thing and human development something different. The point is however that an appreciation of the arts is a *necessary component part of* the final end state of human development or of educatedness. Hence, the language of instrumentality is misleading because of its associations with causality.

The second assumption is also debatable – that something can be causally instrumental and also a final end. I do not want to press this, however, mainly because I believe the entire controversy is misconceived; it seems real only because of the terminology in which it is stated. In short, I wish to maintain that the distinction between an instrumental means and an intrinsic or final end is misleading.

Consider the following example – that of the creation of a painting. In painting a picture the artist will use assorted instrumental means, such as paint brushes, an easel and, say, a model. These are instruments whose justification lies in the final end or product: the painting. They are causally or productively connected with the painting, and when it is completed they have no further part to play (unless of course the painting is being entered for the Turner Prize!). As instrumental means they are only contingently connected with the painting and are removed leaving no trace when it is finished. Are we to think that literature and so on are only causally or contingently or extrinsically connected with producing a flourishing or educated human being, and when they have done their work they will be removed like the easel, etc.? Obviously not! But that is the implication of maintaining a distinction between an instrumental means and an intrinsic or final end.

What then should be said? Let us return to the example of the painting. The paintbrushes, easel, model, etc. are instrumental means to the painting and have no part to play when it is completed. But the canvas, paint and the shapes it creates are also means to the creation of the painting. The difference is that they do have a necessary part in the finished product. We can therefore call them *component* (as distinct from instrumental) *means* to the painting. In Aristotle's terminology, the paint brushes and so on are 'efficient causes' of the painting, whereas the canvas, paint and shapes are the 'material and formal causes' of the painting, which itself is the 'final cause', the ultimate aim of the whole process (Aristotle 1998).

If we apply these distinctions to the question of the relationship between creative writing or the appreciation of the arts, the educated person and the good doctor it might be possible to take the following line. We can say that the enjoyment and practice of creative writing and the arts are activities worthwhile for their own sake, and also that they are means to creating an educated, developed, flourishing human life. But they are not instrumental in that process; they are essential components of such a life. To put it another way: we can say that part of what it means to be an educated developed human being is to be able to enjoy at least some humanities for their own sake. Of course, that is only part of what it means; there are other essential components in the educated life, such as some appreciation of science, some interest in current affairs, some general curiosity, and so on. For the developed or flourishing life other aspects of human life would also be needed: such as friends.

In a similar way creative writing may be a means to a certain sort of therapy, but that 'therapy' means simply that the patient is led to see his or her life in a certain sort of way, as a whole. Both in education and in therapy the point is not to develop feelings. Perhaps an analogy with music might help here. The musician performing a piece of music is not brimming with emotion: he would lose the place if he were! His feelings are, as it were, in his fingers. So with the doctor; his gaze should be outward, away from himself. The doctor needs to be aware of what is on the whole likely to be good for this particular patient and requires sensitivity to the patient's wishes, consent or refusal and so on. In other words, the doctor needs to be able to make considered judgments; and a developed sense of judgment has a humanistic element as a component means (Downie and Macnaughton 2000). In a similar way, the patient may be enabled to look outward away from feelings which may be destructive and toward a more ordered vision of his or her life as a whole. Creative writing, reading and the arts generally can assist in this humanistic project.

Notes

1   www.rcplondon.ac.uk

2   www.dur.ac.uk/cahhm/

3   'A Remembrance of My Friend Mr Thomas Morley' in *Microcosmos* (1602). (Grossart (ed.) 1873)

References

Aristotle (trans. Lawson-Tancred, H.) (1998) *The Metaphysics.* Harmondsworth: Penguin.

Culler, J. (1997) *Literary Theory.* Oxford: Oxford University Press.

Downie, R.S. (1994; 2000) *The Healing Arts.* Oxford: Oxford University Press.

Downie, R.S. (1999) 'The role of literature in medical education.' *Journal of Medical Ethics 25*, 6, 529–531.

Downie, R.S. and Macnaughton, J. (1999) 'Should medical students read Plato?' *The Medical Journal of Australia 170*, 3, 125–127.

Downie, R.S. and Macnaughton, J. (2000) *Clinical Judgement: Evidence in Practice.* Oxford: Oxford University Press.

Forster, E.M. (1946) *Howard's End.* Harmondsworth: Penguin.

Grossart, A.B. (ed.) (1873) *The Complete Poems of John Davis of Hereford.* Oxford: Oxford University Press.

Langer, S.K. (1953) *Feeling and Form.* London: Routledge and Kegan Paul.

Laurillard, D. (1993) *Rethinking Teaching.* London: Routledge.

Mill, J.S. (1962) 'On Liberty.' In M. Warnock *Utilitarianism.* Glasgow: Collins. (Original work published 1863.)

Plato (trans. Lee, H.D.P.) (1955) *Republic.* Harmondsworth: Penguin Books. (Original work published c. 370 BC.)

Southgate, T. (ed.) (1997) *The Art of JAMA: One Hundred Covers and Essays from the Journal of the American Medical Association.* St. Louis: Mosby.

Stenhouse, L. (1975) *An Introduction to Curriculum Research and Development.* London: Heinemann.

Further reading

Bolton, G. (1999) *The Therapeutic Potential of Creative Writing.* London: Jessica Kingsley Publishers.

Brodie, H. (1987) *Stories of Sickness.* New Haven, London: Yale University Press.

Cassell, E.J. (1984) *The Place of the Humanities in Medicine.* Hastings-on-Hudson: The Hastings Center.

Evans, M. and Finlay, I.G. (eds) (2001) *Medical Humanities.* London: BMJ Books.

Greenhalgh, T. and Hurwitz, B. (eds) (1998) *Narrative Based Medicine.* London: BMJ Books.

Haldane, D. and Loppert, S. (1999) *The Arts in Health Care: Learning from Experience.* London: King's Fund.

Hunter, K.M. (1991) *Doctors' Stories.* Princeton: Princeton University Press.

Sontag, S. (1990) *Illness as Metaphor and AIDS and its Metaphors.* New York: Anchor Books.

CHAPTER SEVEN

Fragile Space
Therapeutic Relationship and the Word

Rose Flint

Since childhood I have been both a writer and an artist. I trained as a sculptor but my career took me into teaching creative writing and gradually the visual arts were subsumed by poetry. Then I began dreaming about being back in a studio and realised that I needed to re-connect to this part of myself in some way.

Working with both adults and children in the ordinary, everyday situations of classrooms and residencies I had realised how often I found people who were experiencing distress: a teenage girl whose parents were divorcing, a 10-year-old whose grandmother had just died, a 60-year-old woman trying to cope with life after the death of her husband; a man in his sixties with major unresolved issues with his dying father. These were people who were not 'ill' in the accepted sense of that word, but their levels of distress were often manifested in the grey unhappiness of depression. I knew their stories because they appeared in their creative work – sometimes subtly, delicately, sometimes quite violently – but always demanding some kind of response from me even if I did not know what it was, except that it was on a different level from teaching.

I decided that I needed to know more. I needed to have a broader understanding of mental distress and illness, and how I could meet it in the students I taught. Sometimes I had been able to offer some positive reflection or sympathy but I had often felt helpless, out of my depths, in the face of grief or anger or unexpectedly met psychosis. Sometimes I felt exhausted with the weight of students' troubles. The decision to train as an art therapist seemed natural, part of my own evolution. It took me back into the studio, into re-connecting with my own visual creativity, and it opened me up to a new and challenging way of engaging with the world.

My art therapy training and experience inform the work I have done in writing in health care since 1999. I have found that it may sometimes be appropriate to adopt the strict art therapy paradigm for work with poetry: for instance, working with Alcohol Addiction or Adult Mental Health groups where the security of well-held boundaries provides a safe space for sometimes frail and chaotic minds to explore their inner world. On other occasions, such as with a Women's Group drawn from the community, I work more informally; giving more space to the creative group energy which in itself can provide a safe container for individual expression. This chapter looks at how art therapy perspectives can bring further insights into creative writing in health and social care.

Case and Dalley (1992) remind us that the theoretical aspects of art therapy training are influenced and formed by the precepts of psycho-analysis, including the work of Freud, Jung, Klein, Winnicott and Bowlby.[1] Emphasis is often placed on the exploration of the client's early years and the discovery of unconscious material which affects the present situation, on working with dream or imagery content, and on the relaionship between the therapist and her patients. Various psycho-therapeutic disciplines – Psychodynamic, Humanistic and Behavioural (identified by Rubin 1987) – are all studied to the extent that there is debate in the profession as to whether the term 'art therapist' should be amended to 'arts psychotherapist'.

Although it may be classed with psychotherapy, I don't think that art therapy is a 'talking cure'. While not wishing to minimise the spoken interventions and dialogues of an art therapist, I believe that it is the medium of the art itself that is the therapeutic element and the relation-ship between the patient, the therapist and the art, which provides the space for the healing to take place. Simply defined:

> Art Therapy involves the use of different art media through which a
> patient can express and work through the issues and concerns that

have brought him or her into therapy. The therapist and client are in partnership in trying to understand the art process and product of the session. For many clients it is easier to relate to the therapist through the art object which, as a personal statement, provides a focus for discussion, analysis and self-evaluation. (Case and Dalley 1992, p.1)

One of the most widely held views in the practice is that a great deal of the therapy takes place 'in the transference'. 'Transference' is a term traditionally used to describe the way emotions usually first experienced in infancy or early childhood may be then transferred onto any new situation involving a close relationship with another human being (Schaverien 1992) repeating or replicating the earlier pattern.

All human relations contain elements of transference which are primarily unconscious. Without realising it, the patient or client may find in the therapist an aspect of someone who has had considerable meaning in their early life – father or mother, for instance. The therapist may experience counter-transference: a total response to the patient's reality, who they are, their distress, their creativity and their transference. This counter-transference also contains the therapist's unconscious attitude to their patient; their own transference based in their own history (Schaverien 1992). The therapist may also become aware of 'projection', in which she receives emotions 'projected onto' her by the client. These may take different forms, but a therapist may experience physical or emotional states which are unexpected, unrelated to her life and often both confusing and distressing.

The relationship between a therapist and a patient is never simple, but in art therapy the relationship extends into the wider area of the art materials and the environment itself. We speak of this as a 'container', seeing part of the work of therapy as being to 'hold' a space in which a client can work safely. There are many debates about the most useful nature of this space. It is my experience that many – particularly psychoanalytically influenced – art therapists prefer to keep their art rooms as neutral as possible; the walls blank, the colours muted, the therapist becoming as blank as possible, giving away no details of personality or private life: something that a feminist-oriented art therapist such as Burt (1997) certainly finds detrimental to work with women, for instance. The aim of a neutral space is to provide an area that is uncontaminated by anything which the client can use to describe – either in the art or verbally – their inner feeling, thereby forcing them to go deeper into their own resources. In this model, no direction is ever given to the client and the necessary boundaries or rules which apply to the sessions are set by the therapist and must be rigidly adhered to.

Other more humanistic views such as those described by Case and Dalley (1992) takes a less rigorous path. Art posters or pictures by other clients may be on the walls, the therapist may interact with the patient, setting tasks or making suggestions. As Liebmann (1986) states, boundaries may be negotiated by the whole group and not imposed by the therapist. Most therapists agree that their stance should be empathic, alert, and with the self kept mostly out of the equation.

Art therapy sessions with either an individual or a group take place in an art room or studio if there is one. Many day-care or in-patient facilities now have specific rooms for art and pottery, more rarely music or dance. As described by Case and Dalley (1992) groups may be run in a variety of different ways. Deco (1998) at the beginning of her work with patients in acute psychiatry found an open, drop-in group taking place, and altered it into a more rigorously bounded group to which patients had to be referred by staff. Springham (1998) describes running closed groups for a drug and alcohol programme which ten patients attended for six weekly sessions and, although voluntary, signed contracts which committed them to full attendance and abstinence throughout the six weeks.

The therapist usually does not make any images herself. However, in the setting of an art studio group such as Studio Upstairs, an innovative project running in London and Bristol which provides studio space for clients referred in from the community, the 'therapists' are artists working on their own art, alongside everyone else. Here, the focus is placed firmly on the therapeutic quality of art-making, as it was in the origins of the profession, as traced and recorder by Waller (1991).

Every group is different because of whom it contains and the style of the therapist. The room that holds a group making art is different from any other room; I have known many patients call it a Sanctuary. Even if the therapist tries to keep it as blank as possible, even if the room is used for other purposes such as a kitchen, or day room, the materials themselves – colours of paint, textures of clay, possibilities of paper – are already shouting *this is different*. While it is not possible to set up a 'poetry-room' in exactly the same way, even the addition of poetry books, paper and pens, maybe flowers on the table or poster-poems on the walls, can spell out that *this is different* from group rooms full of chairs set in a ring; from the television room, smoking room or classroom. This implies a mode of being that speaks another language to the rest of the institution. Even the very intention of the patient to enter a group where the making of art or poetry is to happen separates this space from any other.

In my experience, poetry – as distinct from any other form of writing – works, at a therapeutic level, in a similar way to art. The raw materials of poetry, words themselves – the sounds they make, the associations they carry, the images they can construct, their very 'colours' (as in the way words such as *heavy, down*, imply sombre shades or words such as *bicycle, dance*, are light, even glittery) seem to behave in the same way as paints or clay; and poems read out in the session can provide the same kind access to the imagination as a picture. In work with prose, modes of speaking and thought, education and environment can prove too strong a hold on an individual's consciousness, disabling any movement away from the perceived reality of the experienced here and now, or the facts of memory. The very unfamiliarity of both poetry and art to the majority of the clients I have come in contact with enables them to access an extraordinary part of themselves, to go 'deeper' to a self that often surprises them with its clarity of knowledge. This knowledge, held at a metaphoric level, does not always obey the laws of the everyday reality we inhabit; as we make our own inner journey, we may also be affected by the inner journeys of those we are working alongside. When this 'resonance' occurs, both stated or unstated material from other people may become part of our own vehicle of expression. In one session in a Women's Group, someone was responding to a theme of 'dialogue', in which she was given two specific characters to work with. When she began to read out her piece she found that the characters had taken on the roles of two people she knew who had been bereaved that year, one who had lost a grown daughter. She had not been consciously thinking about them, nor had this subject been part of the theme. She exclaimed that she hadn't realised how grieved and helpless she had felt until now. Both the creative action of making a poem and the poem's *content*, which contained the generous and expansive gesture of buying a field of yellow lilies as a memorial, freed her to express her feelings which were witnessed by the group. Much later, she remembered that yellow lilies were the flowers she had sent as a wreath. What she did not remember as she wrote, however, was that another woman, some weeks previously, had told us that she had bought a 'whole grove of trees' to be planted as a memorial to her mother – an action which had arisen directly out of the feelings raised by a poem she had written in the group, about her childhood.

Working with a group or an individual the therapist's attention is a wide-focus lens, noting the way materials are handled, the choices made, the self-sufficiency or lack of it displayed by each patient. Patients' interactions with each other and with the therapist, their responses to the room and the art-making process, are all non-verbal keys to the state of mind of that patient, perhaps just as much as anything they say.

I would suggest it is not possible to create a blank space in which patients are excluded from all experience and stimuli beyond themselves. Nor would I think it desirable to shut out all that touches us; I cannot take myself out the environment, I am a part of it as much as each one of them is a part. I would say rather that the space I would wish to make for a patient holds the awareness of all aspects of the present reality, yet contains them safely and also holds the possibility of a gateway to their own 'inner space', a place of creativity which Franklin (2001) finds very similar to that accessed by the practice of meditation.

Therapist Sandra Robbins describes the care she takes to arrange her room before she sees a client. She makes sure it is clean, that the atmosphere is calm, she may place flowers in the sunlight; she always chooses her clothes with care. She says:

> The room, the clothing I wear and my own therapeutic stance all clearly reflect my belief that everything has its own energetic field and that all fields impact with each other. The healing environment is an integrated whole. (Robbins 1998, p.121)

This integrated healing environment is the 'fragile space' of my title. Philosopher Gaston Bachelard looks at how we experience space on both inner and outer levels, through dreams, art and thought:

The two kinds of space, intimate space and exterior space, keep encouraging each other, as it were, in their growth. To designate space, which psychologists do very rightly, does not however, go to the root of space dreams. The poet goes deeper when he uncovers a poetic space that does not enclose us affectively. Indeed, whatever the affectivity that colours a given space, whether sad or ponderous, once it is poetically expressed, the sadness is diminished, the ponderousness lightened. Poetic space, because it is expressed, assumes values of expansion. (Bachelard 1994, p.201)

I think that in the discovery of poetic space and its expression through the imagistic, metaphoric language of art or poetry, alteration occurs: that which was solid or frozen gains the possibility of movement and fluidity. As change is made on the inner metaphoric level so it will become manifest on the outer, both in the creation of the work and in the feeling which surrounds it. For the therapist, how she holds the paradox between being in the here-and-now, at the same time as giving attention to her own inner space, affects the outcome of each session.

I was first alerted to the possibilities of the therapeutic space as a student when working with a man who had Alzheimer's disease; I'll call him James. He was in his early seventies, looked fit and healthy; his job had taken him all around the world and frequently away from his family. On his late retirement he and his wife had looked forward to enjoying their home and their grandchildren. However, James's illness progressed rapidly and he had become strangely restless and would often just disappear, striding away into the street regardless of traffic. I used to sit in the art room with him for an hour, one afternoon a week, hot sun making me drowsy, James's almost impenetrable silence like a weight.

James never left the room during these sessions. He used white paper and pencil and drew images of his travels, painfully constructing shaky perspectives of streets and once a delicate four-masted boat. In the later sessions whole landscapes began to appear, then slowly colour and finally figures, sometimes including himself.

Whilst James worked I sat quietly watching. One day I picked up a pencil and, just for a few moments, began to draw. I was thinking about a scene I had written in a story, and its setting in a town. I made a quick sketch, defining some details, half aware that I was momentarily *turning aside from* my awareness of James, who continued to draw.

I put my pencil down. James, without looking up, said: 'Where did you go?' Where did I go? I had gone somewhere, into a town located in my imagination. As if for those few moments, I had walked away from the street in his picture, where my attention had been, and turned down a side street into my own. But how did James know?

Another time, when I was working with a woman – Marian – who had an alcohol addiction problem, I had a curious dream about two interlocking gold rings, one with a green stone. The next day, Marian told me about her first marriage – I had not known she had been married twice and said so. She joked that she had been engaged twice too, to her first husband, there had even been two engagement rings, she said; one with a big emerald. How did I know? Or rather, how did my Dreaming Self know?

It seems that the therapeutic relationship is a complex arena of fragile space, inhabited by both the patient and the therapist. It may consist of several elements: past and present experience, understood through memory and mind; the physical presence of the environment, its colour and sensuality; and the shared inner imaginative space, a metaphoric ground which may resonate between individuals.

In contemporary Western culture, lack of health is seen to be primarily a condition of the body. Even types of ill health referred to as mental illness are treated as illnesses of the body in its chemical form. This 'medical model' rules all our care. At adult mental health hospitals where I have worked, the consultants are psychiatrists and their treatments are all drug-based. Psychological assessment and treatment is not automatic. Yet, many of the patients there are ill because of some trauma in their lives such as the death of a loved – or hated – one, post-natal depression, abuse, addiction. While there is no question that drugs alleviate illness and save lives, they do not work in every case and when they fail Electro-Convulsive Therapy (ECT) may be offered.

A more holistic view of illness would allow for the existence of mind and soul alongside body. We are complex beings and there are no silver bullets which will make everything all right for a woman who is shocked with grief at the death of her child, for example. A trauma such as that may be somatised in the body, as depression for instance, but the deep pain simply cannot be fixed with pills, because it is not only in the body, but also in the mind and soul.

At the first Exeter Art Therapy Conference ('Authenticity, Pragmatism and Survival', March 2002) the word 'soul' was dismissed because it had been 'over-used'. But if we work with the concept of soul at all then it is surely important to say so. At the very root of 'psychology' we have the Greek word 'psyche' which translates as *soul*; we also have 'psychosis', translated as *distress of the soul*. How we name ourselves and what we do affects us deeply. Psychotherapist and poet Noel Cobb says:

> For the soul to survive, we must *make something* out of what has happened to us. Poetry according to the ancient Greek root, *poiesis*, means 'making'. In a letter to his brother, Keats wrote: 'Call the world, if you please, "the vale of soulmaking", then you will find out the use of the world.' (Cobb 1992, pp.23–24)

In an art or a poetry therapy session the relationship between the therapist and the patient is loaded with both their experiences of life – memories, knowledge, emotions, sensations – and their inner lives where the consciousness of imagination is interleaved with the unconscious, with its whorls of dreams and archetypes, primal drives and collective memory. Both therapist and patient are part of the world and are affected by society, culture and environment at both conscious and unconscious levels. In the session, then, the space between the two participants, or between the group members, is multi-faceted. I have to make this space safe enough for us all to work and to facilitate patients' own self-expression. By *naming* the session as one where either poetry or art is made I am effectively issuing an invitation: *enter your imagination*.

For some people the imagination is a place full of dangers, monsters, sheer drops and wicked parents. How, then, can I take up a therapeutic stance and say, 'Go on, jump in…'?

The answer is that I don't. If the patient isn't ready I don't push them. If they are willing to make the journey, I understand that my role is to accompany them in some way. This may take the form of using the art materials myself or doing poetry exercises alongside them, but there is also a more subtle declaration: that I too will go to an inner level, as they do. That I will open the gates to my own creativity as I work with them; that I will place myself beside them on an equal footing.

To find common ground I use poems which contain a highly felt landscape or emotion, such as 'The May Tree' by Kim Taplin (Taplin 1989) in which a woman identifies with an old tree the men wish to cut down; or a very well-known poem such as 'Leisure' by William Henry Davies (Davies in Jones 1996) which will often open a gateway to memories. These are read out and I ask for a response from the patients. I chose the poems to fit the nature of each group and individual. For example, a passionately emotional poem is a risky, volatile element to introduce to a group of distressed people, although there are occasions when it may be very appropriate; in the same way the inclusion of poems which reflect something of the patient's own situation must be made with care. I will often try to find something gentle, with an enshrined beauty, or hopefulness, frequently a poem about the natural world, because I believe that asking a patient to make a link – however tenuous – to the outside world, with its changing seasons and promises of perpetual change, is in itself therapeutic.

After the poem has been read there is usually discussion, then each person is asked to write a few lines. In this process each individual is bringing in at least two spheres of experience: outer and inner, here and now, there and then. For example 'Lying in Late' by David Wheatley, a poem about being in bed late in the morning and being aware of missing someone (Wheatley 1997), elected very different responses from three women, all with alcohol addiction problems. One, whose son had taken an overdose, was sympathetic to the male poet: possibly he was addicted and sad. Another woman, who had marital problems, was angry at the picture of male sloth. The third, a repressed and busy housewife with three children, was envious of the luxury of time to waste.

As we discuss it, we have the flexibility to move in any direction; there is no 'right' way to respond, we are not making an academic assessment. We may push the boundaries of the poem to discover hidden layers that resonate within ourselves, by free-associating with a phrase, or trying to describe the feelings the poem raises. It is at this point that the group unites to move into the imaginative space where they each find a pathway lit by a flicker of memory or a juxtaposition of images. As they discuss, remember, argue or fantasise, I interact with them, suggesting, reflecting and listening. They have the task of finding the metaphor on the inner level which will evoke change on the outer, even if they are not conscious of doing so. Poems are written, a 'making' happens, providing a moment of *poeisis* when something new comes into being, the response to the poem becoming creative in itself, a change being made.

Metaphor has become mutative. 'Metaphor' comes from the Greek word 'metaphora', meaning 'the carrying': we can think of this as 'carrying across'. We may think of this work as bringing material from the unconscious into the present or we may have the neuropsychological perspective that 'metaphor integrates the ikonic mode of the right hemisphere and the linguistic mode of the left hemisphere' (Cox and Theilgaard 1997, p.xxvi). Either way, as all this happens I hold onto awareness of my own inner landscape as well as holding onto my awareness of everything that is happening outside myself. I move between the inner world and the outer, maintaining a dual level of consciousness, paradoxically being with the patient and separate from them. The American art therapist Arthur Robbins calls this process 'therapeutic presence'. He says:

> A good therapy session contains many of the characteristics of a work of art. Both share a multiplicity of psychic levels and a release of energy that radiates along the axis of form and content. Therapeutic communication, like art, has both a sender and a receiver and is defined by psychic dimensions that parallel the formal parameters through which art is expressed – he goes on to add – Moreover, the expressive therapist must have the talent to create metaphorical interventions that bridge fantasy, dreams and play, with the world of reality. (Robbins 1998, p.12)

Later, after the session, after the notes are written up, I will go back into my memory and try to reach a mental space of creative introspection and response in which to write or draw as freely as possible how I experienced the session on an inner level. I do this for both the patients and for myself, perhaps in the spirit of *physician, heal thyself.* It not only gives me a deeper insight into the patient's experience, but provides me with a space where I can let go of any projection that I have picked up that does not belong to me. It helps me to separate from the often disturbing content of a session and it enables my search for meaning to go deeper, as I understand more of what affected me in the session. The making of a poem or picture clarifies the counter-transference, and I can then use it as a mirror to reflect back to the process in which the patient or group was engaged. Most important, I can allow my emotions, my creativity, my deep self to be present to witness the mystery and not-knowing of the metaphoric level. After one small group with three very disturbed people, I very quickly wrote:

> The table is sliding sideways and has gone black
> blackness rises from this round ground
> this place where they set their words
> written out in black stammering in breath turning black
>
> I am aware of a desire to catch the table edge
> and force it back against this tide – but I know
> I must let it go on sliding – go further yet
> however seasick I feel.
>
> I use a poem as a pole to right us
> set its strength like a tree trunk against the tide
> so we anchor, but the sea flows round their ankles
> as they walk away.
>
> (Rose Flint 2002)

After this art therapy session, one of the patients relapsed, another committed suicide. I think my deep self knew those events were already in motion when I met the group.

Working as a therapist I am constantly astonished at the gifts I am given by the people I work with, however briefly. Through their recounted experiences and their shared imaginative space they reflect back to me facets of my own life: sometimes shedding new light on dark aspects, often helping me to heal something in myself. And with this giving there is the greater gift still: as I extend my understanding of myself, my understanding of the world and its humanity also grows. When I engage in the process of creative introspection, I often find a deep sense of beauty, of something numinous held at the centre of the group, something utterly human yet transcendent. It is as if the fragile space of the session and a corresponding space within me, acknowledge the blosoming of spirit. Another American art therapist, Shaun McNiff, describes it exactly: '…a sense of beauty is aroused in me when people sincerely strive to express themselves, an effort which evokes an aura of sacredness and authentic presence within the therapeutic space' (McNiff 1994, p.60).

Retrieving experiences, metaphors and images in this internal reflective space is akin to the shamanic journey made to effect a soul-healing. Use of, and familiarity with, the power of imagery and metaphor has always linked poets and artists to healers. In some societies they have been one and the same; the Navaho use sand-painting as a healing tool, the Greek Galen diagnosed his patients' illnesses through studying their imagery or dream content (Achterberg 1985). For the pre-Christian Celts, the Goddess Brighid symbolised both poetry and healing (Matthews and Matthews 1994). Eliade's (1989) exploration of worldwide shamanism shows how the shaman, healing loss of soul, goes into trance to travel through the underworld and to bring back images and story from another reality which will benefit her patient. Achterberg (1985) traces the history of Western medicine right back to the Greek physician Asclepius, who used the interpretation of dreams as his prime healing tool, requesting his patients to dream within the precincts of the temple, the *Asclepia*. Similarly, Matthews's (1991) exploration of the methodology of the Druidic bards shows their use of special sleeping cells in which to receive poetic inspiration and knowledge through dreaming.

As a poet I am familiar with the inner landscape of metaphor, with archetypes and dreams, with symbols, myth and magic. I understand the power of the surrogate, the talisman and the amulet, the strength of wishes, charms and spells, the weight of a curse, the lightness of prayer, the need of invocation. As a poet my job is to be creative, to witness, to reflect and to record. As a therapist my motivating force is to assist patients to heal themselves. As an art therapist I use image and metaphor as a healing tool alongside my stance as poet-artist-therapist.

James Hillman, writing about dreams, says: 'The images are where the psyche is. People say…"I've lost my soul"… To me the place to look when you feel that way is immediately to the images that show where you are with your soul in your dreams' (Hillman 1990, p.75). So too, the images that surface through art or poetry. Consequently, I liked being called a 'Poet for Health' when I worked with both individuals and groups at a doctors' surgery in Bristol, during a six-month residency; awarded as a Poetry Place, by the Poetry Society. Not therapist or tutor – but *poet* for health. As an art therapist I am also called a 'clinician', my work is spoken of as 'treatment', the art becomes a 'medical record'. If I take on only these words, this medical model of my work, they pull me towards a generalised pathologising which holds that distress is a symptom of mental illness and must be eliminated for healthy living, that a state of defined wellness is preferable at all times and that if symptoms cannot be eradicated then they must be suppressed. For many medical practitioners, psychiatrists, doctors or nurses, their training suggests that alleviation of pain is always a goal, a priority. Yet, I believe that what happens on an inner level can alter the outer and I also know that sometimes the most difficult place to get to, the most distressing place, the darkest hour, is where the pearl of great price is hidden. To be allowed to make the journey to that painful place and to be supported until insight and real change are affected is vitally important.

The words we use matter. They shape what we are. We say, 'I give my Word… I keep my Word… I take your Word for it… Word of Honour… I am as good as my Word': all expressing the way the Word has been seen as something deep and sacred within us. W.B.Yeats referred to poetry as the voice of the soul and used the words *soul*, *self* and *imagination* interchangeably (Ellmann 1960). It seems fitting to use poetry to heal soul. If the psyche is sick, distressed, traumatised, grieving, perhaps the only way it *can* be healed is for the voice of the soul to be raised, and heard. Echoing Bachelard's 'expansion', Cobb sees the poetry in images which:

> release the imagination into life, making those connections upward to the realm of the spirit and downward into the realm of the body – connections which have been lost, atrophied, ruptured or paralysed…something has struck home, an image in the heart lifts up its head and comes alive, something vibrates in the soul, sounding its voice and resounding with the experience of being touched, awakened, moved.

He continues:

> I see the true heart of psychotherapy as a 'making' akin to the work
> of poetry, as a 'psychopoiesis', or what Keats called a 'soul-making'.
> Like Hillman, I see psychotherapy as a work which should model
> itself on the crafts and should take its analogies from the arts rather
> than from medicine, physics or technology. No 'cure', no
> 'treatment', no 'repair' or 'adjustment of faulty functioning,' but
> something crafty and seaworthy, imaginative and well-fashioned, as
> well as aesthetic and deft. A work on the imagination, for
> imagination. (Cobb 1992, p.25)

If I separate myself from my patient by raising the blank wall of clinical
practice between us I can't fully enter the fragile space where the
soul-work must be done. If I enter the space of the therapeutic
relationship holistically, I can carry much more; my body is as physically
present as the room, my mind still contains what I have learned; my
medical knowledge and therapeutic training, the gifts of insights given
by patients, by nurses and doctors and books, all are present. If I bring the
willingness to be beside my patients in their inner world, then I am also
committing my soul to the work, and I must name this as working as a
healer. To take on this word profoundly affects how I meet every patient
and how they meet me, and I believe helps me to establish a strong
holding ground within the space of the work.

In my training I worked with an art therapist who taught me to *trust
the process* and to allow the *not-knowing*. While I am infinitely richer for all
the methodology and analysis I have learnt, these two precepts still seem
to be the very basis of therapy; there is the possibility of healing in both
the process of engagement with the therapeutic relationship, and in the
process of going to the inner world to creatively make something that
had no previous existence and bring it back to the here and now,
changing the world.

Note

1   For an overview of the relevance of Freud, Klein, Milner, Winnicott, and Jung
     to Art Therapy, see Case and Dalley (1992), Rubin (1987); for more depth see
     also Bowlby (1971), Milner (1955) and Winnicott (1971).

References

Achterberg, J. (1985) *Imagery in Healing*. Boston, MA: Shambhala.

Bachelard, G. (1994) *The Poetics of Space*. Boston, MA: Beacon Press.

Bowlby, J. (1971) *Attachment and Loss*. Harmondsworth: Pelican.

Burt, H. (1997) 'Women, Art Therapy and Feminist Theories of Development.' In S. Hogan (ed.) *Feminist Approaches to Art Therapy*. London: Routledge.

Case, C. and Dalley, T. (1992) *The Handbook of Art Therapy*. London: Routledge.

Cobb, N. (1992) *Archetypal Imagination*. Hudson NY: Lindisfarne Press.

Cox, M. and Theilgaard, A. (1997, first published 1987) *Mutative Metaphors in Psychotherapy*. London: Jessica Kingsley Publishers.

Davies, W.H. (1871–1940) 'Leisure.' In G.R. Jones (ed.) (1996) *The Nation's Favourite Poems*. London: BBC Books.

Deco, S. (1998) 'Return to the Open Studio Group.' In S. Skaife and V. Huet (eds) *Art Psychotherapy Groups*. London: Routledge.

Eliade, M. (1989, first published 1964) *Shamanism*. London: Arkana, Penguin Books.

Ellmann, R. (1960, first published 1948) *Yeats: The Man and the Masks*. London: Faber and Faber.

Franklin, M. (2001) 'The Yoga of Art and the Creative Process.' In Farrelly-Hansen (ed.) *Spirituality and Art Therapy*. London: Jessica Kingsley Publishers.

Hillman, J. (1990) *The Essential James Hillman: A Blue Fire*. London: Routledge.

Liebmann, M. (1986) *Art Therapy for Groups*. Beckenham: Croom Helm.

Matthews, C. and Matthews, J. (1994) *The Encyclopaedia of Celtic Wisdom*. Shaftsbury: Element Books.

Matthews, J. (1991) *Taliesin*. London: The Aquarian Press.

McNiff, S. (1994) *Art as Medicine*. London: Paitkus.

McNiff, S. (1998) *Art Based Research*. London: Jessica Kingsley Publishers.

Milner, M. (1955) *On Not Being Able to Paint*. London: Heinemann.

Robbins, A. (1998) 'Introduction.' In A. Robbins (ed.) *Therapeutic Presence*. London: Jessica Kingsley Publishers.

Robbins, S. (1998) 'The Healer as Therapist.' In A. Robbins (ed.) *Therapeutic Presence*. London: Jessica Kingsley Publishers.

Rubin, J. (1987) *Approaches to Art Therapy: Theory and Technique*. New York: Brunner Mazel.

Schaverien, J. (1992) *The Revealing Image*. London: Routledge.

Springham, N. (1998) 'The Magpie's Eye.' In S. Scaife and V. Huet (eds) *Art Psychotherapy Groups*. London: Routledge.

Taplin, K. (1989) 'The May Tree.' In A. King and S. Clifford (eds) *Trees be Company*. Bristol: Common Ground.

Waller, D. (1991) *Becoming a Profession: The History of Art Therapy in Britain, 1940–1982*. London: Routledge.

Wheatley, D. (1997) 'Lying in Late.' In D. Wheatley *Thirst*. Loughcrew: The Gallery Press.

Winnicott, D. (1971) *Playing and Reality*. London: Tavistock.

CHAPTER EIGHT

Writing and Reflexivity
Training to Facilitate Writing for Personal Development

Celia Hunt

The Postgraduate Diploma in Creative Writing and Personal Development has been running at the University of Sussex Centre for Continuing Education since 1996. The only postgraduate programme of its kind in Britain, it provides an introduction to the use of creative writing as a developmental or therapeutic tool, whether in relation to one's own personal development or to working with others in health care, therapy or education. At the time of writing the Diploma is changing from its one-year two-course format to a two-year, five-course MA, making this an appropriate moment to reflect on some of the main features of the programme. In this chapter I will be looking at students' experiences of engaging in their own self-exploratory creative writing, the changes and developments they report in their sense of self, and what they learn from this for their work with others.[1] In particular I will be focusing on the value of fictional autobiography in enhancing students' reflexivity, attempting to understand how this is achieved through a range of writings on the self in psychotherapy, cognitive psychology and neurophysiology.

In Course 1 of the Diploma – 'Writing for Personal Development' – students undertake their own autobiographical creative writing following the suggestions of the tutors. Over the years we have used a wide range of individual and group exercises, including Peter Elbow's 'freewriting' (1973), Ira Progoff's 'positioning yourself in the present' (Progoff 1992), Graham Hartill's 'web of words' (Hartill 1998), Cheryl Moskowitz's split-selves exercise, 'self as source' (Moskowitz 1998), and my own 'writing with the voice of the child' (Hunt 1998) and 'imagining the reader in the writing process' (Hunt 2004). All these exercises use fictional or poetic techniques to convey memories, images of self and aspects of the writing process, which means that, rather than capturing autobiographical 'facts', students are being asked to fictionalise themselves and their experience. Of course, any autobiographical writing will contain an element of fiction; as research has shown, memory is more a process of re-creation and reinterpretation of the past than accurate recall (Neisser 1993). However, there is a significant difference between autobiography and fictional autobiography. When we set out to write an autobiography, we enter into a 'pact' with our readers that to the best of our ability we will tell the truth of ourselves (Lejeune 1989, pp.119ff). If we consciously use fictional or poetic techniques in our autobiographical representations, then we are abandoning that pact with the reader, but we are implicitly (at least in a personal development context) making a pact with *ourselves* that we will allow our material to emerge as freely as possible, allow themes and characters based on ourselves to develop and take on a life of their own, even if we don't like what is emerging.[2] In making this pact, we accept the possibility of encountering aspects of ourselves that lie beneath our conscious awareness and of capturing – and conveying to others – a deeper and more personal or emotional truth of our experience, whatever its nature.

This difference between autobiography and fictional autobiography for self-developmental purposes can be summed up as follows: when we write an autobiography we *reflect* on ourselves and our past, and try to capture on the page what we know about ourselves, as a way of making sense of our lived lives. When we write fictional autobiography we suspend our familiar sense of who we are and engage in a *reflexive* relationship with ourselves, opening ourselves up to the possibility of learning things with which we are not so familiar, and of being changed in the process. Let me unpack this distinction between 'reflection' and 'reflexivity' a little more closely, with the help of Donna Qualley. When we reflect on something, we think about things that are in the main readily available to us; we 'take thought', as the saying goes, with its implication that those thoughts are there waiting to be taken. Reflection does not necessitate a change in the person reflecting (although the results of our reflections may lead to change), nor does it necessarily involve an engagement with another person (although we may reflect *with* others). Essentially, reflection is an individual activity that takes place independently of others (Qualley 1997, p.11).

Reflexivity is a different process and potentially a deeper one. At its heart is a particular kind of 'engagement with an "other"' (Qualley 1997, p.11), whether another person or oneself as 'other'. Where reflection could be said to involve taking something into oneself – a topic, an event, a relationship – for the purpose of contemplation or examination, reflexivity involves putting something out in order that something new might come into being. It involves creating an internal space, distancing oneself from oneself, as it were, so that one is both inside and outside of oneself simultaneously and able to switch back and forth fluidly and playfully from one position to the other, giving oneself up to the experience of 'self as other' while also retaining a grounding in one's familiar sense of self. In the social sciences reflexivity implies an awareness of the power of language and discourse to colour or distort our attitudes towards others and the attempt to distance ourselves, even if only temporarily, from the prejudices of our particular culture or upbringing when we are engaging in field work, as well as an awareness of the bias that our own prejudices are likely to have on the results of our research (Plummer 2001, p.208). It implies a move away from a view of self as fixed and one-dimensional, to an open engagement with others as far as possible on their own terms. If we apply this to our relationship with ourselves, then reflexivity involves an increased awareness of the rigidity of our ways of thinking about *ourselves* and our ways of being in the world, and the ability to distance ourselves from them in order to allow the voices of the muffled or silenced parts of ourselves to be heard.

The idea that writing fictional autobiography can enhance our reflexivity, and give rise to developmental or therapeutic benefits, underlies Course 1 of the Diploma, 'Writing for Personal Development'. One of the core books students read is Marion Milner's *A Life of One's Own* (1952, first published 1934). This is a record of her seven-year self-exploration, through journal writing, of 'what kinds of experience made me happy' (p.13), in an attempt to alleviate a background sense of unhappiness and inadequacy. Through this exploration Milner discovered that she was locked into a way of being that was contrary to the tendency of her own nature (p.14). This 'false attitude' drove her always to be 'good' and unselfish so that others would be pleased with her (pp.23, 29, 37). She realised that it was her reason and intellect, armed with a narrative of 'oughts', that drove her relentlessly along these tramlines (p.52), and that consequently she was not sufficiently in touch with what she really liked (p.23). Karen Horney calls this way of being a 'life solution' of the 'self-effacing' variety. A 'life solution' is a powerful self-concept containing a narrative of 'shoulds' that drives a person to try to fulfil an unrealisable 'idealised image' of herself. (See Horney 1951 and Paris 1994).

Milner's journal enabled her to notice things about herself, feelings mostly, of which she was only vaguely aware: 'Exulted in my body and clothes and red skirt and freedom to do as I chose on Sunday morning' (p.40). It also revealed uncomfortable things which contradicted her dominant idea of herself as 'good': 'I realized how completely untrustworthy I am in personal relationships, how I take one attitude when with one person and an opposite one with the next person, always agreeing with the person present' (p.46). Rather than the journal helping her to find out what she wanted to do with her life, she was discovering a different way of relating to herself. It involved an 'internal gesture of the mind' (p.69), a shifting of her attention from the narrow focus of her dominant thinking mind to the wide focus of her feelings and their location in her body. It was a kind of psychosomatic expansion: 'that fat feeling' (p.74). With 'wide attention' she was able to *observe* herself engaging in her life, feeling the pleasure of an activity for its own sake rather than being propelled towards some glorious goal. It wasn't that she was relinquishing her will altogether, rather that it became more benign, like a traffic policeman who provides a safe space for the traffic to flow freely (p.102). This reflexive stance – in which she was both the observer of herself and the observed – wasn't always easy to achieve. It was easier to slump into 'blind thinking' (pp.111ff.), which was associated with narrow vision and the 'search for glory' (See Horney 1951, Chapter 1).

But with the help of her writing which, like a 'net', captured the 'shadowy form' of things sensed rather than known (p.68), she was increasingly able to develop the 'internal gesture' and to tolerate herself as fluid, multiple and complex, rather than driving herself to achieve a particular self-concept that ultimately made her unhappy.

Milner's approach did not involve conscious fictionalising and so differs from the kind of writing that students do on the course 'Writing for Personal Development', but the same principle applies: writing is used to shift attention from dominant and sometimes unhelpful self-concepts or ways of being to what it *feels* like to be oneself, both physically and emotionally, and in so doing to develop a greater degree of reflexivity. Indeed, there is a striking similarity between Milner's experience and that of some of the students who have taken the course.

Emily is one such example. Through her journal and freewriting exercises in the early part of the course she 'became aware of feeling "stuck", of lacking movement' in her life, and recognised a deep anxiety about her future and a 'fear of moving forward in any direction'. This manifested itself physically as well as emotionally, in that her 'lower back had also literally become "stuck" or "locked"' and she had embarked on chiropractic treatment. In the afterglow of the 'deep muscular relaxation' of the treatment she found that she was much more able to experience Milner's 'wide attention', which stilled her mind and allowed her to write freely and intuitively and 'to access subconscious thoughts'. This increased awareness of herself as a physical/emotional being enabled her to start exploring, through poetry, her different senses of self which seemed to be attached to different parts of her body: her fearful, stuck adult-self located in the skull ('I am in bed but never asleep/My closed eyelids see the blue/of breathing/and the red red throb/of silence'); her freely dancing child-self located in the pelvis ('...my arms are swinging/and my feet are slithering/in their red silk across the shining mimbos'[3]). These poetic explorations of her felt, bodily self, in conjunction with the chiropractic treatment, made the different parts of herself feel more fluid and accessible.

Later in the course the 'self as source' exercise helped her to clarify further these different parts of herself and to bring them closer together. This exercise requires choosing a 'role identity' and 'an area of conflict or polarity' within it (Moskowitz 1998, p.39). Emily's indecision over an exciting job offer overseas led her to choose the identity of 'seeker', and to focus on the polarity between the 'good seeker' who is free and unencumbered and can go bravely out into the world, and the 'bad seeker', who is scared and clings to home and domesticity. Brainstorming these polarities through metaphor and imagery in order to develop them into 'self-characters', Emily found herself confronted again with the conflicting images of 'stuckness' (bad/scared) and 'flow' (good/brave) that had emerged in her earlier freewriting. However, as she developed her self-characters and moved towards the culmination of the exercise, in which these characters meet and exchange something of value, she found that the stark contrasts between them softened into a new image, where home and domesticity associated with the 'bad/scared' seeker were not a 'velvet trap but a source of beauty and comfort', and that staying at home rather than fulfilling the idealised image of the 'good/brave' seeker, was what she actually wanted. Like Marion Milner, Emily found that it was her *felt bodily sense of self* that ultimately determined what she wanted and what made her happy, rather than the compulsive drive to fulfil the self-concept of the independent, career woman who goes bravely out into the world.

Another student, Esther, starts her essay similarly with images of 'stuckness' and fragmentation, as she searches for a way of 'positioning herself in the present', Progoff's exercise, which involves 'stretch[ing] the present moment back as far as it needs to go in order to include as much of the past as is still an active part of the present' (Progoff 1992, pp.46–47). She wonders whether her child-self, who looks at her from the photo that sits on her desk as she writes and who feels 'like a stranger', is still somehow 'within' her, or whether we simply become different people as we move through time, discarding past selves. These thoughts bring to mind an autobiographical poem she wrote some years earlier at a painful turning point in her life. In the poem she captures her flight from emotional turmoil in an image of herself as 'a refugee from a war-zone' propelled into a new country who, unable to let go of the past, looks back and, like Lot's wife, is turned into a pillar of salt. This image of self-paralysis conveys to Esther the difficulties of 'mov[ing] freely between one's past landscape and one's present', while the Progoff exercise calls for locating oneself 'in the movement of our life' (p.48). Paradoxically in the poem there *is* movement of a kind, for 'at night my pillar of salt casts a shadow that creeps back across [the] frontier', but this movement only leads to pain and fragmentation because the dark shadow-self 'lies on stony ground/Caught on the wire, barbed and fixed'. Esther's sense of self here is represented as stuck on both sides of the border, in the past and in the present, and in the piece of writing she eventually comes up with for the 'finding the present' exercise this 'stuckness' is linked to the difficulties she senses of moving into the future with her work as a playwright and coming to terms with the physical changes taking place as she enters middle age and becomes aware of her mortality.

The 'self as source' exercise gave Esther an opportunity to explore different images of self, the 'good sister' and the 'bad sister' at a time when she was unexpectedly in conflict with her brother. Exploring the 'bad', angry side of herself she found particularly liberating, but she ended up feeling unclear about the extent to which the characters she had created captured an authentic sense of herself or were simply fictional constructs, and she felt 'unable to unmesh these threads' on her own. This was not the case however with another exercise that required creating a future self as well as an as yet unknown person who would be significant in that future.[4]

The future self that emerges out of Esther's imaginings is a 70-year-old woman who lives in the countryside (rather than the city where the real Esther lives) and who is part of a collaborative theatre ensemble where she makes plays with others rather than writing in isolation. The as yet unknown person who acts as catalyst for these changes turns out in fact to be two people, a young couple from Eastern Europe, who arrive on her doorstep one day in search of shelter. The creative, collaborative relationship that develops under their influence teaches the older Esther how to integrate the different aspects of herself – how to renew contact with her playful child self, how to embrace the realities of aging, how to develop her playwriting in relation to others – and find harmony. This piece of writing, Esther says, 'was a positive way of highlighting the negative aspects of my life at present by pinpointing some of the missing dimensions...a way of working creatively with people, a new way of play-making and a greater integration of the different aspects and forces within me'. Essentially, she continues, it is 'about letting go' of concerns about youth and beauty and worldly ambition, 'but a letting go that does not relinquish the desire to create and to relate', core drives both for her and her imagined future self.

In both of these examples we see a marked shift in the sense of self from fixity and lack of connection between different aspects of self, towards a greater awareness of multiplicity and the possibility that the different aspects of self can work together, moderating each other's extremes. This is not necessarily easy: as Esther says, while she (like Milner) started her writing imagining that she would find her one 'real' self and feel more whole, she discovered that the real Esther was much more complex, trickier to handle. For both Emily and Esther this shift to multiplicity involves confronting uncomfortable aspects of themselves, notably the recognition of worldly, ambitious drives.

The theme of uncovering and embracing new and uncomfortable aspects of self features significantly in the students' work I read in preparing this chapter. For Rose, my third example, it is the main theme of her experience of the course and provides a focus for her long-felt sense of fragmentation:

> I have always been plagued by the conflict between different selves
> to the point of feeling internally attacked by them and unable to
> make decisions. One voice will undermine the other, which will in
> turn be incompatible with a third.

The exercise 'writing with the voice of the child' made her aware of a critical voice that tended to dismiss what she saw as her more creative child voice with its fictionalising of spontaneous memories. She had always regarded this critical-analytical side of herself 'as inferior and tried to squash it rather than include it and work with it'. It was the controlling side of herself, associated in her mind with her mother who resorted to it when faced with situations that evoked difficult feelings. Rose identifies in herself this split between her critical self, which is associated with control, and her creative self, which is associated with freedom. But freedom is also associated with her 'bad' child-self, with her loss of control as a teenager and indulgence in sex, drugs and wild abandon, which she prefers not to think about.

This split in herself became clear in the 'self as source' exercise where she chose to focus on two images of herself: the 'bad child' and the 'good child'. The exercise resulted in a short story, 'Please Re-Direct', in which a teacher and single mother struggling to keep control of her two rebellious teenage daughters receives through the post, without explanation, a bag, a flimsy nylon hold-all, presumably belonging to a boy in her class. The contents of the bag, a CD of heavy metal rock music, several violent videos, some half-eaten junk food, and a soft porn magazine, evoke powerful memories of her own wayward youth and the parts of herself associated with it – her sexuality and loss of control. These powerful messages from the past distract her from her mothering role and in bed at night erupt in a nightmare of demonic possession. The following day she throws the bag and its contents into the garbage, expecting simply to be rid of it, but the lingering smell of junk food on her fingers is more difficult to erase.

Reflecting on the story in her essay, Rose realises that the split in herself between freedom and control is related to her own difficulties with parenting: her attempt to control her daughters' behaviour – to be a 'good mother' – is a rejection of the 'bad child' she herself was. Exploring this conflict through the exercise 'provided me with the opportunity to…acknowledge how unintegrated I felt. The expressing of both sides of myself in this [exercise] led to a sense of self-awareness which gave me the security to develop a piece of fiction based on the conflict.'

Here again, an aspect of the psyche that was repressed comes into sharper focus and is acknowledged as part of a more complex self, even though there is a strong desire, as indicated by the ending of the story, to keep the troublesome part at a distance. The theme of loosening the control of the critical faculty that features in the other two examples is also visible here, as is the increased awareness of the importance of the body in the sense of self, its feelings and emotions, its innate drives and tendencies.

The experience of Emily, Esther and Rose is typical of a significant number of those who have taken Course 1 of the Diploma: a move away from a sense of fixity or 'stuckness' in one or more dominant self-concepts, an increased awareness of spontaneous bodily feelings and emotions, and a more reflexive relationship between different aspects of themselves. It raises the question as to why fictionalising ourselves and our experience can have such a powerful effect. The answer, I believe, lies in the relationship with ourselves that is facilitated by the writing exercises and the context in which they are undertaken. Let me explain what I mean.

According to the cognitive psychologist Ulric Neisser, there are five main ways in which we know ourselves (Neisser 1988): through our sensed relationship with the physical world (our 'ecological self'), through our relations with other people ('interpersonal self'), through our memories of the past and anticipations of the future ('narrative' or 'extended self'), through our dreams and private thoughts ('private self'), and through our various socially and culturally constructed self-concepts, e.g. 'mother', 'playwright', 'beautiful', 'intelligent' ('conceptual self'). Of these, the latter is the most dominant, as:

> our self-concepts typically include ideas about our physical bodies, about interpersonal communication, about what kinds of things we have done in the past and are likely to do in future, and especially about the meaning of our own thoughts and feelings. (p.54)[5]

As demonstrated by the four examples discussed in this chapter, there is a strong tendency for us to become dominated by self-concepts containing powerful narratives of how we *should* be in the world and which drive us to live up to unrealistically high ideals: 'good girl', 'successful career woman', 'successful playwright', 'good mother'. When this happens, our authentic bodily feelings and emotions – a central part of what Karen Horney calls our 'real self' (Horney 1951, p.17) – can become repressed.

The notion of a 'real' or 'true' self underlying or pre-existing our linguistically and culturally created sense of self has been rejected by the humanities and social sciences as indicating a fixed, unitary entity or 'homunculus'. (See Damasio (2000) pp.189–192 on the 'homunculus'.) It is still dominant in the public mind, however, as Esther's use of this term indicates. However, Horney's 'real self' is not a homunculus; it certainly has a genetic element – a set of 'intrinsic potentialities' (p.17), some of which may develop given favourable circumstances – but primarily it is the source of deep, spontaneous feelings, 'the alive, unique, personal center of ourselves' (p.155).[6] Horney did not develop her idea of the 'real self' in detail, but Christopher Bollas's idea of the 'idiom' or 'aesthetic of being' (Bollas 1995, p.151) helps to take it further. The 'aesthetic of being' ('aesthetic' here denotes a 'feeling-state' such as we might experience when immersed in a novel and our familiar boundaries have dissolved) is a felt sense of 'me', different from the experience of the 'I' that guides and governs the psyche; it is a 'dense inner constellation, a psychic texture' (p.152), much less graspable than our self-concepts. It consists not only of the 'given' elements of our nature but also the felt traces of the many 'experiential episodes in which [our] essential idiom meets up with its fate in the domain of lived experience' (p.152). This 'internal object...that can be felt, even though it has no voice' (p.152) is 'unknowable as a thing-in-itself' (p.165), but 'when one senses that it is there, it gives a person a sense of being the author of his existence' (p.166).

It is this 'real self' or 'aesthetic of being' underlying our dominant self-concepts or narratives of self that students are encouraged to access through the writing exercises they undertake on the course. There are, in fact, two different kinds of exercise (although there is some overlap between them): those which use rhythm, rhyme and sound, metaphor and freewriting to capture feelings, and those which involve characterising and bringing into dialogue different aspects of ourselves. Students undertake the first kind before moving on to the second. Because of its emphasis on what one might call 'semiotic'[7] literary devices, the first kind of exercise shifts the writer from a primarily cognitive relationship with herself (what sort of person am I? what do I want to do with my life?), to a more affective relationship (what does it *feel* like to be me beneath my usual self-conceptions?). This shift of attention to feelings and emotions prepares the ground for the second kind of exercise, in which the writer 'plays' with her dominant self-concepts in the imaginative space, entering into a dialogue between different parts of herself and practising reflexivity, as it were, within the text.

This is, needless to say, a precarious process, as opening people up to what might be difficult or uncomfortable feelings and emotions can provoke vulnerability and insecurity. Whether the process works depends to a large extent on the nature of the group (some groups 'gel' better than others) and the way the group is facilitated. In order that students should feel as safe as possible in undertaking this work, they are divided up into small groups for the purpose of reading and discussing the writing that results from the exercises, and they remain with these groups for the whole of the course, spending some 80 minutes together on each of the five six-hour day-schools. The groups are given guidelines for how to give feedback on the written work, and individual group members determine what kind of feedback they want, whether 'personal' or 'critical'. At their best, these small groups develop quickly into tightly constructed 'holding' spaces where feelings and emotions can be expressed and explored safely. These small groups are part of the larger 'holding environment' (Winnicott 1971) of the whole group, where two tutors are always present so that one of them can observe what is happening and be available to deal with difficulties that arise. All the tutors are experienced facilitators of writing groups or have formal counselling or therapy training.

The idea that a 'real self' accessible primarily through feelings and emotions underlies our dominant self-concepts and narratives of self has recently been given added impetus by the work of neurophysiologist Antonio Damasio. Strongly countering the view that our sense of self is solely a product of language, society and culture (Damasio 2000, p.108), he suggests, on the basis of many years' work with people suffering brain damage, that a pre-linguistic, bodily 'core self' experienced through feelings underlies and indeed gives rise to our memory- and lanuage-based 'autobiographical self' (p.196). Like Horney's 'real self' and Bollas's 'aesthetic of being', Damasio's 'core self' is not a fixed unitary entity, since it is constantly undergoing change as a result of encounters with the environment. Essentially it is a second-order, neural mechanism, a felt, bodily awareness of a ceaselessly generated 'narrative without words' (p.168) taking place in the organism (the body and the nervous system) beneath the level of consciousness (in the area Damasio calls the 'proto-self'). This non-verbal narrative occurs when the organism interacts with an 'object' – this might be a physical object (a person) or a sense impression (a melody) or a memory – causing a change to take place in the organism. This interaction, together with its emotional concomitants, is experienced in the form of felt, bodily images, e.g. 'a sound image, a tactile image, the image of a state of well-being' (p.9), and because it occurs continuously in pulse-like fashion it gives rise to 'an image of knowing centred on a self', or 'the sense of self in the act of knowing' (pp.171–176), which Damasio calls the 'core self'. This, however, is not a reflexive consciousness.

Reflexivity develops as autobiographical memories accumulate and the 'core self' becomes connected to a broader canvas, so that 'the sense of self in the act of knowing' is enriched by a growing knowledge of past events and the feelings and emotions associated with them. This 'extended consciousness' (pp.195–233), with its ability to 'hold images active over time' (p.198), makes the organism aware of its knowledge, thus facilitating planning, creativity and problem solving. It heralds the arrival of the 'autobiographical self' (p.196). Language, which arrives in human evolution very late, enables us to translate felt knowledge into words, and contributes significantly to the further development of 'extended consciousness' (p.108). However, extended consciousness is wholly dependent on core consciousness, which carries out the relentless work of neurally reactivating and enhancing autobiographical memories and making them explicit as *felt images*. This development of consciousness, from core to extended, and from feelings to words, is, in Damasio's view, a direct consequence of the evolutionary advantage to us of knowing about our emotions, which allows us 'to plan novel and customised forms of adaptive response' (p.285).[8]

Damasio's self-schema gives us a detailed neurophysiological understanding of the bodily felt sense of self which underlies language and which, drawing on Horney and Bollas, I am calling the 'real self', and of its crucial importance in consciousness and our relationship with ourselves.[9] It also helps to understand why the writing exercises we use in 'Writing for Personal Development' can be so effective in enhancing that relationship. By creating a framework for the 'internal gesture of the mind' (Milner 1952, p.69) – the temporary suspension of our familiar self-concepts and narratives of self – they provide a space in which our 'real self' becomes more readily accessible, strengthening, on the one hand, our relationship with 'core consciousness' and, on the other, providing an authentically felt ground from which we can enter into a more reflexive relationship with our narratives and self-concepts that form part of 'extended consciousness'. It seems paradoxical that words on the page can be employed in a task that is essentially about getting beyond language, but if we think of them as part of the framework that holds the space open for change to take place, then we begin to understand one important aspect of the therapeutic role of writing.

I sub-titled this chapter 'Training to Facilitate Writing for Personal Development', and it has taken me a long time to get to this part of what I wanted to say. In fact it is quite simple. I mentioned earlier the view in the social sciences that a reflexive relationship with others, in which we suspend – or at least become more aware of – our own prejudices and preconceptions is a helpful stance in carrying out field work, as it enables us to engage with other people and other cultures on their own terms rather than through the fixed and distorting lens of our own. A similar point applies to the facilitation of writing for personal development, where the facilitator has to suspend her own needs and tendencies (for example, the desire to please others or have power over them) and to sense intuitively when to distance herself and be quietly observant and when to intervene and be assertively active. Moving smoothly back and forth between these two states – now giving the group its head and now reining it in and containing it – she will create a framework within which people can feel not only *free enough* to engage with their own feelings and emotions, but *safe enough* to do so. It is my view – and feedback from past students of the Diploma indicates that this is the case – that increasing our reflexivity in relation to ourselves through autofictional writing is an excellent training for the reflexive skill of facilitating writing for personal development.

Acknowledgements

I am grateful to Fiona Sampson, Phyllis Creme and Bernard Paris for their helpful comments on a draft of this chapter. I am also grateful to the Diploma students of years 1998 and 1999 who gave me permission to quote from their portfolios of creative writing and self reflective essays. All names have been changed.

Notes

1   Unless otherwise stated, quotations are from students' essays and portfolios of creative writing.

2   See Hunt (2000) pp.157–165 for a fuller discussion of this point.

3   From Emily's poem 'Red Chiropractic'.

4   I am grateful to Cheryl Moskowitz, who devised this exercise, for permission to discuss it.

5   Eakin (1999) discusses autobiographies that illustrate Neisser's modes of self-knowledge.

6   See Paris (1999) for a discussion of Horney's model of the self.

7   'Semiotic' is a term coined by Julia Kristeva (1978) to denote the pre-linguistic realm in which the baby is 'merged in' with the mother, experiencing rhythm, sound, and bodily sensations; separation from the mother takes the child into the 'symbolic', the realm of language and the 'law of the father'.

8   Lodge (2002) discusses Damasio's ideas in relation to the development of the novel.

9   I am grateful to Andrew Tershakovec for sharing with me his unpublished book, *The New Cognitive Model of the Mind and Its Implications for Psychotherapy*, which has been invaluable in enabling me to clarify my ideas on the connection between Horney's 'real self' and Damasio's 'core self'.

References

Bollas, C. (1995) *Cracking Up: The Work of Unconscious Experience*. London: Routledge.

Damasio, A. (2000) *The Feeling of What Happens: Body, Emotion and the Making of Consciousness*. London: Vintage.

Eakin, P.J. (1999) *How Our Lives Become Stories: Making Selves*. Ithaca and London: Cornell University Press.

Elbow, P. (1973) *Writing Without Teachers*. Oxford: Oxford University Press.

Hartill, G. (1998) 'The web of words: Collaborative writing and mental health.' In C. Hunt and F. Sampson *The Self on the Page: Theory and Practice of Creative Writing in Personal Development*. London: Jessica Kingsley Publishers, pp.47–62.

Horney, K. (1951) *Neurosis and Human Growth: The Struggle toward Self-realization*. New York: Norton.

Hunt, C. (1998) 'Writing with the voice of the child: Fictional autobiography and personal development.' In C. Hunt and F. Sampson, *The Self on the Page: Theory and Practice of Creative Writing in Personal Development*. London: Jessica Kingsley Publishers, pp.21–34.

Hunt, C. (2000) *Therapeutic Dimensions of Autobiography in Creative Writing*. London: Jessica Kingsley Publishers.

Hunt, C. (2004) 'Reading ourselves: Imagining the reader in the writing process.' In G. Bolton, S. Howlett, C. Lago and J. Wright (eds) *Writing Cures: An Introductory Handbook of Writing in Counselling and Therapy*. London: Brunner/Routledge.

Hunt, C. and Sampson, F. (1998) *The Self on the Page: Theory and Practice of Creative Writing in Personal Development.* London: Jessica Kingsley Publishers.

Kristeva, J. (1984) *Revolution in Poetic Language.* New York: Columbia University Press.

Lejeune, P. (1989) *On Autobiography.* Minneapolis: University of Minnesota Press.

Lodge, D. (2002) *Consciousness and the Novel.* London: Secker and Warburg.

Milner, M. (1952) *A Life of One's Own.* Harmondsworth: Penguin (first published 1934 under pseudonym Joanna Field).

Moskowitz, C. (1998) 'The Self as Source: Creative Writing generated from Personal Reflection.' In C. Hunt and F. Sampson, *The Self on the Page: Theory and Practice of Creative Writing in Personal Development.* London: Jessica Kingsley Publishers, pp.35–46.

Neisser, U. (1988) 'Five modes of self-knowledge.' *Philosophical Psychology 1*, 1, 35–58.

Neisser, U. (1993) 'Self-narratives: true and false.' In Ulric Neisser and Robyn Fivish (eds) *The Remembering Self.* Cambridge: Cambridge University Press, pp.1–18.

Paris, B. (1999) 'Karen Horney's vision of the self.' *American Journal of Psychoanalysis 59*, pp.157–166.

Paris, Bernard (1994) *Karen Horney: A Psychoanalyst's Search for Self Understanding.* New Haven and London: Yale University Press.

Plummer, K. (2001) *Documents of Life 2: An Invitation to a Critical Humanism.* London: Sage.

Progoff, I. (1992) *At a Journal Workshop.* New York: G.P. Putnam's Sons.

Qualley, D. (1997) *Turns of Thought: Teaching Composition as Reflexive Inquiry.* London: Heinemann.

Tershakovec, A. (with John Kerr and Bernard Paris) *The New Cognitive Model of the Mind and its Implications for Psychotherapy.* (unpublished manuscript).

Winnicott, D.W. (1971) *Playing and Reality.* London: Tavistock Publications.

CHAPTER NINE

Any-angled Light
Diversity and Inclusion Through Teaching Poetry in Health and Social Care

Dominic McLoughlin

This chapter looks at how poetry can be used as an educational tool for promoting cultural diversity and social inclusion in health and social care. My account aims to sidestep any argument about whether the use of the literary arts in this context is either art or therapy by seeing it primarily as an educational activity. It assumes that the art form can be kept intact as it crosses the boundary into health care. In this view, the challenge for the facilitator is to stay in role as a writing teacher, albeit one who may have counselling skills or particular forms of awareness. This allows clients to pick up and use poetry in many diverse ways according to their own developmental and educational needs.

There are pressures for poetry practice, in particular, to become something different when presented to vulnerable clients, perhaps because this is a literary art from which readers can often feel excluded; but it is this *literary* quality itself that makes poetry effective as a tool to consider differences between and within individuals. Despite such intrinsic difficulties – and the challenges faced by clients in receipt of clinical or social care – this chapter aims to support Kenneth Koch's view that: 'It is better to teach poetry writing as an art than to teach it – well not really teach it but use it – as some form of distracting or consoling therapy' (1977, pp.43–44). I will describe a rationale for writing in health care; look at how poetry writing can help individual participants and groups; and examine the role of the tutor-facilitator. Throughout I will draw on my experience of running workshops in hospice and mental health care, and give practical examples. I will also refer to some ideas from psychodynamic counselling, which I have recently studied in order to help me understand some of the processes involved in this work.

A rationale for teaching poetry in health care

My first premise is that poetry is, on the whole, is a good thing. As Randall Jarrell has put it, 'Poetry doesn't need to be defended, any more than air or food needs to be defended' (Jarrell 1955, p.19). The only real question is how it can be taught safely in a health care context. This account assumes that the process of writing poetry does not have to change, as it crosses the threshold into a health care environment, into a question of catharsis or self-expression. But what are the properties of poetry that makes it appropriate as an educational tool in any context? Poetry is such a huge and diverse subject area that each writer in health care has to make up his or her own mind about this. I will start by examining some of the aspects of the craft that ring true for me: *making; concentrating; investigating; playing.*

Making

In a recent talk Australian-born poet Peter Porter stressed how writing a poem is crucially about making something. Porter asked his audience to think of a poem as a made object like a sculpture or a barrister's speech in court; he reminded us of the derivation of the word poetry from the Greek verb *poiein*, to make (Porter 2003). This emphasis is in contrast to the view of poetry as being about *feeling* something, which may be familiar and therefore more appealing for the new writer but which in the end offers fewer rewards. The American poet Elizabeth Bishop wrote a pertinent letter along the same lines to the editor of a college textbook *The Harper Anthology of Poetry* at the very end of her life. She writes of her students that 'they mostly seem to think that poetry – to read or write – is a snap – one just has to feel – and not for very long, either' (Bishop 1994, p.639). In Bishop's own work it is evident that poetry helps us to express both personal and universal truths. Her point is well made that in order to achieve this self-expression on its own is not enough.

Concentrating

The second principle is that poetic form allows us to tolerate difficult thoughts, and to concentrate in a particular way. Seamus Heaney gives a compelling account of poetic concentration in *The Government of the Tongue* (1988). As Helen Vendler has underlined (1995), Heaney quotes the Gospel of St John Chapter Eight in which the scribes and Pharisees bring to Jesus a woman who was taken in adultery; her accusers ask Jesus whether she should be stoned, as Mosaic law commanded. Before Jesus proclaims that 'He that is without sin among you, let him first cast a stone at her', he 'stooped down, and with his finger wrote on the ground, as though he heard them not'. It is never revealed what Jesus wrote in the sand, but in this act Heaney finds an allegory for poetry:

> The drawing of those characters is like poetry, a break with the usual life but not an absconding from it … Poetry holds attention for a space, functions not as distraction, but as pure concentration, a focus where our power to concentrate is concentrated back on ourselves. (Quoted in Vendler 1995, p.199)

Investigating

Another fruitful starting point for writing a poem is to take up the spirit of philosophical investigation. The task then becomes not so much to say what we know, but to wonder how we know what we know. With this sort of approach 'show not tell' is not only a helpful device, but also a stance towards the world and to the work. Through the use of given forms, sonic effects, imagery, diction, syntax and other literary devices, the writer and the reader are constantly learning something new.

Playing

In *Sunbathing in the Rain* Gwyneth Lewis describes the poetic impulse as the need to play with words, and as a means of forgetting the self. 'Poetry for me has always been a sacred place, where I allow myself to express my true feelings however absurd, exaggerated, or 'uncool'... The best reason I can give for writing poetry is that there's nothing in it for me' (2002, p.35).

Given these properties of *making, concentrating, investigating* and *playing*, the writer in health care's aim may be to facilitate an experience of reading and writing that will help the participant learn some of the skills which make up these processes. However, it may be the case that the client is too vulnerable to have the necessary objectivity to learn about a topic in this way. They may not want to undertake an activity that is not solely generated either by them (as a letter or reminiscence would be) or by an imperative of their clinical care. This 'third thing' – literature – might appear to be an irrelevant or even persecutory intrusion at a time of crisis. Where this is the case the activity may not be appropriate, and for this reason its participants need to be self-selecting; but for many the fact that writing in health care asks participants to learn about the topic and about themselves at the same time is in itself helpful. In *Counselling in Education* (1999) Elsa Bell has shown how learning relies on students being able to be dependent on their sources of knowledge such as teachers and books. They need to be able to take in facts and to remember them, but they also need to develop an ability to play, to make links, to think, to express ideas using metaphorical language. To master a subject a student will need to manipulate ideas, engage with subject in external world, see that 'it is not completely within their control, but nor is it outside their control' (Bell 1999, p.8). Taking place in the transitional space, studying and learning is an opportunity to play. This idea of the 'transitional space' is linked to Winnicott's notion of the 'in-between space' which is neither inside nor outside. As a paediatrician Winnicott developed his theory from the study of infants, who must learn to accept the reality of their loss (of their primary creativity), and to bear the frustration of not having their needs met instantaneously. For Winnicott the task of reality acceptance is never entirely complete. The transitional object[1] – which in adult life can take the form of art and cultural life – goes on to provide an enduring source of relief from 'the strain of relating inner and outer reality' (Winnicott 1971, p.13).

This concept suggests why art activities are popular with patients who have to negotiate between the internal reality of their own thoughts and feelings and external realities such as doctors, family and the challenges of facing illness. The notion of the transitional object also helps to privilege the subject matter, which is placed squarely between the teacher and participant. The temptation for this learning framework to be jettisoned for the comfort of participants and facilitator could arise if the subject is found to be too difficult, or if the client was too vulnerable (or if the writer in health care perceives them to be so). Without it the group may be doing many things: writing, learning about themselves, and enjoying a shared activity; but they will not be learning about poetry in the way this chapter argues can be most useful.

How writing poetry can help individual participants

Paradoxically, writing gives us the chance to both go towards the self, and to escape from it. It is sometimes assumed that writing in health care will encourage the former over the latter impulse. But Alison Marks gives a lively account of a property of poetry that writers in health care fully utilise. She writes, 'Poetry…demonstrates – indeed enacts – what contemporary theory suggests about "the post-modern": that identity is not unproblematic, given or unified' (2000, p.68). She goes on to discuss how poetry has an ancient pedigree in allowing and encouraging diversity:

> From its earliest incarnations in epic, in all the languages I know of, poetry has been plurivocal, ventriloquising a range of figures including all genders, sexes, sexualities, races, ethnicities, classes and conditions, the non-human, and immortals, gods and demons. (2000, p.68)

On the workshop floor, as it were, taking this understanding forward entails encouraging students to write in the many languages of poetry, bearing in mind the traditions and strategies it makes available. The idea of a fragmented and problematic core identity can be a painful one for some people at some times. For such people the idea of writing from a self that is knowable and known is more comfortable and stimulating. For others, however, the idea of drawing directly on personal memories for creative writing can be equally painful and restricting. In psychodynamic terms what is required is a certain amount of ego strength for an individual or group to be able to appreciate their own diversity. Where this is not present, writing may be utilised in a different way, to create and present a unified self, perhaps defined on the basis of gender, race, sexuality, disability or another differentiated aspect of identity.

Sujatta Bhatt's poem 'Search For My Tongue' (1988, pp.63–70) is a popular resource in workshops. It is written in both English and Gujerati, and as it unfolds it moves towards a resolution of difference for someone who has a mixed cultural identity. Harmony is found not in one language or the other, but in music and in the sort of linguistic music that poetry allows us to play. It is clear that aspects of difference that exist in the writing in health care group and in the wider society – such as those of ethnicity, culture, sexuality, and religion – need to be reflected in the teaching materials used. Nevertheless, the facilitator also has to be wary of making assumptions about the kinds of difference that are important to an individual's sense of identity. In the mental health setting which is described more fully in the next section one client, L.S. was a man who regularly drew on reggae rhythms and Rastafarian idioms in his work. He also liked to start each session by reading from a play or poem in the Complete Shakespeare and he enjoyed a wide variety of contemporary poetry. Among the work which we read over the years, one which most delighted him was Simon Armitage's poem 'The Phoenix' (1997, p.62), written in Yorkshire dialect. Although I was very aware of L.S.'s Caribbean heritage, I had not been aware that he had grown up in Yorkshire, nor of how Armitage's poem would find a resonance with that part of his history.

Another case history worth mentioning here is from the hospice context. It shows how poetry can unlock different parts of the self at a time when one's identity is threatened by the onset of serious illness. G.H. was a man who, in his retirement, had hoped to so some gardening and woodwork until he found he had been 'struck down' by cancer. On his visits to the hospice day centre he joined the poetry group. One of G.H.'s early poems was based on an exercise devised by Kenneth Koch (1977, pp.139–141), in which participants are invited to follow the example of John Keats' sonnet 'Bright star' and to speak to the moon or the stars. G.H. wrote: 'The star of yore/ Keep where you are/ Evening star/ Very useful to mariners'. This lyric proved to be a good start for G.H., and the more he came to trust the process of writing the more he allowed himself flashes of inspiration and self-awareness. On another occasion we looked at Stephen Spender's 'To My Daughter' (1985, p.137) and the theme of touch was suggested. G.H. wrote 'At Guy's Hospital':

> You touched me when I was feeling low
> It is surprising how some of your strength
> Seemed to pass to me.
> We said a prayer together and I felt a lot better.
> This is an incident I shall always remember.
>
> (G. H. 1992)

In this way, G.H.'s writing came to feature more emotional content, and to be more playful. After a beginning when he was understandably nervous although willing to take a risk, he told me later that the poetry group had 'opened up a whole new world' for him, and that he 'sees things differently now'.[2]

How writing poetry can help groups

In this section two health care settings are described from which practical examples can be drawn. Each of them has a specific relevance to the issues of inclusion and diversity.

Hospice day care

One of the fundamental principles of modern hospice care is to welcome patients with open arms and to cherish each one of them until the moment of their death. Hospice care aims to welcome those with terminal illness whether they are of any religious faith or none. As Dr Cicely Saunders has put it: 'You matter because you are you, and you matter until the last moment of your life and we will do all we can, not only to help you die peacefully but to live until you die' (Saunders 1999). The examples which follow are from a writing group for patients at a hospice in south London from 1990–1997, where I was employed on a sessional basis to attend the day centre once a week for two hours.[3] The day centre staff made referrals to the group from the patients who came to the day centre from home or from the wards. The format for the group was: the introduction of new members; handing out of the previous week's work which had been typed; reading of a poem for inspiration; discussion of the reading; the suggestion of a way into writing; a quiet time for writing; time to read out; gathering in patients' work.

Each weekly writing workshop in the hospice setting was self-contained – that is, although patients did attend over a number of weeks and months and in some cases years, the sessions were prepared bearing in mind that it might be any patient's only chance to attend. There was rarely a time when the composition was exactly the same as the week before. Nevertheless, as there were some long-standing members, a group culture did form, and at certain times conventions and idioms would take hold. One member, P.H., had been a committed member of the group but after a time decided to continue her writing outside of it. She was writing a series of elegies for people she had met in the hospice. Here is one of P.H.'s poems, 'Sheila':

Her smile was warm and bright
Like a candle glowing in a dark corner.
Her body still – unmoving –
Like the candlestick beneath the flame.
Remarkably her sense of humour still remained
And we often shared a gentle joke.
Slowly and relentlessly her body
Closed down
Unable to perform a simple movement
But as it faded the smile remained in working order
Only the smile – just like the cat in Alice.

(P. H. 1994)

In this way the group's activities were defined by the writing that was produced outside it as well as inside. The series of poems P.H. wrote about friends in the day centre were later published in the day centre newsletter and read out at memorials and other hospice events.

P.K. was a woman in her seventies who came to the hospice day centre for a year or so from 1993. She had never learned to read and write but wanted to join the poetry group. A volunteer would sit in the group with her and she would dictate her stories. She was a natural storyteller and had a great way with titles. One morning she sat back having dictated a particularly vivid account of life with her husband. She was asked what she wanted to call it and she replied emphatically, 'This is My World'. P.K.'s experience in the writing group is a good example of a patient using writing to gain some control at a time when her illness and home life were presenting her with many uncertainties. It was notable how the rest of the group cherished P.K. and her contributions. The way that she thrived in the group is a good example of how tolerance of difference and the promotion of equal opportunities had developed as part of the group's collective identity.

Day care for mentally disordered offenders

From 1997 to 2001 I worked at a central London housing project for men who were ex-offenders with mental health problems.[4] The primary aim of the project as a whole was to re-introduce clients into the community by stabilising their health and equipping them with life skills. The poetry group was part of a wider provision of education and training conducted in a facility that also offered art, woodwork, basic literacy skills, computer training, and photography. The educational activities were provided to include clients socially at a time when they were in transition following time in a secure mental hospital or prison. Many clients had special educational needs resulting from a lack of literacy skills and a history of low educational achievement. They were also often learning to cope with enduring mental health problems in this new context. Others had an ambivalent attitude towards groups and to any kinds of authority, sometimes due to their experience of compulsory group work in hospital or prison. In format, the class was run very much along the same lines as the hospice group. I started the writing group with a poem read for inspiration. There was then time for discussion; a suggested poetry idea, and time for writing. This group was well attended, long lived, and productive.[5]

In contrast to the hospice setting where each session was self-contained, this group had a built-in sense of continuity from one week to the next. A sense of achievement and progression, even in small steps, was an important part of the learning environment. For those whose literacy skills were poor, poetry could be used to teach close reading skills and new vocabulary. Participants often had a limited concentration span as one of the side effects of medication. At times participants would wander off in the middle of the session, or find they had to get up and walk around and then come back. In common with other group activities in the organisation the poetry group had the effect of normalising the condition of mental illness and allowing group members to give voice to other aspects of their lives. From time to time there would be conflicts, but group members also displayed much mutual sympathy, compassion and tolerance.

The composition of the group changed over the years, but one member was V.W., a man in his late thirties who had a talent for singing and spinning stories. He was also very troubled and at times he suffered from psychotic episodes. When his mental state allowed it, the working stance of the poetry group may have helped him to be more grounded and focused. The group also had a socialising effect, allowing him to show respect for and interest in others and to have this returned, where in everyday life the impact of his illness could mean his behaviour was hard to live with. V.W. often didn't follow the suggested writing exercise. However, the format of the group, in which we read a poem first then had a quiet time for writing, offered some structure for his thoughts. His poems often contained mistakes in grammar and syntax and so on, but he had an unmistakable writing voice which he and others in the group enjoyed. The following poem 'It's a Far Cry' gave its title to an anthology of poems produced by the writing group in 1997:

> The poem of the eye is to cry something sweet
> Love is a far cry from what people say it is
> The answer to love is the intelligence of feelings
> The boat goes out to distant shores
>   and falls in love with other feelings.

> The path of mysteries is a symbol to a wise man
> The pain is a root in man's history
> The place of love is a symbol for all men to see

> but then it is a place for there to be, nurtured in the land
> of surprise and accomplishment of abilities.
>
> (V. W. 1997)

When he was asked what was distinctive for him about the process of writing V.W. replied, 'No-one can write a poem for you, you have to do it for yourself.' In the health care context, where there is often a great deal of distress in evidence, it is helpful to think of learning about poetry as *work*. The more sober, less mystical, statements that poets make about their work can be salutary: for example, W.H. Auden's: 'Poetry is not magic. In so far as poetry, or any other of the arts, can be said to have an anterior purpose, it is, by telling the truth, to disenchant and disintoxicate' (1975, p.27). Moruslav Holub meanwhile points out, 'one must decide whether to be uplifted by one's conception of creation or whether to try to understand it; whether to be enchanted with oneself or to try to learn about oneself' (Holub 1990, p.117).

The role of the tutor-facilitator

A common thread between these creative writing projects, at the hospice day centre and the project for ex-offenders with mental health problems, and with my teaching in 'mainstream' classes, has been the use of published work as a starting point for creative writing. This does not always entail using writers as models, but allows the development of what Kenneth Koch has called, 'poetry ideas' (1996, p.122). While not a bibliotherapist, Koch has been hailed as a writer who taught in a way that leads to 'self-emancipation' (McCarty Hynes and Hynes-Berry 1986, p.189). He has described wanting to bring to the classroom the sorts of processes that he was familiar with as a writer. These would include:

> reading other poets and being influenced; trying new forms; like sestinas, say, or poems with only one word in each line; collabo-rating with other poets; writing about dreams; writing stream of consciousness; deliberately writing things that didn't make sense; and so on. All these things I turned into assignments. (Koch 1996, p.155)

This approach seems to me to respect both creative writing as a process, and the autonomy of the participants in choosing what they want to write. The workshops described below come with the caveat that it is impossible to know what will stimulate someone else's imagination. I try to avoid offering a template for how to write a poem (as if such a thing existed) but offer a range of possibilities from which individuals in the group can choose. Poems brought in to the writing group for inspiration came from as wide a range of sources as possible, from Shakespeare to dub poetry, from surrealists to post-modernists. We looked at forms such as the haiku, sonnet, and villanelle. I would bring in anything that I found had opened up possibilities for my own writing.

Often reading two poems side by side suggested a 'third idea' that the group could then explore. For example in one workshop we read two poems featuring bridges: Wordsworth's 'Composed upon Westminster Bridge' (1975, p.115) and Lavinia Greenlaw's 'From Scattered Blue' (1993, p.13). It was effective to have a contrast in times and styles between the two pieces, giving the group a chance to make distinctions and have preferences. Group discussion focused on the symbolism and associated meanings of the word 'bridge'; the idea emerged that a poem is itself a kind of bridge in terms of communication, and that the writer needs to bear in mind the reader he or she is trying to reach. After the discussion it was suggested to participants they write about walking across a bridge, using the first person. In other workshops, poems were coupled together in a similar way. For example Seamus Heaney's 'A Kite for Michael and Christopher' (1984, p.44) and Simon Armitage's 'Any distance greater than a single span' (1993, p.11) with their shared imagery of the kite and the anchor. And Jean 'Binta' Breeze's 'Spring Cleaning' (1992, pp.12–14) which was read alongside Psalm 23, on which her poem draws. In this workshop it is suggested that participants make a feature in their own poem of any text – song, rhyme, prayer – which they may have learned by rote, to explore how texts learned by heart are carried with us.

At a recent summer school for students involved with creative writing and hospice care[6] we examined at another pair of poems for inspiration: 'No. 3 Greenhouse, 7.30 a.m.' by Sarah Maguire (1997, p.36), and 'Come In' by Robert Frost (1973, p.195). When we had discussed the poems I suggested that students take a central image both poems share – the threshold – and explore this in their own writing. In our discussion the idea came up that a threshold was often a line marking a beginning or an ending and was suggestive of transition or change. Students were asked to think about the first line of their writing as a kind of threshold that the reader would have to cross to enter the newly created world of their poem. This exercise led to some very interesting pieces of work. In the discussion afterwards we talked about whether 'Come In' in particular is a work that would be appropriate to bring to patients in hospice, with its dark imagery of the woods representing death. As Deryn Rees-Jones has said: 'Writing poems is a negotiation of loss, a way of capturing time in the moment of writing' (2000, p.58). In this respect the activity of writing a lyric poem leads us to think about loss no matter what the poem's overt subject matter. Creative writing groups do not aim to set the agenda by pursuing topics for writing in a prescriptive way. Ideally, they provide opportunities for writers to use language to make something new in any way that seems right to them at the time.

Inevitably some participants in writing workshops, such as P.H. in the example from hospice above, will want to use writing to explore the impact of their illness directly. The challenge for the writer in health care is to be open to such impulses, and not to end up denying the reality of why participants are receiving care in the first place. For this reason the writer in health care needs some means of reflecting on their practice at a time when the issues raised may be hard to bear. For example, it can be helpful to ask difficult questions such as: What are my motivations for doing this work? How is it making me feel? What are the implications for my own writing? Counselling training may be useful in this context. Some key concepts from psychodynamic theory, such as *projection* and *transference*,[7] can help the writer to understand what might be going on when strong feelings are being expressed which do not seem to belong entirely with the writing group or its leader. Such training also gives an appreciation of the importance of maintaining the boundaries of time and space, and of the dynamics between the staff and clients in health care.

Theoretical perspectives, such as the psychodynamic, on how groups work may also be illuminating. For example Wilfred Bion (1961) showed how a group's ability to work effectively is influenced by all the emotions and irrational feelings of its members. This analysis also showed how a group's behaviour can speak volumes about its overall health: for example, how the group deals with a leader's absence, how it deals with change including welcoming new members, and how well it is able to tolerate and express differences. The psychodynamic theory of organisations also has a lot to contribute. Intuitively the writer in health care knows that the better the support and the safer the setting, the more creative the facilitator and participants can be. Several chapters in Obholzer and Zagier Roberts (1994), and de Board (1978) help to show why this might be. De Board's summary of general systems theory, for example, explains the benefits to all parties in an organisation of having a shared 'primary task', a concept itself derived from Bion's work on groups (1978, pp.86–111).

For the writer in health care there is a need to agree with the host institution some means of thinking through the impact of the work. This could either be through a formal system of supervision or a more flexible arrangement according to changing circumstances. The host organisation meanwhile has a responsibility to manage the boundaries of the group, for example, by making appropriate referrals, ensuring there is a suitable room, providing a member of staff, where needed, to assist clients with special needs, and so on. This support provided at the managerial level is vital to ensure the safety and effectiveness of the writer in health care, thereby enhancing the quality of service that can be offered to their clients.

Conclusions

Since the 1970s the creative writing movement has done much to democratise the teaching of English, inviting readers into literature as an experience in which we can take part as active participants. The development of the use of the literary arts in health and social care has widened access to the study of literature to include many people from outside the academy. At the same time, health and social care providers have come halfway to meet this activity as they search for ways to allow their clients to be autonomous and empowered.

The Arts Council, England's support for promoting literature amongst groups who are socially excluded as a result of economic disadvantage or cultural difference has given strength to the case for the use of the literary arts in health and social care, and has helped provide the resources to develop its practice. One of the implications of this for writers is that training is becoming essential to enable them to take up a role in which they are in an unfamiliar setting working with vulnerable students.[8]

Historically, writers in health care have taken responsibility for their own safety and ethical practices. Now they can also draw on others in the field for support: the membership organisation Lapidus has a key role to play in encouraging best practice, by providing the means for writers to meet and exchange ideas. Current Lapidus initiatives include: development of an ethical code; compilation of a bibliography to map the field; establishment of special interest groups; research; support for writers who are disabled.[11]

In this chapter I have conceived writing in health care as a form of education rather than art or therapy, and have stressed the need for a capacity for work by the participants, the facilitator and the host organisation to make sure that writing groups can be diverse and inclusive. More research needs to be done to substantiate this position, and to evaluate exactly what it is about writing poetry that patients in different settings find helpful, and how this compares to the experience of nascent writers other contexts, for example, higher education.[12] However, I would like to finish with an example of poetry at work. Philip Larkin might not be the first writer who comes to mind when we think of diversity and inclusion. In fact his themes tend to centre on loneliness and exclusion. For example 'The Importance of Elsewhere' in *The Whitsun Weddings* (1964, p.34) suggests how much we are defined and disturbed by our differences. Nevertheless, as Seamus Heaney shows in 'The Main of Light', Larkin's poetry is also at times concerned with 'joyous affirmation' (1988, p.21). A good example of this is in 'Water' from the same collection, where there is an image of unity that seems to be generated by poetry itself. The opening lines state in a matter of fact tone, 'If I were called in/ To construct a religion/ I should make use of water', but it is the last stanza that presents the reader with a rather mystical and beautiful image:

> And I should raise in the east
> A glass of water
> Where any-angled light
> Would congregate endlessly
>
> (Larkin 1964, p.20)

In a workshop readers might be asked how they respond to the poem. How does the poem achieve its effects? Do you feel excluded or included by the imagery of water and light? Through such an engagement with the text, poetry can be an inspiration, and therefore a means of emphasising our common humanity, while also helping to acknowledge the real differences that exist between us.

Acknowledgements

The poems by patients quoted here have been published elsewhere – in either a day centre newsletter or a specially produced pamphlet – with each of the authors' full permission. As it has not been possible to contact all the patients' relatives regarding their use here, initials have been used to protect confidentiality.

Notes

1   The transitional object is useful to the infant who is learning to discover what is 'me' and what is 'not-me'. It typically takes the form of a cuddly toy or blanket. Paradoxically, the object is both created by the child, and exists before the child created it and was waiting to be found. The object will not act or retaliate, and is able to survive all the powerful feelings the child expresses in relation to it. The transitional object facilitates play and allows the child to become independent of the 'original object', the mother. See Winnicott (1971, pp.1–25); Gray (1994, p.155); Noonan (1983, p.74).

2   The advent of the creative writing group was one regular activity which led to the inauguration of a monthly *Day Centre Newsletter* beginning in 1992. Both of G.H.'s poems here were published in the *Newsletter* in November of that year.

3   This project took place at St Christopher's Hospice in Sydenham, London SE26. The project was funded through the day centre's budget for employing

sessional tutors in the arts; the project was set up and managed by the then Day Centre Manager, Anne Gibson and was developed by her successor, Cyndy Kennett. Tribute should also be paid to volunteer hospice workers and nurses who contributed their time to supporting clients within the writing group; Joy Elias-Rilwan in particular was a long-standing volunteer helper.

4   This writing project took place at the Effra Trust, then based at Effra Road, Brixton, London SW2. My role as creative writing tutor was part of my broader general role as a four-day-a-week support worker; colleagues in a similar role often helped to co-facilitate the group.

5   The group ran from 1997 to 2001 in various configurations. The average attendance was four clients; it was run as an open group, with new members being welcomed each week even if on a one-off basis; writing produced by group members was regularly displayed at the Effra Trust's annual Open Days.

6   A seminar on 22 June 2002 as part of 'Writers in Healthcare', a short course offering professional development for writers at the University of Sussex, Centre for Continuing Education.

7   *Projection* is a process by which we manage unacceptable thoughts and feelings 'whereby we expel feelings, qualities or wishes so that they are relocated in another person' (Gray 1994, p.152); *transference* is the 'transfering or placing of qualities of someone else (usually someone from the past) onto the counsellor and then responding to her as if she were that person' (Noonan 1983, p.86). Both are seen as universal phenomena not restricted to occurrence within a formal therapeutic setting.

8   Several initiatives are underway in this area, including the *Creative People* project set up to foster continuing professional development for all artists including writers, and *literaturetraining*, a newly formed agency providing information and advice.

9   Inclusion and diversity is not just an issue among participants but also amongst writers in health care themselves who may have special needs that need to be met to help them do their work. This is area of work that is being pursued by Lapidus along with other partner organisations in the literature sector such as the National Association of Writers in Education and *writernet* (see for example, Meth 2000).

10   Mark Robinson (2000) has indicated a way forward which is likely to be fruitful.

References

Armitage, S. (1993) 'Mother, any distance greater than a single span.' In *Book of Matches*. London: Faber.

Armitage, S. (1997) 'The Phoenix.' In *CloudCuckooLand*. London: Faber.

Auden, W.H. (1975) 'Making, knowing and judging.' In *The Dyer's Hand*. London: Faber.

Bell, E. (1999) 'The role of education in the role of counselling.' In J. Lees and A. Vaspe (eds) *Clinical Counselling in Further and Higher Education*. London: Routledge.

Bhatt, S. (1988) 'Search for my tongue.' In S. Bhatt *Brunizem*. Manchester: Carcanet.

Bion, W.R. (1961) *Experiences in Groups*. London: Routledge.

Bishop, E. (1994) *One Art – The Selected Letters*. (R. Giroux (ed.)). London: Pimlico.

Breeze, J. (1992) 'Spring cleaning.' In *Spring Cleaning*. London: Virago.

de Board, R. (1978) *The Psychoanalysis of Organizations – a Psychoanalytic Approach to Behaviour in Groups and Organizations*. London: Routledge.

Frost, R. (1973) 'Come in.' In *Selected Poems*. London: Penguin.

Gray, A. (1994) *An Introduction to the Therapeutic Frame*. London: Routledge.

Greenlaw, L. (1993) 'From scattered blue.' In *Night Photograph*. London: Faber.

Heaney, S. (1984) 'A kite for Michael and Christopher.' In *Station Island*. London: Faber.

Heaney, S. (1988) 'The government of the tongue.' In *The Government of the Tongue*. London: Faber.

Holub, M. (1990) 'Maxwell's dream, or on creativity.' In *The Dimension of the Present*. London: Faber.

Koch, K. (1977) *I Never Told Anybody – Teaching Poetry Writing in a Nursing Home*. New York: Random House.

Koch, K. (1996) *The Art of Poetry*. Ann Arbor: University of Michigan Press.

Jarrell, R. (1955) *Poetry and the Age*. London: Faber.

Larkin, P. (1964) *The Whitsun Weddings*. London: Faber.

Lewis, G. (2002) *Sunbathing in the Rain – a Cheerful Book about Depression*. London: Flamingo.

Maguire, S, (1997) 'No 3 Greenhouse 7.30 am.' In *The Invisible Mender*. London: Cape.

Marks, A. (2000) 'Writing about writing.' In A. Marks and D. Rees-Jones (eds) *Contemporary Women's Poetry – Reading/Writing/Practice*. London: Macmillan.

McCarty Hynes, A. and Hynes-Berry, M. (1986) *Bibliotherapy: The Interactive Process: A Handbook*. Boulder, CO and London: Westview Press.

Meth, J. (2000) 'Disabled writers mentoring scheme – a report on a pilot training and development project.' London: *writernet*.

Noonan, E. (1983) *Counselling Young People*. London: Routledge.

Obholzer, A. and Zagier Roberts, V. (eds) (1994) *The Unconscious at Work*. London: Routledge.

Porter, P. (2003) A talk to students of the Certificate in Creative Writing at Birkbeck, University of London, 22 March.

Rees-Jones, D. (2000) 'Nothing that is not there...' In A. Marks and D. Rees-Jones (eds) *Contemporary Women's Poetry – Reading/Writing/Practice*. London: Macmillan.

Robinson, M. (2000) 'Writing well: health and the power to make images.' *Journal of Medical Ethics in Medical Humanities 26*, 79–84.

Saunders, C. (1999) Personal communication.

Spender, S. (1985) 'To my daughter.' In *Collected Poems 1928–1985*. London: Faber.

Vendler, H. (1995) *Soul Says: On Recent Poetry*. London: Harvard University Press.

Winnicott, D.W. (1971) *Playing and Reality*. London: Routledge.

Wordsworth, W. (1975) 'Composed upon Westminster Bridge.' In W. Davies (ed.) *William Wordsworth: Selected Poems.* London: J.M. Dent.

Further reading

Carpenter, E. (1999) 'The Arts and inclusion – evaluation of London Arts Board's 1998/99 Regional Challenge Programme.' London: London Arts Board.

Coren, A. (1997) *A Psychodynamic Approach to Education.* London: Sheldon Press.

D'Ardenne, P. and Mahtani, A. (1989) *Transcultural Counselling in Action.* London: Sage.

Koch, K. (1998) *Making Your Own Days – The Pleasures of Reading and Writing Poetry.* New York: Touchstone.

Lapidus at www.lapidus.org.uk.

Literaturetraining at www.literaturetraining.com.

McLoughlin, D. (2000) 'Transition, transformation and the art of losing – some uses of poetry in hospice care for the terminally ill.' In *Psychodynamic Counselling 6,* 2, 215–234.

Orr, G. and Bryant Voigt, E. (1996) *Poets Teaching Poets – Self and the World.* Ann Arbor: University of Michigan.

Sansom, P. (2000) 'Reading for writing.' In L. Jeffries and P. Sansom (eds) *Contemporary Poems, Some Critical Approaches.* Huddersfield: Smith/ Doorstop.

CHAPTER TEN

Notes towards a Therapeutic Use for Creative Writing in Occupational Therapy

Nick Pollard

Despite considerable interest in the use of writing as a creative and therapeutic medium, few occupational therapists have investigated the theoretical grounding for such work (Jensen and Blair 1997). Although some research has been carried out by writing practitioners, Wright and Chung's (2001) review suggests a similar omission in the field of counselling. The authors of articles in occupational therapy journals have rarely been clinicians and have been concerned more with praxis than theory (e.g. Foster 1988; Dynes 1989; Inglis 1993). Yet the emerging discipline may prove to be as complex as dramatherapy, art therapy or music therapy.

In this chapter, therefore, I hope to explore some proto-therapeutic issues concerning writing produced by groups of people who, as mental health service users, may be marginalised by society. In doing so I am drawing on my background of involvement in the Federation of Worker Writers and Community Publishers (FWWCP),[1] whose belief, outlined in their publicity material, is 'that writing and publishing should be made accessible to all'.

The history of community writing and publishing has to some extent been one of exclusion from the mainstream of literary culture[2] and the attendant problems of finding a context for its serious evaluation. I feel that it therefore reveals lessons for the treatment of writing produced in a therapeutic milieu. There are now several community publishing groups, for example, Survivors' Poetry,[3] which are specifically organised around mental health issues. The opportunities for developing and participating in such groups are increasing, and with them a body of emergent literature.

New writers are frequently advised to write about what they know (Doubtfire 1978; Sparrow 1980; Sansom 1994). In worker, or 'proletarian' writing, a literature based in autobiography, experience is paramount: 'When they write *I*, they are witnessing' (Lucien Jean, cited in Ragon 1986, p.26).

Foucault thought that intellectuals should be informed by the lives of workers and then act as a mirror by which workers' experiences are transmitted (Eribon 1993). However, though this may be relevant for the FWWCP, the lives of a few people from the marginalised group of people with mental health problems cannot stand for all. The direct relationship of 'witness' writing to the experience it records is both its weakness and its strength when it is subjected to a critical process that demands an external coherence. Experience is often particularised rather than universal (Ragon 1986), and in the exploitation of a few examples to represent social history the individual creative voice may be lost or devalued.

Accommodating lived reality within the disciplined straitjacket of received literary form requires adjustments that often do not sit easily with the writer on the margins. Foucault's intellectual can never offer more than a partial reflection of a culture, interpreted as if by a colonial explorer who is 'not from round here'. Many FWWCP writers have felt that, in the process of acquiring intellectual discipline, the capacity for expression was 'educated out' of them, or was something they were never given credit for possessing. For example:

> the teachers were remote as hell. They understood nothing whatsoever of us kids. They knew how to keep a class in order. They knew the curriculum by heart. They knew how to put a lesson over. But all this was to no effect because there was something they didn't know about. Something to do with us. (Barnes 1976, p.151)

Learning disabled writers identify a parallel experience of having being alienated from their capacity to express their own feelings, or from the written word itself (McDowell 1998). Although, generally, occupational therapists recognise clients as artists or writers, and the quality of their productions are judged on their own merits (Jensen and Blair 1997), sometimes clients' writing has been considered purely as a data source and intellectual property rights have been ignored (Francis 1997).

In recent times opportunities for expressing individuality through writing appear to have increased through comprehensive education and greater access to Higher and Further Education. Night classes in English, literacy classes and Workers Education Association writers' workshops have all encouraged people to write about themselves and their communities. In describing the emerging FWWCP, Worpole (1983) hailed the new expressionism developing in working-class writing and community publishing and looked forward to a literature of post-modern multiplicities across which individuals must move in their own experiential paths. I suggest that today community publishing continues to offers this diversity, this arena of re-definition, from which writers practising in the therapeutic context can learn.

Actualisation and participation

I would argue that the roots of creativity are in the expression of individuality, which Rogers links with the 'curative force in psychotherapy – man's tendency to actualise himself, to become his potentialities' (Rogers 1970, p.140). Although this same goal of actualisation motivates involvement in the arts and the development of participatory arts projects, the *essential* character of creative expression has rarely been connected with social impact (Matarasso 1998). However, many therapeutic practitioners suggest that the activity of writing can extend to a process of self-discovery and development; and from group participation into parication in the activities of the wider community, such as adult education and other writing groups (Foster 1988; Dynes 1989; Hartill 1993; Inglis 1993; Pollard 1993; Brewer *et al.* 1994; Bryant 1995; Bolton 1999).

In other words, this work towards self-actualisation may have a political dimension as well as therapeutic applications. Learning to articulate and express the self is a therapeutic objective along a continuum toward assertion of one's citizenship, taking up one's democratic rights to write, publishing and sharing in 'the pleasures of the text'. As Barthes (1990) suggests, this pleasure is that through which one reads, within which the reader is reinvented and rewrites the text. The community-based writing group to which I belong developed from this idea the maxim that 'readers should be writers' (Heeley Writers 1981).

To *read* and to *write*

Sampson (1998) discusses how an editor or reviewer may think about imaginative writing as 'product', yet it cannot be divorced from a 'process' of writing which is both personal to the author and part of the shared community through which our personal use of language is understood. The test for our experience is not so much to rise to Ragon's (1986) universal, but to eclipse the intellectual's 'trick with mirrors', as Bradford (1996, p.262) calls it, so that the cultural expression of the individual writer's *spirit*[4] is undiminished by someone else's stereotyped packaging.

Yet, writing is often not primarily a creative activity. We may use it predominantly for the production of lists and letters (Heath 1983). Sometimes in a therapeutic programme it is seen as a secondary or transferable skill (Denton 1987). The idea of a one-way process of *cultural* production is manifested in official satisfaction at levels of writing and reading skills which merely enable information to be assimilated and reproduced (Hughes 1991). We may experience writing as an elite practice, its purpose didactic, which we can consume rather than use for creative self-expression (Williams 1975; Morley and Worpole 1982; Sutton-Smith 1986; Birch 1990). Many people are taught writing and reading, but not how to write and how to read *for themselves*.

Friere (1990) argued that a true literacy enables people to *read* the society they live in. Active choice and knowledgeable participation require the ability to read between the lines of the texts society produces, to evaluate critically, and to appreciate the experiences we have produced ourselves (Hughes 1991).

The use of written pieces interspersed within the oral narrative is a key element of this book. Arthur has been writing since the age of thirty, both fact and fiction, sometimes combining the two...because writing has been, and still is, very important to Arthur it seemed appropriate to use the material in some way...

I hoped that these two sources would complement each other and provide a richer story, to show the contradictions and possible tensions at play in his story, and to provide more detail about feelings or events which Arthur was reluctant (or unable) to explore in the interviews. (L. Sitzia (2002) 'Introduction' in Sitzia and Thickett, *Seeking the Enemy*, pp.12–13)

If the aim of occupational therapy is 'to maintain, restore, or create a match, beneficial to the individual, between the abilities of the person, the demands of his/her occupations and the demands of the environment, in order to maintain or improve the client's functional status and access to opportunities for participation' (Creek 2003, p.14), writing may offer a practical and creative way of relating experience and understanding to the rehabilitation process and the maintenance of gains made.

This view of the individual as situated in the world of meanings and experiences restates some of the occupational therapy values defined by Yerxa (1983):

- productivity requires a personal meaning to be valuable;

- occupational balance (Wilcock 1999) entails productive participation in leisure, play and social activities as well as work;

- a client centred rather than an objectivated approach to client's expression;

- the prime source of information about the client is the client, and understanding their perceptions of themselves, their world and their interests is a precondition for the therapeutic process.

Writing activities fit well with Creek's more recent exploration of core values (2003) in client-centred practice which set out the need to listen to and explore the contextual world of the client and the need for occupational therapists to reflect on their own values in relation to the interventions offered.

Occupational therapy has often viewed writing in functional terms, in other words in terms of the *physical* components of such tasks as producing meaningful marks on paper: hand-eye co-ordination, spatial awareness and the fine motor skills required to produce handwriting or manipulate a keyboard. This, as much as issues of grammar and 'correct' use of English, militates against the free-thinking creative process indicated by psychotherapeutic concerns. The FWWCP's view of 'writing' and 'publishing' – which accommodates performance, tape recordings and video as well as the written word – is intended to enable the inclusion of members with writing difficulties or without English as a first language. This approach thrusts 'writing' very much back to what Vaneigem (1983, pp.153–156) calls 'the purity of its moment of genesis'; to the Greek *poiein*, or 'making': in other words to a 'lived poetry', 'the word in action'. Writing becomes:

> the protector par excellence of everything irreducible in mankind, i.e. creative spontaneity. The will to unite the individual and the social, not on the basis of an illusory community, but on that of subjectivity – this is what makes the new poetry into a weapon which everyone must learn to handle by himself. (Vaneigem 1983, p.156)

This suggests that the writer seeks insight through discovering what is 'hidden' not only *within* himself but as it were from partial reflection in society's mirror. Sometimes it may be necessary to seize this mirror and reposition it. As writers in the community, particularly when working alongside people with mental health problems, we must discover what has been marginalised and sequestrated. It is important to regain the things we have hidden from ourselves and to confront our disempowerment, our difficulty in engaging with our individual creativity.

Creativity and compliance

One way to live creatively through the healthy expression of the self is to resist (textual) compliance (Camus 1971; Winnicott 1971). Sometimes a client's artistic integrity, their free expression, may *appear* to conflict with the aims of therapy (Clayburn, Natzler, Silcock 1998), because of the suicidal or depressive content of what they write. However, these clients may need to use writing to defuse their feelings.

Furthermore, Thomas (1997) describes a schizophrenic client using a journal to come to terms with her voices and learning to control their influence. These auditory hallucinations relate to people and significant life events in the narrative of the individual's past and present experience, and tell the hearer how to act, or not act: most of the time in mundane contexts. The controlling effect they have often disempowers the client and limits their free expression. Art derived from such a psychosis may be artistically interesting yet be described by a traditional medical establishment as pathological (Boyle 1990). Yet, an individual's free expression depends upon empowerment, upon an understanding and recognition of the artistic integrity of their work, and this in turn depends upon insight, gained a little at a time through discipline; and a gradual realisation, practice of and familiarity with tenets of writing practice. The occasional mainstream publication of such volumes as *Beyond Bedlam* (Smith and Sweeney (eds) 1997) may represent the rehabilitation of writing about mental illness, perhaps led by a rising number of mental health system survivors acting as readers, writers and researchers; and it appears to support Boyle's view (1990) that the acceptability of what may elsewhere be determined hallucinatory or deluded depends on social context. *Beyond Bedlam*'s contributors represent themselves as artists and poets who have suffered and survived, and to do this effectively, as Post (in Smith and Sweeney 1997, p.14) says, requires 'very special gifts and hard work'.

However, part of the role of insight is to allow the artist is to project a *recognisable* portion of reality. A tension exists between what is depicted and what must be left out of the frame (Camus 1971). Expression is at once free and constrained by particular choices. Furthermore, insight and recognisability are qualities of *texts* and recognised by *readers* whatever the *writer*'s intentions. Therefore, an element of conformity, of the hard work of effecting a compromise with rebellion, is necessary. Moreover, where a writer does try something new, their experiment may serve only to reinforce the norm (as writing in dialect reifies the received English of other texts).

The mental health client may have difficulty with this compromise. Illness and medication may impair memory and cognitive ability, or clients may have lost out on learning opportunities, and perhaps have restricted literacy as a result. The ability to grasp abstract ideas may be poor or even absent (Borikar and Bumstead 1988; Dynes 1989). In previous opportunities to use creative writing clients may have actually been prevented from writing about their feelings, with detrimental effects on their capacity for free expression (McDowell 1998).

As Sampson (1998) suggests, both politically and in the psychoanalytic theories that may underpin our therapeutic approaches individuation requires the ability to symbolise the self. Someone who is unable to do this through a medium which is societal (such as language) cannot express the self in a way which others can recognise. On the other hand, to label expression as merely symptomatic is to discount the individual who is doing that expressing.

A few years ago, when I was working in a long-stay psychiatric unit, a patient with dementia regularly stationed herself near the staff offices. She shouted, 'Poison in the food...they're Nazis in this hospital...this is a German concentration camp', intending this to be heard by people whose job it was to deliver care in the hospital, and against whom she was daily rebelling. While this might be dismissed as symptomatic babble, once it is written down it becomes a text in which the concentration camp theme functions as a metaphor for her experience of (lack of) care and choice. The 'Nazi' epithet relates to the client's own experience as someone who lived through the 1930s and the war. Sampson (1998) has described a similar process in which coherence in a client's verbalising can be derived from context. Through recording, and sometimes even publication, individual written accounts have the opportunity to acquire universalisable meanings.

Stuart (1998) applies this sense of the individual and societal to the construction of the self. The social marginalisation of the past two centuries produced proletarian writers, but the FWWCP's 'worker writers' and 'community publishers' have to redefine an oppositional writing based around the political possibilities that have emerged over the past 20 or 30 years. People who may previously have thought of themselves as worker writers (or not) can acquire new identities based on race, sexuality, disability, or being survivors. I suggest this process is analogous to the one Stuart (1998) identifies in his discussion of Lyotard: the social classification or naming process is fundamental to self-identification. The story of how something or someone acquires a name or classification becomes in turn the story of a cultural location or context which might easily incorporate the concept of occupational (working) role (for example, 'I'm Nick, an occupational therapist from Sheffield').

Stuart is less concerned with the nature of a 'true self' to be expressed through a creative medium than with the *interactions* which are represented through writing. These are themselves based on marginalisations, multiple positionings which occur as a consequence of the power possessed by certain groups. She draws on Barthes' essay on 'The Death of the Author' (1977), which describes the reader moving across the text (or texts) and becoming a repository for their assembled meanings, or perhaps a site of interaction for a multiplicity of readings.

A double-edged pen

Literacy students frequently cite the linguistic hurdle of 'teacher's red pen' in their experience of writing and their reluctance to express themselves through it. This is a major barrier to making literature and even the experience of reading available to large parts of the population (Hughes 1991). In writing, these internalised and unresolved disempowerments result in a strong set of idealised imperatives which an author may feel she must uphold, even when the conflicts they produce for the characters (as the author's *real selves*) are unrealisable (Hunt 1998). Rather than the real self of the author the text exhibits only those aspects of the self which the author's inner conflicts and self-alienation will allow her to show. When the inconsistencies of this idealised image are irrevocably exposed, a counterpart, the despised image, is revealed.

Hunt's discussion of these issues resonates not only with the multiplicities suggested by Barthes, but also with questions of otherness signified by different uses or registers of language. Minority language users in both Britain and the Irish Republic and those whose first language is English where Welsh or Gaelic are emphasised have found that linguistic inclusiveness for some can facilitate others' exclusion

(Bolger 1986; Williams 1985; Bardon 1992). The ability to use linguistic markers of social status has implications for self-esteem or gaining social access (and is a question of oral facility as well as literacy).

Bakhtin was also interested in the multiple voices of literature, in particular quotation – seen primarily as the use of another person's words – which permeates and creates a dynamic in all aspects of language use (Pomorska 1984; Morris 1994). As Bakhtin and many of his contemporaries in Stalinist Russia knew, a dominant mode of expression can exclude or constrain what can be said or written. In his discussion of Rabelais' *Gargantua and Pantagruel*, Bahktin (1984) considered how attempts to regulate the folk culture survivals in the language of the common people reinforced its ability to expressly reject an official code which regarded them as sacrilegious. The language in which Rabelais and his contemporaries described their Renaissance world reflected the marketplace rather than ecclesiastical officialdom.

To sum up, I suggest that our capacity for free self-expression may be inhibited and constrained through false idealisations originating in the external world, but these problems also contain the key to our empowerment. Therefore, an exploration of the therapeutic uses of language might perhaps be usefully directed towards the goal of realising true verbal expression and restoring appropriate self-acceptance.

From self-acceptance to a public acceptance?

Although new technology has made publication a relatively easy and accessible process, it does not provide an alternative way in to the ranks of the *literati*. In fact community publishers experience great difficulty getting reviewers and other gatekeepers of the literary establishment to recognise the achievement their books represent (Hughes 1991).

One reason may simply be that popular uses of language do not translate well into 'serious' expression (Bahktin 1984, p.422). Sociolinguistic studies on style-shifting which examine the relationship between prestige and vernacular dialects show a tendency for prestige dialects to be valued over or dominate the vernacular in formal situations. A certain amount of social ability appears to depend on the individual's ability to be 'bi-dialectual', able to switch appropriately from vernacular to formal codes (Labov 1970).

Bakhtin (1981) argued for a recognition of these social languages within a national language: for the recognition of a 'dialogic' multiplicity of expression. Oral language is dialogic because it is directed to a listener, and an anticipated answer, while the learned language of officialdom is a mandarin for the passing of edicts and instructions. To answer is to answer back, to transcend the authority of the statement. Like Bakhtin, Palfrey (1996) argues that vernacular and accessible language used in protest can have a galvanising effect; this can be found in much of the work produced by members of Survivors' Poetry. While there have been official calls for the recognition, in a mental health context, of 'different uses of English and modes of communication' within our cultures (Reed 1994, p.16), this is only a partial answer to the problem: 'different uses' are still constructed as *other* than received English.

On the other hand, being *other* provides a base for challenge. In *The Hidden Ireland* Daniel Corkery (1967) describes a rough peasant holding a Latin text upside down in an eighteenth-century bookshop and asking the price, to be told he can have it *if* he can read it. At once he rights the book and demonstrates the outcome of a clandestine hedge-schooling in Gaelic[5] *and* the classics. In this model, though, success depends on the *other* establishing a degree of proximity to the accepted and official.

I suggest that artistic expression works through a web of multi-layered tensions between conformity and creativity. The 'mad' and the 'artistic' are perceived as *other*, as possessing a mystery which society's demand for conformity cannot tolerate. Chetcuti *et al.* (1993) identify links between the vilification of dissident artistic expression and of mental illness in a society and its inability to accommodate or even permit innovation unless it can be tamed. Clients producing a magazine for their day hospital may find that it has to pass 'quality control' and bear the Trust logo and Charter Mark before it can be circulated. If their sense of ownership, with attendant therapeutic benefits, is somewhat dented by this, the threat of their independence has nevertheless been curtailed.

As this demonstrates, effective outcomes depend on a familiarity with the mechanics of normalisation. Friere (1990) calls for a process of 'conscientization': for individuals to act in an informed way to transform and liberate society. He advocates recognition of the dialogic; for the world to be transformed and recreated through the word which names it.

Like Bahktin and Foucault, Friere requires that dialogue be established to admit the new, rather than have it oppressed by a hostile 'truth' or order. The recovery of dialogue is a process necessary to the recovery of humanity; an officialdom which denies dialogue denies what is human; to begin the dialogic process we have to begin with our perceptions of ourselves and the world in which we exist (Friere 1990). This is the *word-in-action*, an open and poetic process which is 'the most complex and concentrated response that can be made with words to the total experience of living' (Longley 1996, p.121)

The empowering word

As I have already suggested, one difficulty with which the use of creative writing as therapy has to engage is that of being framed in a therapeutic context where the therapist represents part of the psychiatric establishment, and therefore of those very contradictions to which the patient/writer may be witness. Changing the term 'patient' to 'client', 'consumer' or even 'member' fails to disguise this power relationship. Ultimately, clients' productions will be evaluated not in terms of literary quality but, perhaps, in terms of ability to participate, or of non-specialist versus clinical language.

The client may be aware that 'confidentiality' carries the proviso that certain things may have to be communicated to other clinicians: sometimes leading to pressure for behavioural changes. If a writing group in a health care setting aims to 'produce writing of quality', clients may find themselves engaged by another authoritative – *literary* – discourse.

These issues suggest there may be advantages to a writing group's being convened by a non-therapist. Clients may have the space to discuss problems they could not address elsewhere (Inglis 1993). Post (1997) sees this as particularly true of poetry writing activities. However, health care contexts put pressures on activities which are not carried out by clinicians, therapists or nurses. Inglis (1993) found she needed to refer difficult issues to a nurse. The provision of a writing group which, as Jensen and Blair (1997) suggest, does not easily lend itself to justification through scientific investigation may have low priority in a therapeutic programme. We might question to what degree a once-weekly creative writing group provides real opportunities for a group of people whose problems include poor prognosis, marginalisation and loss of control.

To achieve writing of quality it is important to make the most of that time, unless the group's members are able to undertake homework. Many factors may work against this: disruptions in home life or on the ward in addition to memory, concentration or cognitive problems, particularly for the most disturbed clients with poor coping skills; high expressed emotion; or over-involved relatives. Clients can be simply overloaded (Bebbington and Kuipers 1992).

In my experience of working with service users in enduring mental health settings these issues have been a particular difficulty, although some of the most disabled clients have worked on material between sessions. Describing the uses of therapeutic writing by counselling practitioners, Wright and Chung (2001) find several authors who base their work around on-line contact, or letters from clients, and note that this format is popular with shorter-term service users who can perhaps use writing for immediate benefit in home situations. I suggest that situations like these show how it may be possible to move beyond current social limitations to a living art, a word in action, centred on the person; the dialogic possibilities arising from collisions of the new may continually be created or re-invented.

In the emphasis on the quality and production of a group's writing which Jensen and Blair (1997, p.529) advocate, psychotherapeutic benefits occur 'covertly' as a side effect of a 'here and now' approach. They include: 'improved well-being in the form of worth, self esteem, clear identity and confidence' arising through a group context of 'encouragement, constructive criticism, trust, mastery and feelings of competence'. Clients gain through listening to each other, reading, and sharing their work: benefits which are also identified with writing groups outside the psychiatric setting (Foster 1988; McDowell 1998; Pollard 1993).

It would be facile to see this as the completion of rather than as a stage in the process of rehabilitation towards lived poetry. Our clients may decide to 'leave the bus' at this point, since 'at the same time as many people acquire their first typewriter, they also acquire their first suitcase' (Worpole 1983, p.94). The challenge of a lived poetry may be too demanding; they may feel they have already said all they want to say, or else, like many working-class writers, it is materially and psychologically necessary to break away from their class in order to write (Cherry 1996). Some psychiatric service users attending a day hospital poetry group with whom I worked responded to an encounter with the local Survivors' Poetry movement by saying they felt that there was more to their lives than being mentally ill, and they therefore did not want to take on the politics connected with the movement.

I suggest that the future of therapeutic writing could nonetheless take a lesson from Corkery's *gairmscoile*[6], a repository of culture able to comment on and maintain an objective relationship to prevailing reality, in which participants find an esteem and recognition they may not have found elsewhere; whose simplicity of organisation allows easy survival and a line to the community in precarious times. This is how writing groups in the community have endured, and how their writing has never quite become the property of anyone else, an occupational role marginalised but never sequestrated: a therapeutic writing beyond therapy, enjoyed for its own sake.

Notes

1   The Federation of Worker Writers and Community Publishers was formed in 1976, and now has a membership of over 65 independently organised writers' workshops, community publishers and organisations in Britain and around the world. It is an umbrella organisation for those who wish to share their skills and work with their communities. For more information write to: The FWWCP, Burslem School of Art, Queen Street, Stoke on Trent, ST6 3EJ, or E-mail thefwwcp@tiscali.co.uk.

2   However, the FWWCP has for many years been supported by the Arts Council of England, as well as having specific projects funded by other grants, such as the National Lotteries Fund.

3   Survivors' Poetry is a registered UK charity that promotes 'the poetry of survivors of mental distress...both those who consider themselves "survivors" and those who have empathy with their experiences'. It has a large membership (around 2,500 people) made up of both those who consider themselves 'survivors' and those who have empathy with their experiences. E-mail, phone, or write to: Survivors' Poetry, Diorama Arts Centre, 34 Osnaburgh Street, London NW1 3ND Tel: 0171 916 5317 Fax: 0171 916 0830 E-mail: survivor@survivorspoetry.org.uk.

4   By which I mean the essential personality of the writer, as communicated through artistic expression.

5   During this period Gaelic was suppressed, but still taught by itinerant teachers in gatherings which could quickly disperse, hence 'hedge schools'.

6   The *gairmscoile* was a bardic challenge in which poets would exchange extemporised verses in shebeens on popular subjects. This practice kept alive the traditions and skills of the court bards who had been deprived of their living following the flight of the Irish nobility in 1603.

References

Bahktin, M. (1981) *The Dialogic Imagination* (trans. C. Emerson and M. Holquist). Austin: University of Texas.

Bahktin, M. (1984) *Rabelais and His World* (trans. H. Iswolsky). Bloomington: Indiana University Press.

Bardon, J. (1992) *A History of Ulster*. Belfast: The Blackstaff Press.

Barnes, R. (1976) *Coronation Cups and Jam-Jars*. London: Centerprise.

Barthes, R. (1977) 'The death of the author.' In S. Heath (ed. and trans.) *Image-Music-Text*. London: Fontana, pp.142–148.

Barthes, R. (1990) *The Pleasure of the Text* (trans R. Miller). Oxford: Blackwell.

Bebbington, P. and Kuipers, L. (1992) 'Life events and social factors.' In D.J. Kavanagh (ed.) *Schizophrenia: An Overview and Practical Handbook*. London: Chapman and Hall.

Birch, K. (1990) 'The growing phenomenon of working class writing on Merseyside.' In (ed. unattrib.) *Don't Judge this Book by its Cover*. Liverpool: Merseyside Association of Writers' Workshops.

Bolger, D. (1986) (ed.) *The Bright Wave: An Tonn Gheal*. Dublin: Raven Arts.

Bolton, G. (1999) *The Therapeutic Potential of Creative Writing: Writing Myself*. London: Jessica Kingsley Publishers.

Borikar, A.M. and Bumstead J.M. (1988) 'Literacy/numeracy provision and its effectiveness in psychiatric hospitals.' *British Journal Of Occupational Therapy 51*, 11, 395–396.

Boyle, M. (1990) *Schizophrenia: A Scientific Delusion?* London: Routledge.

Bradford, G. (1996) 'Media: Capital's global village.' In H. Ehrlich (ed.) *Reinventing Anarchy, Again*. Edinburgh: AK Press, pp.258–271.

Brewer, P., Gadsden, V. and Scrimshaw, K. (1994) 'The community group network in mental health: A model for social support and community integration.' *British Journal of Occupational Therapy 57*, 12, 467–71.

Bryant, W. (1995) 'The social contact group: An example of long term group work in community mental health care.' *British Journal of Occupational Therapy 58*, 5, 214–218.

Camus, A. (1971) *The Rebel* (trans. A. Bower). Harmondsworth: Penguin.

Cherry, M. (1996) 'Towards recognition of working class women writers.' In S. Richardson (ed.) *Writing on the Line*. London: Working Press.

Chetcuti, M., Monteiro, A.C.D. and Jenner, F.A. (1993) 'The domestication of art and madness and the difficulties for the outsider.' In F.A. Jenner, A.C.D. Monteiro, J.A.

Zargalo-Cardoso and J.A. Cunha-Olivera (eds) *Schizophrenia – A Disease or Some Ways of Being Human?* Sheffield: Sheffield Academic Press.

Clayburn, A., Natzler, C. and Silcock, A. (1998) 'Discussion and debate (responses to "What are the advantages and disadvantages of the medical model, which addresses the therapeutic benefits [of creative writing] and seeks an evidence base for the intervention").' *Lapidus News 6.*

Corkery, D. (1967) *The Hidden Ireland.* Dublin: Gill and Macmillan.

Creek, J. (2003) *Occupational Therapy Defined as a Complex Intervention.* London: College of Occupational Therapists.

Denton, P.L. (1987) *Psychiatric Occupational Therapy, A Workbook of Practical Skills.* Boston: Little, Brown and Co.

Doubtfire, D. (1978) *The Craft of Novel Writing.* London: Alison and Busby.

Dynes, R. (1989) 'Using Creative Writing.' *British Journal Of Occupational Therapy 52,* 4, 151–152.

Eribon, D. (1993) *Michel Foucault* (trans. Betsy Wing). London: Faber.

Foster, L. (1988) 'Writers' workshops, the word processor and the psychiatric patient.' *British Journal of Occupational Therapy 51,* 6, 191–192.

Foucault, M. (1971) *Madness and Civilisation* (trans. Richard Howard). London: Routledge.

Foucault, M. (1972) *Histoire de la Folie.* Saint Amand: Gallimard.

Foucault, M. (1987a) *Mental Illness and Psychology* (trans. Alan Sheridan). Berkeley: University of California.

Foucault, M. (1987b) *Death and the Labyrinth* (trans. Charles Ruas). London: Athlone.

Francis, G. (1997) 'The use of a patient diary in health care research.' *British Journal of Therapy and Rehabilitation 5,* 7, 302–304.

Friere, P. (1990) *The Pedagogy of the Oppressed* (trans. Myra Bergman Ramos). Harmondsworth: Penguin.

Hartill, G. (1993) 'With the mind's eye: The world opened up by reading.' *Reading Therapy Newsletter 5,* 1, 8–9.

Heath, S.B. (1983) *Ways with Words.* Cambridge: Cambridge University Press.

Heeley Writers (1981) *Down to Heel.* Sheffield: Heeley Writers.

Hughes, V.M. (1991) *Literature Belongs to Everyone.* London: The Literature Panel of the Arts Council of England.

Hunt, C. (1998) 'Autobiography and the psychotherapeutic process.' In Celia Hunt and Fiona Sampson (eds) *The Self on the Page.* London: Jessica Kingsley Publishers, pp.181–197.

Inglis, J. (1993) 'Reading for pleasure: An experiment using fiction with psychiatric patients.' *British Journal of Occupational Therapy 56,* 7, 258–261.

Jensen, C.M. and Blair, S.E.E. (1997) 'Rhyme and reason: The relationship between creative writing and mental wellbeing.' *British Journal Of Occupational Therapy 60,* 12, 525–530.

Kristeva, J. (1984) *Revolution in Poetic Language* (trans. M. Waller). Columbia: Columbia University Press.

Labov, W. (1976) 'The study of language in its social context.' In J.B. Pride and J. Holmes (eds) *Sociolinguistics.* Harmondsworth: Penguin.

Longley, M. (1996) 'A tongue at play.' In T. Curtis (ed.) *How Poets Work.* Bridgend: Seren, pp.111–122.

Matarasso, F. (1998) 'Use or ornament.' *Federation 12*, 3–7.

McDowell, A. (1998) 'Creative writing: How it is viewed by adults with learning disabilities.' *British Journal of Therapy and Rehabilitation 5*, 9, 465–467.

Merleau-Ponty, M. (1994) *The Phenomenology of Perception* (trans. C. Smith). London: Routledge.

Morley, D. and Worpole, K. (eds) (1982) *The Republic of Letters: Working Class Writing and Local Publishing*. London: Comedia Publishing Group.

Morris, P. (ed.) (1994) *The Bahktin Reader*. London: Arnold.

Palfrey, S. (1996) 'Writing and the Miners' Strike.' In S. Richardson (ed.) *Writing on the Line*. London: Working Press.

Paterson, D. (1996) 'The dilemma of the peot.' In T. Curtis (ed.) *How Poets Work*. Bridgend: Seren, pp.155–172.

Pollard, N. (1993) 'On doing the write thing.' *Reading Therapy Newsletter 5*, 2, 8–9.

Pomorska, K. (1984) 'Foreword.' In M. Bahktin *Rabelais and his World*. Bloomington: Indiana University Press.

Post, F. (1997) 'Foreword.' In K. Smith and M. Sweeney (eds) *Beyond Bedlam*. London: Anvil.

Ragon, M. (1986) *Histoire de la Littérature Prolétarienne de Langue Française*. Foche a Mayenne: Albin Michel.

Reed, J. (Chairman) (1994) *Review of Health and Social Services for Mentally Disordered Offenders and Others Requiring Similar Services, Vol 6: Race, Gender, and Equal Opportunities*. London: HMSO.

Rogers, C.C. (1970) 'Towards a theory of creativity.' In P. Vernon (ed.) *Creativity*. Harmondsworth: Penguin, pp.137–151.

Sampson, F. (1998) 'Thinking about language as a way through the world.' In Celia Hunt and Fiona Sampson (eds) (1998) *The Self on the Page*. London: Jessica Kingsley Publishers, pp.129–141.

Sansom, P. (1994) *Writing Poems*. Newcastle upon Tyne: Bloodaxe.

Sitzia, L. and Thickett, A. (2002) *Seeking the Enemy*. London: Working Press.

Smith, K. and Sweeney, M. (eds) (1997) *Beyond Bedlam: Poems Written Out of Mental Distress*. London: Anvil Press.

Sparrow, G. (1980) *How to Get Your Book Published*. London: Bachman and Turner.

Storr, A. (1991) *The Dynamics of Creation*. Harmondsworth: Penguin.

Stuart, M. (1998) 'Writing, the self, and the social process.' In C. Hunt and F. Sampson (eds) (1998) *The Self on the Page*. London: Jessica Kingsley Publishers, pp.142–152.

Sutton-Smith, B. (1986) 'Children's fiction making.' In Theodore Sarbin (ed.) *Narrative Psychology*. New York: Praeger Publishers.

Taylor, P.V. (1993) *The Texts of Paulo Friere*. Buckingham: Open University Press.

Thomas, P. (1997) *The Dialectics of Schizophrenia*. London: Free Association Books.

Vaneigem, R. (1983) *The Revolution of Everyday Life (Traite de savoir faire a l'usage des jeunes générations)* (trans. D. Nicholson-Smith). London: Left Bank Books/Rebel Press.

Wilcock, A.A. (1999) 'Reflections on doing, being and becoming.' *Australian Occupational Therapy Journal 46*, 1–11.

Williams, G.A. (1985) *When Was Wales?* Penguin: London.

Williams, R. (1975) *The Long Revolution*. Harmondsworth: Penguin.

Winnicott, D.W. (1971) *Playing and Reality*. London: Routledge.

Worpole, K. (1983) *Dockers and Detectives*. London: Verso.

Wright, J. and Chung, M.C. (2001) 'Master or mystery? Therapeutic writing: A review of the literature.' *British Journal of Guidance and Counselling 29*, 3, 277–291.

Yerxa, E. J. (1983) 'Audacious values: The energy source of occupational therapy practice.' In G. Kielhofner (ed.) *Health through Occupation: Theory and Practice of Occupational Therapy*. Philadelphia: F.A. Davies.

CHAPTER ELEVEN

Evaluating Creative Writing in Health and Social Care Settings

Some Principles[1]

Fiona Sampson

Like the rest of the book, this chapter focuses on creative writing in health and social care settings. It does not examine other activities, however suggestive or analogous,[2] except insofar as they contextualise the field. This is significant because I would like to argue that, if it is to be useful and effective, evaluation must develop a clear sense of *what* it is evaluating. Otherwise, it will not reflect the particular project or practice it is being asked to look at, but rather some notional way of going on, with imagined criteria and virtual activities. To put it another way, in trying to define our practice itself – as Part Two in particular of this book has tried to do – we get nearer to defining the uses and forms of evaluation for that practice.

In this chapter, therefore, I will think through the question of evaluation in three ways. First, I would like to think a little about what writing in health and social care is. Second, I hope to tease out from this some implications for what evaluation of the practice does and does not consist of; and, third, I would like to run through some practical suggestions for appropriate forms of evaluation.

First, then, what is writing in health and social care? For the purposes of coherence in this chapter, I will be looking at the paradigm of writing in health care, a model on which writers in social care activities already can and do structure themselves.[3] I will use the term to mean an *arts*-led practice: creative writing and literature activities which take place in the British National Health Service (NHS),[4] *insofar as they are appropriate* to this setting, but which, though they take place in the clinical context, are not part of a therapeutic programme.

Let me unpack this a little. First, I should stress that this is not a model of what I argue the practice of writing in health and social care *ought* to be, but about the limits beyond which it becomes another kind of thing, such as a part of psychotherapy or an addition to clinical notes. I have discussed elsewhere (Sampson 2001, pp.107–149) the value of under-defining a practice which is itself characterised by obliquity and uncertainty. I take the ways poetry positions itself *in contradistinction to* other ways of using language (such as naming, defining, arguing, representing) as a paradigm of how creative writing and literature may act in any setting, but particularly in the setting of clinical discourse and its authority. Writing in health care, I am suggesting therefore, is particularly concerned with creating some 'play' in the confined terms in which someone receiving that care can talk and be talked about. Because, whether an individual is on a *one-off* visit to a general practitioner, makes *series* of trips to see a consultant, or has to some degree become institutionalised – has internalised the health care version of themselves – by having to *live* in some sort of care unit, health care is about a particular set of certainties. Indeed, we ask it to be. We ask our carers to be certain that what they are doing will produce the best outcome for us. We ask that they are experienced: that what we are 'presenting' them with comes to them not as a novelty to be explored but as something familiar and bounded, something with which they can deal.

That certainty takes the form, as Robin Downie has pointed out (Downie 1997), of a discourse in which what each individual experiences is recorded neither as unique nor indeed as *experience* but simply as one example of a repeated clinical phenomenon, something which *shows itself* to the clinical observer. In this 'horizontal' view of illness and treatment, *knowledge* is precisely *not* seeing a set of experiences as entire to themselves, in their own terms. The individual receiving care is the *object* of this knowledge, not what used to be called the *subject*: the one *having* the experience (the 'vertical' view).

It is not difficult to work out how this way of thinking about the individual 'case' can seem to play out as a lack of humanity. Here is Sam Moran on a bad experience in occupational therapy (O.T.):

O.T.

And they sat there
Counting letters
Shuffling words
Killing time
Like squashed
Dark flies
Ducking outside
To draw
Deep harsh drags
On pencil thin
Cigarettes
Avoiding the group
The game
The sad slow chat
That is only
A reminder
That they've been asked
To participate
To throw the fluffy
Die
Or discuss
Incoherent ideas
That are veiled
In current affairs
As if they'd know
Or even care
When like white noise

There are voices
And distraction
And low deep pain
Hot knives
And cold numb existence
That persuade them
That the medicine
Is merely a placebo
And the sharp clear edge
Of reality
Draws blood
Every time
They take a breath.[5]

(Sam Moran 2000)

Sam herself writes the 'sharp clear edge of reality'; yet even her insight cannot sum up the *whole range* of experiences of occupational therapy, let alone of health care. In other words it is the *underdetermined*, flexible character of writing such as this – the non-scientific, non-totalising character of this *arts* practice – which makes it appropriate to health care when that is viewed as a series of 'vertical' individual – and changing – experiences.[6]

The idea of the underdetermined character of creative writing and literature is itself underdetermined and supported by a range of ideas rather than a single argument:

- It makes the familiar strange.

- The numinous idea is developed and recorded (see Killick in Chapter Two).

- The imagination has an escape route from what is going on in the material world of pain, illness and fear.

- It has a special vocabulary and register of ideas, one that resonates with aspects of our *selves* which are not everyday and that allows us to glimpse ideas, principles and emotions which may be profoundly important to us (see Eriksson in Chapter One and Downie in Chapter Six).

- Its obliquity makes it a good medium in which to explore and maybe only half-form ideas about difficult social and existential issues (see Prokopiev in Chapter Three).

- It is personal in some way.

- It is hard, pleasurable work (see McLoughlin in Chapter Nine).

- In being about language itself it allows us to escape the realist illusions of other ways of thinking, ways that call themselves forms of knowledge.

Jan Alford's 'Seed Words', for example, uses an extended metaphor for writing which moves across several of these ideas:

Seed Words

A blank page *must* be filled.
It's a compulsion.
Put down something,
Anything,
Then pause.
A fallow moment.

I see a garden plot
Waiting to be turned over,
A forkful at a time.
How long it takes
Depends much on the soil:
Whether there's loam
Beneath the weeds, or stones
Or builders' rubble.

Nothing can grow
Until the earth is turned.
Planting must wait
Until the plot is cleared.

It's hard labour.
Back-breaking.
Mind-breaking
Sometimes.

But then sun warms the soil
A robin comes to feed
On new mined worms;
A wildflower offers up
Its gentle scent;
A bird sings after rain.

One sense wakens another,
Raking up memories.
The words arrange themselves
The plot's revealed.

(Jan Alford, in Sampson 1999, pp.78–79)

Like Jan, and like several of this book's contributors, I have found *poetry*
works particularly well in writing in health and social care settings. It
offers a concentrated paradigm of creative writing, making overt –
performing – what many of these ideas suggest: that this is a particular
way of going on, with particular opportunities and rewards. This concentration of experience is particularly important in the short weekly
sessions, of one or two hours each, in which many projects are delivered.

Perhaps analogously, I am using 'writing' here as a shorthand for a
range of activities – poem-posters and hospital radio, reading and discussion, the publication and performance of project participants' writing –
of which the actual experience of writing, or we might say *composing*, is
the paradigm. My argument for this is that not only does 'writing' have
the double sense, in English, of *text and process*: but it also names the
intimate form of experience – the old idea of learning through doing –
which *doing* writing, making a text, provides.

There is no space here to develop or critique any of the ideas about
the character of creative writing I listed above. I would suggest that it is
significant, though, that they *are current*, not only in the field this book

addresses, but in contemporary British society.[7] In other words, 'creative writing' *names* a particular set of activities which have been given the responsibility or privilege of carrying these out meanings and enacting these roles in society.

All these kinds of ideas 'pull to the left' – that is to say, they move away from fact-centred or systematising approaches. They allow for partiality, personality and evocation rather than representation. Even ideas about the deeply personal nature of creative writing and literature – or its role in catharsis – see such writing as something *creative*, something *made*, rather than as pure symptom. They pull away, in short, from the idea that creative writing and literature, *as* creative writing and literature, is reducible to something *quantifiable within* the framework of clinical discourse.

How, then, can evaluation – which seems to name an objective, systematic and disinterested understanding of a particular practice – capture the individual experiences and underdetermined nature of writing in health care? Before I address that question directly, I want to turn briefly to the clinical context. At the outset of this chapter I defined as writing in health care activities which, 'though they take place in the clinical context, are not part of therapeutic provision'. I also talked about a practice which is context-*appropriate*. In other words, these activities bear *some* relation to clinical ways of doing things and values, even though they are not clinical interventions themselves. Other non-clinical, context-appropriate activities in health care settings include the hospital chaplaincy and the portering, cleaning and catering services. All these activities – leading prayers, cooking lunches, moving heavy loads – take place in other contexts too; but in a health care setting they take place *within* a set of clinical values and practices. For example: they fit round the timetable of the operating theatre; if someone in one of these roles were to betray confidentiality they would be violating clinical care conditions.

Similarly, to work against the grain of clinical values and practices, as some writers visiting health care units have suggested they might, is to work *outside* the clinical context. It is to not be part of the work that is going on in a unit. It is also dangerous and inappropriate, since it breaks the contract with the patient, that they will receive *clinical* care in that particular setting.[8] In short, it is to do writing, maybe: but not writing in health care.

All this being the case, the evaluation of writing in health care needs to pay attention to a number of things:

- the specific, irreducible character and role of creative writing and literature including its links with particular and individual forms of thought;

- the potential for the clinical discursive context to be reductive or authoritative while the experience of receiving clinical care is necessarily individual and may be disempowering;

- writing *process* as the paradigm of creative writing and literature;

- the contribution and limits of language practices which take place within a clinical context, yet are not themselves clinical interventions.

Terry has an image I would like to borrow to illustrate the confusions which can come about when we muddy these waters: when, for example, we try to evaluate counsellors' uses of writing within therapy in the same way as an arts-funded writing project in a hospital unit:

Here and There

The ground slipped away with amazing speed
Though there was no sensation of movement.
There was stillness despite the rapid ascent.
What was close and immediate suddenly became but a memory
and far away.[9]

(Terry 2000)

This chapter has itself 'slipped' straight into the question of *how* to evaluate writing in health care, without pausing at the problem which seems to have been raised, of whether or not we *should* evaluate writing in health care. One reason for this is that the field, and so this book, finds itself within a context of expectation that evaluation will take place. Contemporary arts work, especially work with people, is carried out in a

'world of work' and alongside educational paradigms increasingly preoc-
cupied with planning, assessment and outcome. Evaluation, as a practice
separate from whatever it evaluates, is becoming increasingly significant. In
other words, this discussion is not quite about the kind of evaluation
which is a necessary *part* of reflective, accountable practice.[10] Such
practice includes: clinical supervision; project steering; informal as well as
formal feedback, in particular by practitioners and participants; planning;
practitioner reflection; record keeping and documentation. This is
despite widespread agreement that evaluation has a direct and intimate
relationship with every stage of planning and implementing a project
(Woolf 1999). To conclude, evaluation itself is part of the context for
writing in health and social care: and therefore must be taken into
account in same way as the field's other defining limits.

A closer look at two possible arguments against evaluation suggests
that they evaporate whenever *good* evaluation practice is posited. These
arguments are: one, that evaluation might violate the terms of a *particular
practice*; and, two, that the terms of *writing in health care itself* might be especially violated if what is unparaphrasable and unique is reduced, under
some systematising impulse, to a set of outcome patterns or case histories.

The first of these arguments is the easier to unpick. Just as writing in
health care must be context-appropriate if it is to occupy that context, so
evaluation – like book reviewing – will only have anything to say about a
writing in health care project if it accepts the terms of the particular
project and discipline it reviews. It seems an obvious point[11] that writing
in health care, although it is capable of review and development and will
certainly continue to change and grow in the years to come, is *not* counselling, art therapy or lecturing; and that to evaluate it as if it were is a
waste of resources, time and trust. It is also poor evaluation practice.
After-the-event *bolt-on* evaluation is also weaker than evaluation *built-in*
to a project: for example, *measures of success* can be planned for each aim
and objective from the outset. Thinking in this quite concrete way can
help clarify those aims and objectives[12] as well as the shape of a project
before work even starts.

A measure of success might work something like this. A project in a
day-care unit might *aim* to develop awareness, in the local community, of
the voices, talents and skills of people with learning difficulties. One

objective through which the project might plan to achieve this aim might be a broadcast of participants' writing on local radio at a certain stage in the project's life. A *measure of success* for this objective might be that at least two individuals who have never made a creative text before have their work included in such a broadcast. This measure is orientated towards individual achievement and the development of skills. However, another measure of success might be positive feedback from the broadcast, such as the invitation to repeat the process or listener feedback. That's a community-orientated and product-led measure of success. A third measure might be conspicuous literary merit. A fourth, more context- and process-led, might be a high level of awareness in the host unit, beyond the writing group, of the broadcast. And so on. None of these measures of success conflict with each other: but not *all* are necessary in order to measure success in any one set of terms. In other words, measures of success do not only need to be *identified with* a project's aims and objectives: they themselves *express* aims and objectives for the work.

This is an example of how evaluation, even when it is built into a project, cannot be value-neutral. *Evaluation has its own aims and objectives.* There are aims and objectives for each evaluation of a particular project: to find out whether to develop existing work by adding a publication element or to confirm suspicions that user uptake is low, for example. However, evaluation with a capital 'E', evaluation itself before it is *applied* to any particular project, also has its own aims and objectives. These may include a systematising impulse, a commitment to accountability or a belief in demystification.

Significantly, in other words, for a field which is still in its comparative infancy and has occasionally proved controversial, there is no value in evaluation carried out by individuals who cannot accept the basic tenets of writing in health care or of a particular project. There is a profound difference, for example, between an evaluation which concludes that a project has not managed to demonstrate ways in which poetry can be used with older people, and one which concludes that the project is invalid because it only uses poetry with older people.

A more positive way to formulate this is to suggest that evaluation cannot be expected to make a case on grounds outside those of whatever it is evaluating. Evaluation is a form of contract with, and an acceptance of the principles of, the practice it evaluates. It has to work with, or modify from the *outset*, the basic aims and objectives – reasons for working and, in principle, methods – of that practice. Evaluation is *necessarily parasitic* on what it evaluates.

This brings me to the second possible argument against evaluation: that writing in health care will be 'especially violated if what is unparaphrasable and unique is reduced, under some systematising impulse, to a set of outcome patterns or case histories'. Once we speak *for* the experience of participants, staff and other protagonists, we are speaking *instead* of them. To paraphrase or analyse what people 'report' is to make something very like a case history. To treat what and how people write as a symptom of well-being or illness is to move away from a transformative, flexible and personal role for creative writing and litera-ture into a clinical model where individuals are objects of experience. Most of all, to try to build proofs of systematic curative or palliative effects of writing in health care, in order to 'sell' the practice to NHS managers and make the case for its inclusion in therapeutic provision, is to claim that an arts activity works *in the same way as* a therapy. As I and as other contributors have argued elsewhere in this book, this is only one of several possible ways to think about the practice; and it is one with inherent risks and limitations.

Yet evaluation is important. Good-quality practice is important (see Paul Munden's Introduction to Part One and Stewart's Introduction to Part Two). Some projects do work better than others (Hartill undated). Practitioners, providers and partners need ways to think through and talk about good practice. They also need to be able to use *some of the same terms as* funders, clinicians and educators. More radically: if writing in heath care is writing which is *appropriate* to the clinical context, it would be sig-nificant to be able to make the case for this appropriateness through the incorporation of writing in health care into clinical policy. Even though this might initially be at unit level, such an incorporation would *map* possible relationships between the arts activity and its care context; would formalise a *contract* of respectful practice between complementary ways of working; and might have significant *practical benefits* in terms of planning, management, and support at all levels, from the nursing 'floor' to financial responsibility.

What might these terms be? Natalie Goldberg tells the story of a friend who, when she was mugged, threw up her arms and yelled 'Don't kill me, I'm a writer!' (Goldberg 1986). Goldberg tells this story to point out that, although we do not need to write – or write well – in order to be worthwhile people, we often think we do. Plainly, as Christina Patterson points out in her Foreword to this book, writing, whatever its rewards, does not either solve or trump every aspect of human life. On the other hand, exploring and demarcating their own version of experience is something which does place writing in health care participants at the centre of their own picture. It is here that the field of writing in health and social care overlaps with the contemporary clinical theory and practice of person-centred care.

Person-centred health care works to put the individual and their experiences at the centre of care.[13] In doing so it tries to shift care practice – if not the forms of clinical knowledge – away from the objectifying 'conveyer-belt' of symptomatic similarities towards individualised human difference.[14] This practice reflects a form of Kantian ethics in which I (the clinician or carer) recognise in the other person – who is receiving health care – another self; and so respect their humanity in order to respect my own (Kant 1989, first published 1787). Person-centred care is delivered by clinicians; but it is *also* delivered by those other members of a team who can help to place the individual receiving care at the centre of their own experience. These include: the social worker who visits the hospital unit to talk to that individual about his future housing options; the dietician and catering team who co-ordinate their efforts so that every client has their nutritional needs met; portering and cleaning staff who offer the people they are working with respect by, for example, ensuring their privacy; and those 'value-added' activities, such as visits by schoolchildren, which add to the human quality of life on a unit. Person-centred care, in other words, is *both* about putting the *individual* client at the centre of his own picture – able to have a voice in the institutional context, be involved in decision-making about his care, and have a fuller range of his personal needs met – *and* about humanising the entire *unit*, thus supporting care staff in their own human needs. Person-centred care activities such as writing in health care also open up a practical and discursive space which may afford additional *therapeutic opportunities.* Writing in health care may open up the *opportunity* for something measurable in terms of clinical benefit to take place – such as a temporary reduction in participants' requests for painkillers or the emergence of a topic which is key to a group psychotherapeutic process – even though that measurable something is not a direct *objective* of any such arts activity.

What has this to do with evaluation? It makes the crucial connection between care provision and writing in terms which contemporary clinical practice and policy can understand, without compromising the character of writing in health and social care. So, an evaluation of writing in health care which takes its lead from the practice itself, but which mediates between it and the worlds of clinicians and funders by demonstrating measures of success and accountability, can be built on this paradigm, the paradigm of a person-centred practice. To put it in practical terms: writing in health care does not need to be evaluated in terms – which as I've already argued are inappropriate – of symptom outcome or demographic patterning to make a coherent and appropriate case for its relevance to the clinical context.

So much has been written on evaluation that it seems unnecessary to restate first principles of that discipline itself. However, I would like to end this chapter with a brief overview of some practical examples of evaluation methodology which make explicit the central importance of the personal and creative character of the activity they examine. In particular, these methods seek to learn from participants' experiences expressed *in their own words*. These methods fall into two main groups: the retrospective and the continuous. All have advantages and disadvantages, and none of these is suggested as a single recipe for 'successful evaluation'. Like the practice it evaluates, sensitive and appropriate evaluation must work piecemeal, albeit to rigorous practical and ethical standards.

Forms of retrospective evaluation might include the following:

1. Participants (who may include staff) work with another enabling writer than their usual facilitator, in order to explore and record their experiences of the project through *creative genres* such as fictional reinvention, role-play, myth and metaphor. In this activity the project itself becomes another starting point for creative activity: a kind of 'creative

recycling'. This may be particularly good practice when another project – for example, one using visual arts – is to start after a writing project has finished, in order to re-establish group work and provide participants – as well as providers – with an opportunity to think about differences and continuities between different stages of provision.

Apart from the risk involved in making the original writer practitioner feel to some degree isolated from or abandoned by a critique led by a peer who might be seen as in some way 'usurping' a project, the main challenge in this form of evaluation is to produce genuine arts work which nevertheless contains substantive information about the way the original project worked.

2.   Participants produce *individual* narratives, written or recorded in any of a range of media (sound recording, video, calligraphic text), of their own experiences of the project. Although there might be guiding questions – such as what they remember, how they characterise the project as a whole, what they think are marks of personal and project success and failure – these narratives are best supported with technical facilitation and a minimum of group work, so that genuinely individual accounts can emerge.

This begs the question of whom evaluation is for. Participants who are going to produce genuinely personal narratives need to be protected by a particular form of confidentiality agreement. If this includes a clause which lets project managers or external evaluators, for example, see these individual narratives no matter what they throw up, some participants may exercise an understandable measure of self-censorship. On the other hand, it is likely that individuals' evaluations offer their authors benefits, in terms of making sense of and summing up their experiences, which by themselves justify this process. The practitioner must decide, therefore, whether evaluation is primarily for the benefit of a project as a whole or the individuals who take part in it.

3.   Participants work with relevant *themes* – such as 'writing', 'memory', 'groups' – in writing workshops and/or retrospective discussion of pieces from their 'portfolio' of project writing. This might well be part of the process of ending for a particular project or group and it affords a range of activities – reading and discussion as well as writing – which enable full participation by a project's least as well as its most confident writers.

How is this process recorded? How are questions of confidentiality to be resolved: for example, if a participant wants to say something 'off the record'? More fundamentally, the use of oblique themes to introduce topics of relevance for evaluation must be handled carefully if it is not to seem like a form of 'trick questioning'.

4.   Participants complete *discursive feed-back sheets* using a series of workshops and discussions to think about key questions in depth. This familiar strategy is most useful for work with team members, such as project managers, who have not been involved in the writing activities themselves and so have not gained confidence in creative genres. However, evaluation practice which seems to discriminate between project providers and users and to ask more direct evaluative questions of providers runs the risk of stratifying what may already be widely differing experiences of one piece of work.

5.   *Creative writing* by the facilitating writer and/or staff on themes related to the project (see under 3 above), including topics already used by participants in particular high spots of the project. In this model evaluation becomes a reward *for* project workers, rather than a chore. A link, established between the writer as facilitator and the writer *as* professional writer, is useful for the project but also allows the writer to integrate their own practice. It is difficult, though, in a retrospective evaluation, to make this link accessible to project participants.

6.   Researcher-led discussion between groups unlikely to meet
      during the life of a project, such as providers and participant
      representatives, or clinicians from a range of units, may be
      enabled through a variety of language games and writing
      exercises. The practical difficulties of getting these groups
      together, however, mean that such sessions need to be short
      and tightly focused. Potential participants may well need a
      concrete motivation – such as the promise of a follow-up
      project – to take part.

If retrospective evaluation brings with it some problems of motivation, of
practical execution and of the status and ownership of the accounts it
generates, on-going evaluation, in the following examples, needs to be
carefully and ethically managed if it is to benefit the project and its
participants:

1.   Appropriate built-in *measures of success*, such as numbers of
      participants, with periodic revisions of those measures. The
      number of members in a day centre writing group might, for
      example, fall because of other aspects of the day centre's
      provision. On-going re-evaluation is valuable though it needs
      to be tightly disciplined to resist the management tendency to
      make a project 'top-heavy' with administrative meetings.
      'Top-heavy' projects may fail to keep writing activities and the
      experiences of participants at the centre of the project picture.

2.   Participants keep a *project journal* in one of a range of media.
      This works well with independently motivated, highly skilled
      participants in relatively good health, providing they have
      made a reasonably long-term, and so serious, commitment to
      the project. It is unsuitable for participants in acute care or
      one-off sessions. Keeping a journal of this nature explicitly for
      evaluation purposes may make the participation experience
      overly reflexive; however, keeping it for general reflexive
      purposes may generate evaluative material.

3.   A feedback *suggestions book* may encourage more participants
      and staff to contribute their thoughts on the project, although

issues of confidentiality and anonymity remain, as does the problem of an overly reflexive practice.

4. *Records of work* may include: photographs or videos of events; portfolios of work; a cuttings file; showings of participants' work to a wide audience through radio, posters, exhibitions, publication and public art; and peer review through open days, seminars and publications. This is perhaps the most reliable and transparent evaluative record of a project. It is reliable because it records the project's work itself, and not accounts *of* that work; and transparent because the material has been produced under the project's terms and for the stated writerly aims of that project.

5. Involvement of participants in project planning – through discussion in workshops but also through participant representation – is usual good practice which not only allows participants a voice but generates a form of *action research* in which participants' processes themselves guide the 'loop' of re-evaluation. Transparency is important – for example, it is important that participants know the (perhaps financial) scope within which their ideas can carry influence – if this collaborative work is to be successful.

6. The project, led by or in collaboration with the usual facilitator, makes a short-term move into another medium, such as video work or art, in order to explore questions and themes from another direction. Such additional activities can give a project a boost of extra provision, and enlarge the range of participants' experiences and skills as well as their scope for feeding back those experiences.

It is important to remember that on-going evaluation tends to bring the voices of project *participants*, above all, centre-stage: unlike retrospective evaluation, it is usually facilitated by the writer leading the project and delivered by those protagonists who carry out most of the project's activities: the participants themselves.

In this short list of examples of appropriate ways to evaluate writing in health and social care, material is produced in a variety of media and genres which can nevertheless be recorded and reproduced in evaluation reports. The resulting documents are likely to be unwieldy and sometimes awkward to manage: just as are the highly individual needs, experiences and voices of people in any care setting. It is this untidy, human, ultimately irreducibly idiosyncratic material which writing in health and social care, and so the evaluation which serves it, exists to celebrate and record.

Notes

1   An earlier version of this chapter was given as the keynote address at *The Healing Word* conference, Lapidus/Falmouth College of Arts, September 2000, and published in The Lapidus Newsletter, ed. Victoria Field, 2001.

2   Such as: a written element to counselling; personal journal-keeping (Progoff 1975); autobiographical and life-history work (Chandler 1990, Hoar *et al.* 1994); creative writing in educational settings; or other arts therapies. But see discussion in the Introduction to this book on the development of Poetry Therapy. See also Epston and White 1990; McLeod 1996.

3   In my own practice, for example, I have worked with adults with learning difficulties in weekly sessions to which they were referred by on-the-ground care workers, and used roughly similar material and approaches, whether in: long-stay mental health care units (before the development of community care); day centres jointly run by health and social services; social service-run care homes; or voluntary sector provision.

4   Or in other settings, such as private clinics or specialist day care provided by such voluntary sector organisations as The Alzheimer's Society insofar as they correspond to an NHS model.

5   Written during a session of the Kingfisher Project, Salisbury, at Salisbury Arts Centre, March 2000. Sam Moran discusses her experience of this project in Chapter Five.

6   I find I want to write 'an *overwhelming* series'. Managing staff stress and avoiding compassion burn-out has long been a concern of nursing practice and training. Clinical staff cannot experience 'the sharp clear edge' of the 'reality' of illness and distress, day in and day out, as fully as the individuals receiving care from them. It is possible, however, that the rigidity of the 'mechanical' model of care produces its own stresses; for example, by not allowing individual nurses to express the humanity which, as Downie argues in Chapter Six, is part of their own 'whole' experience, and which may have been one reason for their entering a caring profession.

7   Ideas about the specialness of, for example, poetry and oral literature are widespread in society, in every cultural strand and in each community: from prisons (where poets have particular cachet) to the high street (witness the memorials to Princess Diana). See Sampson 1999, pp.6–11.

8   An additional danger is that the visiting writer does not have a body of training, knowledge and experience with which to replace that of carers and clinicans. Her literary or writerly expertise represents only one half of the *hyphenated* identity of writing in health and social care (see Introduction); which is why it is good ethical and professional practice for practitioners to be line-managed and supervised (in the sense of receiving clinical briefing and debriefing) from within the clinical structure (UKCC 2000). In settings other than formal care, facilitators in this emerging field should be giving serious thought to the ethical code within which they will work. Most relevant is the British Association for Counselling (BAC)'s *Code of Ethics and Practice for Counselling Skills* (BAC 1989). Although writers in health and social care are not counsellors, they work with vulnerable people in some of the same contexts and management structures.

9   Written during a session of the Kingfisher Project, November 2000.

10   A point Sue Stewart makes in her Introduction to Part Two.

11   This is not necessarily obvious to potential evaluation consultants and funders, any more than it may be to the team members practitioners work most closely with: Health Service Managers 'steering' them, for example.

12   Elsewhere, I have referred to this formulation of work in terms of aims and objectives as 'double thinking' (Sampson 2000).

13   'The person-centered approach focuses all aspects of service planning, funding and delivery on the person with the disability (the consumer). It emphasizes and balances a person's needs and preferences rather than trying to fit the consumer into programs.' (South Carolina Disability District Services Network (SCDDSN) 1998)

14   In the British Government's *NHS Plan* of 2000, for example, proposed improvements to provision are described as 'a health service designed around the patient' (British Government 2000). The shift towards person-centred care coincides with a strengthening of the user movement, the name given to a field of largely voluntary activity in which health and social care service users organise themselves to create support and lobbying networks. Especially relevant here is Survivors' Poetry, a registered UK charity which promotes 'the poetry of survivors of mental distress...both those who consider themselves 'survivors' and those who have empathy with their experiences'. The user movement has gathered strength in the UK in recent years, although the first groups were set up in the 1950s. Person-centred care in the UK is also a culmi-

nation of the move towards Community Care, care taking place outside large long-stay institutions and in partnership with the voluntary sector and unpaid family members who act as carers (Skidmore 1994). For an examination of how these changes were enacted, see Seedhouse 1994.

References

British Association for Counselling (BAC) (1989) *Code of Ethics and Practice for Counselling Skills.* Rugby: BAC.

British Government (2000) *The NHS Plan: A Plan for Investment. A Plan for Reform. CM4818 – 1.* London: The Department of Health.

Chandler, M.R. (1990) *A Healing Art: Regeneration Through Autobiography.* New York and London: Garland Publishing.

Downie, R. (1997) 'The wounded storyteller.' Unpublished conference paper. Williamstown, MA: *Arts and the Calling: The Humanities, Healing and Health Care.*

Epston, D. and White, M. (1990) *Narrative Means to Therapeutic Ends.* New York: W.W.Norton.

Goldberg, N. (1986) *Writing Down The Bones.* Boston and London: Shambhala.

Hartill, G. (undated) '*Creative writing: Towards a framework for evaluation.*' Occasional paper no. 4. Edinburgh: University of Edinburgh.

Hoar, M. *et al.* (1994) *Life Histories and Learning: Language, the Self and Education.* Brighton: University of Sussex.

Kant, I. (trans. N. Kemp-Smith) (1989) *Critique of Pure Reason.* Basingstoke: Macmillan Education. First published 1787.

McLeod, J. (1996) 'Working with narratives.' In I. Horton and J.Bimrose (eds) *New Directions in Counselling.* London: Routledge.

Progoff, I. (1975) *At a Journal Workshop: The Basic Text and Guide for Using the Intensive Journal.* New York: Dialogue House Library.

Sampson, F. (1999) *The Healing Word: A Practical Guide to Poetry and Personal Development Activities.* London: The Poetry Society.

Sampson, F. (2000) 'Writing and identity: The British writing in healthcare experience.' Unpublished conference paper. Jarvenpaa, Finland: *Finnish Association of Language Teachers Annual Conference.*

Sampson, F. (2001) *Writing in Health Care: Towards a Theoretical Framework.* Nijmegen: University of Nijmegen.

Seedhouse, D. (1994) *Fortress NHS: A Philosophical Review of the National Health Service.* Chichester: John Wiley and Sons.

Skidmore, D. (1994) *The Ideology of Community Care.* London: Chapman and Hall.

United Kingdom Central Council for Nursing, Midwifery and Health Visiting (UKCC) (2000) *United Kingdom Central Council for Nursing, Midwifery and Health Visiting Code of Professional Conduct.* London: UKCC.

Woolf, F. (1999) *Partnerships for Learning: A Guide to Evaluating Arts Education Projects.* London: Arts Council of England and the Regional Arts Boards.

Further reading

The Arts Council of England (ACE) (1999) *The Arts Council Writer in Residence Guidelines.* London: ACE.

Dickson, M. (ed.) (1995) *Art with People.* London: Artists Newsletter Publication.

Gilbert, T.T. and Scott Taylor, J. 'How to evaluate and implement clinical policies.' In *Family Practice Management.* Leawood, Kansas: American Academy of Family Physicians.

Haldane, D. and Loppert, S. (1999) *The Arts in Health Care: Learning from Experience.* London: Kings Fund.

Miles, M. (1997) 'Does art heal? An evaluative approach to art in the health service.' In C. Kaye and T. Blee *The Arts in Health Care: A Palette of Possibilities.* London: Jessica Kingsley Publishers.

Palmer, T. and R. (2003) *Word of Mouth: Reaching Readers.* Ilkley, Yorkshire: National Association for Literature Development.

Smith, T. (1999) *Live Literature.* London: The Arts Council of England.

South Carolina Disability District Services Network (SCDDSN) (1998) *Person Centered Services.* Columbia, South Carolina: SCDDSN.

The Contributors

Robin Downie is Professor of Moral Philosophy at the University of Glasgow. In addition to philosophical interests he has an interest in using the arts in medical education. He has published widely in this area. Books include: *The Healing Arts: An Illustrated Oxford Anthology* (1994, pb 2000); *Clinical Judgement: Evidence in Practice* (with Jane Macnaughton) (Oxford 2000); *Palliative Care Ethics* (with Fiona Randall) (Oxford, 2nd edn, 1999).

Inger Eriksson is preparing her PhD thesis on Ethics in Poetry Groups in Palliative Care at Lund University, Sweden. Her research grows out of her more-than-twenty-years' experience as a deacon in Lund Hospital Chaplaincy. She has previously published research as a part of Stockholm County Council's research programme, *Arts in Hospitals and Care as Culture.*

Rose Flint is a poet, artist and Art Therapist. She teaches creative writing and works as a poet in a variety of healthcare settings. She is Lead Writer for the Kingfisher Project, Salisbury Arts Centre and Art Care, Salisbury General Hospital. She has worked in Adult Mental Health and Alcohol Addiction for Severn NHS Trust and has been awarded two Poetry Places by the Poetry Society. She has published three collections of poetry, *Blue Horse of Morning, Firesigns* and *Nekyia.*

Maureen Freely was born in New Jersey and grew up in Istanbul. Since graduating from Harvard she has lived mostly in the UK. She is the author of five novels – *Mother's Helper, The Life of the Party, The Stork Club, Under the Vulcania* and *The Other Rebecca* – and three books of non-fiction including *The Parent Trap: Children, Families and the New Morality* (Virago 2000). A regular contributor to several national papers, she is also Senior Lecturer on the Warwick Writing Programme.

Graham Hartill evaluated the Kingfisher Project. He is one of the co-founders of Lapidus and has worked for the last seven years as Lifelines facilitator (with older people) for the Ledbury Poetry Festival. His most recent book was a collection of "transcription poems" from the festival. *Cennau's Bell*, his selected poems, is published in 2004.

Celia Hunt is Senior Lecturer in Continuing Education at the University of Sussex Centre for Continuing Education. She has a special interest in the developmental and therapeutic role of creative writing and is the author of *Therapeutic Dimensions of Autobiography in Creative Writing* (Jessica Kingsley Publishers 2000) and editor (with Fiona Sampson) of *The Self on the Page: Theory and Practice of Creative Writing in Personal Development* (Jessica Kingsley Publishers 1998). She is currently working on a new book with Fiona Sampson called *Creative Writing and the Writer* for Palgrave Macmillan.

John Killick is Research Fellow in Communication Through the Arts at Dementia Services Development Centre, University of Stirling, where he is editing a series of publications. He worked in education for 30 years and has worked with people with dementia since 1993. His books include: *Writing for Self-Discovery* with Myra Schneider (Element 1997), *Communication and the Care of People with Dementia* with Kate Allan (Open University Press 2001) and two collections of poems by people with dementia (*The Journal of Dementia Care*).

Jill Low is the Director and **Catherine Sandbrook** is the Assistant Director of Salisbury Arts Centre which co-manages the Kingfisher Project with ArtCare, Salisbury District Hospital's Arts Service. **Emma Ryder Richardson** is founder and former General Manager of ArtCare and is now Hospital Arts Advisor for Paintings in Hospitals, a charity that has a national collection of original paintings that are loaned to hospitals all over England. **Sister Maria Purse** is a Workforce Developement Officer at Salisbury District Hospital.

Dominic McLoughlin is former Chair of Lapidus, the Association for the Literary Arts in Personal Development. His publications include 'Transition, transformation and the arts of losing: some uses of poetry in hospice care for the terminally ill' in *Psychodynamic Counselling* (2000) and poems in the Poetry School anthology *Entering the Tapestry* (2003). He teaches counselling and creative writing in the Faculty of Continuing Education, Birkbeck, University of London.

Sam Moran is a conscientious writer and poet and has been involved in a variety of different projects. She attended an Arvon course at Lumbank House in 2000. Her poems have been published in the anthology *Strange Baggage* and in DAIL magazine. She has performed her poetry on local radio and radio 4's 'All in the Mind', Ledbury Poetry Festival, the Poetry Society Poetry café, Covent Garden, Bristol and Frome. Her poetry has been used in a short film for an art installation, and she has written and performed her work for theatre – her monologues 'Robert's Fall' have recently been shown at the Merlin Theatre, Frome. She co-runs and comperes Salisbury Poetry Café. She is currently writer in residence at Salisbury Arts Centre and is continuing to write for theatre.

Paul Munden is a writer, editor and Director of NAWE, which has done more than any other UK organisation to support and define the thriving contemporary role of writers working in the community – from universities to prisons. He has worked as a creative writing tutor in a wide range of community and care settings and won an Eric Gregory Award as a poet.

Christina Patterson is Deputy Literary Editor of *The Saturday Independent*. She has worked in bookselling and publishing, as a freelance writer and editor and, for seven years, for the literature programme at the Royal Festival Hall. She joined the Poetry Society in 1998 to run the Poetry Places scheme and took over as Director in March 2000. As a literary journalist and critic, she has written regularly for the *Observer*, *The Sunday Times* and the *Independent* and has contributed to *The Cambridge Guide to Women's Writing in English*. She was chair of the judges for the Geoffrey Faber Memorial Prize for Poetry in 2000 and chair of the judges for the Forward Poetry Prizes in 2001.

Nick Pollard worked as an occupational therapist in psychiatric settings for over twelve years, mostly with people with enduring mental illnesses. He edits *Federation*, the magazine of the Federation of Worker Writers and Community Publishers. Now senior lecturer in occupational therapy at Sheffield Hallam University, this chapter was written while working for and with the support of Doncaster and South Humber Healthcare NHS Trust.

Aleksandar Prokopiev has published 13 books of short stories and essays including *The Young Master of the Game* (1983), *Letter about a Snake* (1992) and *Anti-Instructions for Personal Use* (1996). He has been translated into, among others, English, French, Italian, Polish, Hungarian, Bulgarian, Serbian and Slovakian. A former Balkan rock star with *Idols* and *Mouth to Mouth*, he studied ethno-philology in Paris and has also worked in radio and as Professor of Philology at Ss. Cyril and Methodius University, Skopje. He works as a writer, editor and Director of Balkan Projects at the Institute of Literature at the university.

Fiona Sampson is AHRB Research Fellow in the Creative and Performing Arts at Oxford Brookes University. Translated into 11 languages, her awards include the Newdigate Prize. Her latest poetry collection is *Folding the Real* (Seren 2001). She is Editor of *Orient Express*, a journal of contemporary writing from Enlargement Europe, and of *Context*. A practitioner in the field for 13 years, and founder member of Lapidus, her books on writing in health and social care include *The Self on the Page* with Celia Hunt (Jessica Kingsley Publishers 1998) and *The Healing Word* (The Poetry Society 1999).

Sue Stewart is a poet with wide experience of teaching creative writing in school, university and community settings. As Literature Officer at Arts Council East Midlands, member of the Council of Management of the Arvon Foundation for 15 years and Director of Write2B Ltd (see www.write2B.co.uk for details) she has had responsibility for researching, planning and implementing all forms of literature education and outreach projects. Her books include: *Inventing the Fishes* (Anvil 1997), winner of the Aldeburgh Prize, and *A World of Folk Tales* (Scottish Cultural Press 1998).

Useful Addresses

Academi
www.academi.org
3rd Floor, Mount Stewart House, Mount Stewart Square, Cardiff CF10 5DQ

Apples and Snakes
www.applesandsnakes.org
Battersea Arts Centre, Lavender Hill, London SW11 5TN

Arts Council of England
www.artscouncil.org.uk
14 Great Peter Street, London SW1P 3NQ

Arts Council of Northern Ireland
www.artscouncil-ni.org
MacNeice House, 77 Malone Road, Belfast BT9 6AQ

Arts Council of Wales
www.artswales.org.uk
Museum Place, Cardiff CF1 3NX

The Federation of Worker Writers and Community Publishers
Burslem School of Art, Queen Street, Stoke on Trent, ST6 3EJ
thefwwcp@tiscali.co.uk

Lapidus
www.lapidus.org.uk
BM Lapidus, London WC1N 3XX

literaturetraining
www.literaturetraining.com
literaturetraining, Freepost NEA 12181, Edinburgh EH6 0BR

National Association for Literature Development
www.nald.org
PO Box 140, Ilkley, West Yorkshire LS29 6RH

National Association of Writers in Education
www.nawe.co.uk
PO Box 1, Sheriff Hutton, York YO60 7YU

Scottish Arts Council
www.sac.org.uk
12 Manor Place, Edinburgh EH3 7DD

Survivors' Poetry
groups.msn.com/survivorspoetry/
Diorama Arts Centre, 34 Osnaburgh Street, London NW1 3ND

Subject Index

Author Index

Made in the USA